Contents

Preface		iv
Introduction		v
Chronology of Events		vii
1	Anarchy in Hindustan: India in the Later Eighteenth Century	9
2	Mughals, Marathas and Mercenaries: Indian Military Forces in the Eighteenth Century	16
3	The Man from Savoy: The Making of a Military Entrepreneur	36
4	Building an Army from the Ground Up: De Boigne's First Campaign	41
5	The Army of Hindustan: Organisation, Weapons and Uniforms	56
6	The Army of Hindustan at War: De Boigne's Campaigns	74
7	General Perron Takes Command	97
8	The Widows War and Other Stories	106
9	Mercenaries and Freebooters: George Thomas's War	123
10	Holkar and Scindia: The Civil War in the Maratha Confederacy	141
11	'Their Infantry and Guns will Astonish You' The Last Campaigns of the Army of Hindustan: The Campaign in the Deccan	157
12	Things Fall Apart: The Last Campaigns of the Army of Hindustan: The Campaign in Hindustan	175
13	What Came After: 'Sometimes Pleasure, Sometimes Pain, In The Service of the English'	201
Appendices		
I	Officers of the Army of Hindustan	205
II	A Selection of Other Trained Brigades	210
Glossary		214
Bibliography		216

Preface

The military history of India has fascinated me since the early 1970s when I discovered Shelford Bidwell's book *Swords for Hire* on the shelves of my local lending library. Since those now distant days I have collected books and information upon many aspects of Indian military history, always keeping an eye out for more information on the 'Military Adventurers,' the 'Free Lances' or as we would term them, mercenaries, who provided the rulers of many Indian states with the military know how that they lacked. The result of that collecting bug is this book.

I could not have written this without the help and encouragement of quite a few people. Most notably and always first in my thoughts my wife Carole who had had an awful lot to contend with as I 'gave birth'. The volumes of obscure history that had littered the house as I wrote are now back, more or less tidily, on their shelves, at least for the time being.

I should also like to thank my good friend, historian and author, Mike McNally who nudged me into writing this book in the first place and for reading the manuscript and not infrequently listening to me ramble on about the complexities of eighteenth century Indian history. It would also be remiss of me if I did not thank Dr Andrew Bamford (editor of Helion's From Reason to Revolution series) and Rob Griffith, for keeping me on the straight and narrow during the preparation of this book.

A short note on place names. I have usually used the English variants current at the time and those used by earlier historians of the period. Some Indian place names have changed considerably in the modern era. Thus, Poona is now Pune and Madras is now Chennai, a list of some others is at the end of the glossary.

Introduction

India in the eighteenth century was a place of wonder, adventure, and, if you were lucky and lived long enough, massive profit for the Europeans who had been visiting and sometimes staying since the sixteenth century.

The European merchants, soldiers and administrators were not, as the Victorians would have it, there to civilise the population or to impose order and enlightenment. That idea would not appear for another century or more. No, in the eighteenth century the Europeans were there to make money. They wanted to 'shake the pagoda tree.'[1] By European standards India was seen as fabulously wealthy and every European merchant and trader wanted to cut himself as large a slice of that splendid pie as they could the potential for profit was huge. To take only one example, in 1770–71 the British East India Company, transferred £1,086,255 back to London from its Bengal territories alone, this would be worth perhaps £100 million today.[2] Yet outside of the relatively small coastal enclaves occupied by the French, the British, the Portuguese and the Dutch, Indian life went on as it had for the last century or so – indeed for the small farmers it went on much as it had done a millennia ago.

Therefore, the military history of India in the eighteenth and early nineteenth centuries is not merely the history of British expansion and conquest. Indeed, it can be argued that until the end of the Second Maratha War in 1805, Britain, in the form of the Honourable East India Company, was not the paramount power in the subcontinent. With this in mind, one is forced to wonder what was happening in those parts of India where the British writ did not yet run. The 'Princely States', to use a later term, had armies of their own and fought wars of their own. In the second half of the eighteenth century, while the British and French East India Companies were fighting a small war on the South East coast of India, many miles to the north huge armies were fighting for control of the rump of the once dominant Mughal Empire. Northern India was once again invaded by a large Afghan army and in 1761 the Third Battle of Panipat was fought, wherein perhaps

---

1   Idiom: To become very rich, very quickly. The pagoda was a gold coin used in the Madras Presidency until 1818.
2   William Dalrymple, *The Anarchy: The Relentless Rise of the East India Company* (London: Bloomsbury, 2019), p.221.

as many as 150,000 combatants battled for control of the remnants of that Empire.

Eighteenth century Indian political life was dangerous and bloody. As the Mughal Empire crumbled, successor states fought and manoeuvred for power. Warfare was almost continuous across the subcontinent. The various factions moved, fought, and intrigued on an ever-changing chessboard. The Marathas became the most effective power in the northern half of India – but it was never an uncontested power – as, besides competing with other successor states, they also fought and intrigued amongst themselves. The prestige of the Mughals still commanded respect and possession and control of the person of the Emperor and therefore the rump of the empire, was still a huge political advantage. Into this murderous mixture the Europeans added military know how and a technological edge. Indian rulers were not slow to see the advantages of this. So, it came about that in the second half of the eighteenth century a small but steadily growing and rather disparate group of European military adventurers were scattered across northern India. All those successor states with any pretentions to power had their corps of regular troops formed, trained, and often officered by Europeans. Most of these European mercenaries were either British, Irish or French, but there were also Dutch, Portuguese, Italians, and Germans and at least one American. Many, especially of the British, were, in the euphemism of the time, 'country-born'– the sons of British fathers and Indian mothers. One such was James Skinner, whose father was a Scottish officer of the East India Company's army and whose mother was a Rajput lady. Skinner served with the greatest of the military adventurers and has left us a lively memoir. He also is the James Skinner who raised perhaps the most famous Indian cavalry regiment of all time, Skinner's Horse. Although some of these military adventurers returned home at the end of their service (a few with considerable fortunes) many others stayed on and raised families and made their homes in India. Equally many more died there. Most of these men sank into obscurity but a very few have left accounts of their adventures and of the events that surrounded them.

The aim of this book is to detail the greatest of these 'Regular Corps' and the only one that reached the size of an army in its own right. The Army of Hindustan eventually had five distinct brigades, as well as its own arsenals and munitions factories, and could put over 30,000 men into the field with the most powerful artillery in India.

This is the story of that army.

Chronology of Events

1498	Portuguese explorer Vasco de Gama reaches India. The Portuguese begin trading. They are followed in the next century by the Dutch and later the English
1556	Akbar the Great become Mughal Emperor. His tolerant attitude to religion within his Empire institutes something of a Golden Age over much of the Indian subcontinent.
1600	East India Company founded by English merchants.
1642	The East India Company in Madras begins the building of Fort St. George which has a garrison of 35 Europeans plus the same number of local 'peons'. The Council of Madras is given the legal right by local rulers to dispense justice within its boundaries.
1658	Aurungzeb becomes Mughal Emperor after killing his three brothers. His brutal and intolerant attitude begins the break-up of the Empire.
1670	The Maratha hero Sivaji begins a war of independence against the Mughal Emperor Aurungzeb. His guerrilla tactics wear out and destroy Mughal armies.
1707	Emperor Aurungzeb dies.
1717	The Mughal Emperor allows the English East India Company to trade duty free and to buy land and villages around its trading factories
1720s–1760	Mahratta conquests of former Imperial provinces continues. The Maratha Confederacy becomes supreme in much of Central India and reaches as far north as the Punjab.
1727	Madhaji Scindia born.
1739	Nadir Shah of Persia invades northern India, captures and loots Delhi. Thousands are killed in the ensuing massacre. Nadir Shah then returns home with the loot including the Peacock Throne of the Mughal Emperors.
1740–1748	War of Austrian Succession in Europe.
1746	September. Madras falls to the French after a short siege, despite a theoretical non-aggression pact between the British in Madras and the French in Pondicherry, and the express instructions of the Nawab of the Carnatic, the supposed overlord of both of the European settlements, to abstain from hostilities.

1746	4 November. Battle of St Thome. The Nawab of the Carnatic sends his son, Maphuz Khan, to recover Madras with an army 10,000 strong including artillery. This army is destroyed by a French force consisting of roughly 300 Europeans and around 700 trained *sepoys*. This is the first instance where the superiority of European military training is displayed on an Indian battlefield.
1761	14 January. Third Battle of Panipat. Afghan invaders helped by local Muslim rulers smash the Maratha confederacy armies 80 kilometres northwest of Delhi. The Marathas lose their hold on Northern India. Although seriously wounded Maratha leader Madhaji Scindia escapes capture.
1757–1763	Seven Years War in Europe. In India the British emerge victorious over the French. Former French officers and soldiers take service with local rulers, anxious to strengthen their own military forces as the Mughal Empire continues to disintegrate.
1764	22 October. Battle of Buxar. The British defeat Mir Kassim ruler of Bengal and his 'Trained Brigades' under Walter Rheinhardt – alias Somru. This force is one of the first of the Trained Brigades that are to become an important feature of warfare in Northern India for the rest of the century.
1767–1769	First Mysore War Haidar Ali defeats the Madras presidency of the British East India Company.
1774	Self styled Colonel Rene Madec raises a force of five battalions and 20 guns for the Rana of Gohad. Other European officers are also raising trained forces for various local rulers in Bengal and Oudh.
1775–1782	First Maratha War ends in a stalemate for the East India Company despite tactical military victories, but Madhaji Scindia learns the value of European trained infantry and artillery.
1776–1783	American War of Independence. In India the French land a force under Bussy in the Carnatic, purportedly to support Haidar Ali, but it arrives only after his death.
1778	January. Benoit De Boigne lands in Madras.
1780–1784	Second Mysore War. Haidar Ali defeats the British at first but is then in turn defeated by Lieutenant General Sir Eyre Coote. Ali's son Tipu Sultan continues the war with some French aid. The end of the war sees more French adventurers becoming mercenaries. Pierre Cuillier – alias Perron arrives in India at this time.
1785–1786	De Boigne begins to raise his first two-battalion mercenary force for Madhaji Scindia.
1788–1789	Madhaji Scindia contracts De Boigne to raise and train an army of 10,000 men. By 1790 the First Brigade is in being, the Second Brigade is already forming. The Army of Hindustan is born.

1

Anarchy in Hindustan: India in the Later Eighteenth Century

Imagine, if you will, a patchwork quilt of many varied and often beautiful fabrics, some more sumptuous than others. The best of these fabrics are very rich and costly indeed, and the lesser fabrics look rather tawdry beside them. Imagine further, that each type of fabric was antagonistic towards each and every other type and all of the lesser wanted to be just like the richest and most sumptuous on that particular quilt. This analogy is something like the state and appearance of India in the latter half of the eighteenth century.

When the Mughal Emperor Aurungzeb died in 1707 the fabric of the mighty empire of his predecessors, Babur the Conqueror and most especially Akbar the Great, was already beginning to fray at the edges. The Muslim Emperor Aurungzeb's religious intolerance had pushed many of his Hindu subjects into rebellion against his harsh policies. The Sikhs of the north-west and the Jats to the south-east of the centre of power in Delhi had both rebelled. Yet the most serious rebellion against the Empire was that of the Marathas of south-central India under their great hero Sivaji. In a series of campaigns in the late seventeenth century Sivaji won independence for his people. In the following decades his successors would become de facto rulers of much of the territory that had once been part of the Mughal Empire.

This turn of events was brought about by a collection of political and military factors. The most obvious of these was a succession of weak emperors who, unable to enforce their rule, saw their once more or less loyal satraps break away to form independent successor states. These successor states were militarily strong enough to resist any imperial forces likely to be sent against them and while the person of the Emperor, and the idea of the Empire, would still retain enormous cachet into the next century, it was rather as a political pawn in the endless and bloody game of power constantly being played out in the Indian subcontinent, than as a powerful piece in his own right, that made the Emperor and the Empire valuable.

As the eighteenth century wore on the Empire continued to disintegrate as its successor states accrued more power unto themselves. The northern

'THEIR INFANTRY AND GUNS WILL ASTONISH YOU'

India in the late eighteenth century. Britain was by no means the paramount power in the country at this time.

half of the subcontinent especially became a warring snake pit of states competing for power and territory at each other's expense. Warfare was endemic. The borders of individual states and territories fluctuated and merged as the cycle of conquest and rebellion continued in a seemingly never-ending continuum. Political life was unstable and frequently blood soaked, the various bodies politic, both Imperial and successor state, seethed with continual plot, counter-plot, and conspiracy. The strong, clever, and ruthless survived – if they were lucky. The weak, trusting, or foolish died – frequently in unspeakable pain. This period of Indian history is known as the *Gardi ka Waqt*, or time of troubles.[1]

However, for men of an adventurous stamp the spawning of new states and empires would provide a series of opportunities for wealth and power the like of which would never be seen again. This was true of rulers large and small. As is always the case in such anarchic periods anywhere in the world, the chief sufferers were the agricultural peasants – in India the Ryots – who tilled the land and hoped, often in vain, for the various 'tax-gatherers', often no more than mere plunderers, to stay away long enough for them to raise and harvest a crop.

The various successor states varied widely in size and power. Some, such as Hyderabad in the south, could put many thousands of troops into the field and held territories of thousands of square miles. It is a mistake, however, to think of these successor states as without problems of their own. Each of these states was, in effect, the Mughal Empire writ small with exactly the same problems. Essentially, each state was a collection of lesser feudatories ruled or overawed by a stronger ruler. A strong dynasty might well command obedience and a more or less stable state emerge – as it did at Hyderabad, and for a time in Mysore further to the south and, on a smaller scale, in Oudh and Bengal in the north-east. This period also saw the emergence of the Jat state around the great fortress of Bhurtpur. However, borders fluctuated, and many areas were plagued by constant rebellions, which might be as simple as the withholding of tax revenue or tribute to see if those demanding it were strong enough to enforce their demands, or which might be complex wars of succession when a ruler died and the various claimants to the vacant throne made a bid for power. The whole makeup of society was basically feudal in nature and even benevolent despots were plagued by robber barons. It was a truism of the time that:

> The good old rule, the ancient plan,
> That he who has the power shall take,
> And he shall keep who can.[2]

This was the only real political creed. Collecting enough revenue – at whatever level – to sustain their rule was the major occupation of any ruler, from minor *poligar* or *zemindar*, to great *raja*. Some succeeded spectacularly and became incredibly wealthy. Asaf-ud-Dualah, the *nawab-wazir* of Oudh amassed at

---

1 John Lall, *Begam Samru* (New Delhi: Roli Books, 1997), p.1.
2 Shelford Bidwell, *Swords for Hire* (London: John Murray, 1971), p.5.

least £8 million in jewels (at eighteenth century values, close to £990 million today) as well as 20 palaces and other riches by 1782.[3] By comparison with other states Oudh was relatively peaceful – but also comparatively small.

The Rajput states of the nearer north-west amongst them Jodhpur and Jaipur had maintained a vassalage under the Mughals and despite Aurangzeb's bigotry still felt some kind of loyalty to the Empire. Their principalities, under their Hindu *Rajas* had endured for many generations by the standards of much of the rest of the subcontinent they were also comparatively stable but for the constant internecine feuding of the various noble clans. Nevertheless, these Rajput States usually managed to stand somewhat together against outside interference especially from the rising power of their fellow religionists the Marathas.

The most energetic and rapacious of the successors to the Empire were the Marathas of western and south-central India. Since winning their independence from the Mughals the Maratha Confederacy had expanded until it laid claim to much of northern and central India. These claims were far from undisputed, but the Maratha claim to raise *chauth* (traditionally a 25% tax on goods and wealth) from those lands it deemed theirs were frequently backed up by devastating raids from the swarms of irregular light cavalry which usually composed its various armies. Such raids even penetrated as far north-east as Bengal by the 1740s once again showing how feeble the Mughal Emperor in Delhi had become.[4] *Chauth* was little more than a protection racket, though in theory it did entitle the victim to actual protection from other robber barons – after all you do not allow other gangsters into your territory.

This Confederacy was, by the latter half of the eighteenth century, more a loose alliance of like-minded chieftains than a collection of states. This had not always been so. Initially the Marathas had been ruled over by the *peshwa* – a kind of head man or first minister who normally resided in Poona. However, the disastrous defeat at Panipat in 1761 irretrievably weakened the position of the *peshwas*. The various chieftains were frequently little more than bandits on a large scale, who sometimes, when politically desirable or convenient, remitted a share of the *chauth* to the *peshwa's* government in Poona and sometimes not. Maratha cavalry also fought as mercenaries or allies when lucrative opportunities presented themselves. Clive had up to 4,000 of them as his allies in 1750–51 in his campaign around Trichinopoly against the French and their allies, in the far south of the subcontinent.[5] They were often the most numerous troops in the small armies operating in those campaigns.

So, Maratha power grew as that of the Mughal Empire waned. The Marathas defeated the Mughals in battle as early as 1737 and the Portuguese the following year. In 1752 the Emperor even entered into a defensive alliance with this rising power. By the late 1750's the Marathas had effectively taken over the whole of the remaining rump of the Mughal Empire. This rump, the last province, if you will, was known as Hindustan.

---

3   Desmond Young, *Fountain of the Elephants* (London: Collins, 1959), pp.51–52.
4   Major P. Sensarma, *The Military History of Bengal* (Calcutta: Naya Prokash, 1977), pp.176–181.
5   Col. J.P Lawford. *Britain's Army in India* (London: Allan and Unwin, 1978), pp.120–123.

Keene provides a description of its extent:

> The country to which the term Hindustan is strictly and properly applied, may be roughly described as a rhomboid, bounded on the North-West by the rivers Indus and Sutlej, on the South-West by the Indian Ocean, on the South-East by the [rivers] Narbadda and Son and on the North-East by the Himalaya mountains and the river Ghagra.[6]

However, the Marathas received a severe check on their ambitions when, once more, India was invaded via the traditional route from Afghanistan. This northern invasion route into India was a well-trodden one; through the northern passes from Afghanistan into the Punjab and on into the heart of Northern India. In 1739 Nadir Shah of Persia had invaded, destroyed the defenders, and put Delhi to a fearsome sack and massacre. The city barely had time to recover from this calamity when the founder of the Afghan state, Ahmad Shah Dourani, began a series of invasions of India which detached the Punjab from the Moghul Empire and overran Kashmir. In 1756 his hoard swept up to Delhi and only an outbreak of cholera in his army forced a temporary retreat. While the Marathas filled the temporary power vacuum thus created, they were not prepared when the Afghans returned, and in a bloody day-long contest with a total of over 150,000 combatants they smashed the Maratha forces at the Battle of Panipat in January 1761. The Marathas lost around 30,000 men including most of their high command. One of the few to escape was Madhaji Scindia. The Maratha power in the north of India was pushed back below the River Chambal and all the gains of the previous decades were wiped out.

Meanwhile, far to the south, small yet eventually momentous, campaigns were being fought.

The almost continuous warfare between Britain and France in eighteenth century Europe spilled over into the Indian subcontinent. The early successes of the Portuguese and Dutch in the sixteenth and seventeenth centuries had waned and by the 1740's the major European powers were the British and French in the form of their respective trading companies. This did not at first appear evident to local Indian rulers who seemed to regard these small bands of European traders as another source of income and latterly a source of aid in their own wars with their local rivals. It would be some years before they were to be convinced of their collective errors of judgement.

At first both of the trading companies were content merely to drive trade and pocket an often exorbitant profit. However, from the 1740s onwards mere commercial rivalry became open warfare. To start with the French were by far the most successful, capturing the main British settlement at Madras after a short siege in September 1746 in which the British defenders were notably incompetent. The French had embarked upon this operation despite the *Nawab* of the Carnatic, upon whose sufferance both the British and French settlements existed, abjuring both parties to refrain from warfare

---
6   H.G. Keene, *The Fall of the Moghul Empire of Hindustan* (Driffield: Leonaur, 2009), p9.

within his territories. Their disobedience caused the *Nawab* to send his son Maphuz Khan with a 10,000 strong army to assert his rights in this matter and recover Madras. Upon the French commander of Madras, one Jacques Duval d'Espremenil, a civilian official rather than a soldier, declining to deliver the settlement without instructions from his superiors in Pondicheri, Maphuz Khan encamped his army and laid the town under a rather leisurely siege.

Meanwhile in the French settlement of Pondicheri, the governor, the very able and imperially minded Dupleix, decided against giving up his gains. He therefore sent an engineer officer, M. Paradis with 300 European troops and 700 French trained Sepoys to relieve d'Espremenil. Maphuz Khan had already raised the siege after d'Espremenil had sent out a sortie of 400 men and two field guns (half of his garrison) to secure his water supplies. This sortie on 1 November had been attacked by a party of Maphuz Khan's cavalry which it promptly routed, emptying 70 or so saddles. This same sortie then routed the Khans accompanying infantry and captured two guns which they found so useless that they dumped them down a well on the way back to Madras having suffered not a single casualty.[7]

More than a little abashed by this unforeseen setback, upon hearing of the approach of Paradis' relief force, Maphuz Khan deployed his army in traditional Mughal style in front of the formerly Portuguese settlement of St Thome on the northern bank of the river Adyar on 3 November 1746. His heavy guns – though perhaps the medieval term of bombards might be more appropriate – in front, interspersed with irregular infantry, mostly matchlock musketeers, and sword and spear armed rabble. The cavalry were behind and possibly on the flanks. The guns seem to have been dug in behind earthen ramparts and were effectively completely immobile. Maphuz apparently decided to fight defensively since the French force needed to reach Madras to achieve its only and obvious objective of relieving the garrison. After dawn on 4 November Paradis' little command appeared on the south bank of the river. Despite being outnumbered by almost 10 to one he deployed his force into line, Europeans in the centre with *sepoys* on either flank, and advanced to attack. His force consisted entirely of infantry with no field guns or cavalry.

Robert Orme, a contemporary historian who served later with Clive, takes up the story:

> The river was fordable and they passed it without loss, notwithstanding they were exposed to the fire of the enemy's artillery, which as usual was very ill served. As soon as they had gained the opposite bank they gave a general fire of their small arms and then pressed on to attack the enemy with their bayonets. The Moors unaccustomed to such hardy and precipitate onsets gave way and retreated into the town where they again made a show of resistance from behind the pallisadoes which they had planted in different parts of the south side of the town. The French continued to advance against them in good order and no sooner fired from 3 or 4 platoons than the Moors gave way again …[8]

---

7 Robert Orme, *A History of the Military Transactions of the British Nation in Industan* (New Delhi: Today and Tomorrow's Printers and Publishers, 1985), Vol.1, p.76.
8 Orme, *Military Transactions*, Vol.1, p.77.

As the French followed up, the narrow streets of St Thome became clogged with panic stricken fugitives, and when the first mob of Maphuz Khan's routed horse finally got through the town they were met by a late arriving sortie from Madras, which poured more fire into them. The victorious French took Maphuz Khan's camp and all his guns. Their victory was both sudden and complete.

While the present author would not go as far as Malleson's overcooked statement that the Battle of St Thome was: '… so memorable is that it was the very first of its kind, that it proved, to the surprise of both parties the absolute and overwhelming superiority of the disciplined European soldier to his Asiatic rival'.[9] This especially as Maphuz Khan and his brother Mohammed Ali were to administer two small defeats to the French in the following weeks with the same troops as were defeated at St Thome.[10] The battle is still of considerable interest as it was the first time that Indian troops trained in the European manner had – with European aid – given such a heavy defeat to another Indian ruler.

Fighting continued for several years with the British and French trading companies supporting one or another local ruler in the south of India in order to frustrate and defeat their national rivals. Equally, local rulers sought to use these new potential allies for their own ends. By the standards of the more northerly Indian states these campaigns were simply small local scuffles many miles to the south. They did not often impinge upon events near to the centre of power in Delhi.

Yet these comparatively small campaigns were to have an influence well beyond the size of the battles or length of the butcher's bill, for it was here in the south of India that the first locally raised, but European armed and trained, infantry were to demonstrate their battlefield superiority over traditional Indian armies. The use of European style discipline and training was to have a major effect on the armies of Indian states further north. From the 1760s onwards almost every Indian prince worth the name would want his 'trained brigades' of European style infantry.

The conditions existed for a new kind of military force to flourish in the almost continuous warfare of eighteenth century India. The lack of strong central authority and collections of mutually hostile competing states, coupled with the visible success of these new trained and organised forces, gave the various Indian rulers grave cause for concern. For it was not to be allowed that one ruler should gain sway over his fellows. However, these rulers were, by the mid eighteenth century, also becoming more aware of the wider availability of new types of arms in the form of lighter mobile artillery and flintlock muskets in quantities which had formerly been beyond their reach, as the result of the increasing contact with these European trading companies. All that was needed was a collection of men to raise and train these new forces for the service of these princes and *rajas*. The day of the European 'Free Lance' or mercenary entrepreneur was close at hand.

---

9   Col. C.B. Malleson, *History of the French in India* (Edinburgh: John Grant, 1909), p.195.
10 Orme, *Military Transactions*, pp.80–84.

2

Mughals, Marathas and Mercenaries: Indian Military Forces in the Eighteenth Century

We have already seen how it is a mistake to think of any such institution as an 'Indian Army' in the period preceding that of the British Raj. It is far more accurate to think of separate armies under various rulers and of various states which, while they had common elements, also had very substantial differences in style and tactics. Equally, although the Mughal armies which had conquered most of India in the sixteenth and seventeenth centuries had been fairly efficient organisations, by the eighteenth century they had declined considerably until European observers considered them frequently little more than an ill-disciplined rabble. While this is an overly harsh judgement, it did have a very firm basis in fact. The sometimes-contemptuous ease with which European trained and led forces defeated these traditional Indian armies gave rise to this opinion. That other factors were often at work does not seem to have troubled the European observers, or even some later historians, in the least. Therefore, a brief overview of the major traditional armies of India seems in order, together with the changes that occurred in the years before the raising of the force that became known as the Army of Hindustan.

Traditional Armies

The Mughals
There were several reasons for the decline in the quality and quantity of Mughal troops. The most obvious being the falling away of provinces which in the past had provided enough revenue to pay for a centrally controlled standing force of regular troops. This simple fact underpinned all the other reasons. As pay became infrequent the regular troops deserted Imperial service for greener pastures, often under local warlords who had until

recently been Mughal officials themselves. Ties of duty became more local and feudal as the various successor states sought to build up their own forces against their rivals. This instability meant that military leadership was almost entirely personal and military service virtually feudal in nature. The death of a leader in battle, or by murder, usually lead to the disintegration of that leader's following.

In the 'time of troubles' every ruler needed troops. This meant that the overall quality of these troops declined. The almost continual cycle of civil wars and wars of succession was also a major factor. The Empire had no law of primogeniture, as many European states had, so upon an Emperor's death civil war was almost inevitable as his sons and relatives fought for the throne – assuming they had not already died bloodily in the equally inevitable palace intrigues. Between 1707 and 1754 there were no less than nine Emperors, with the years 1712 and 1719 both having three each![1]

Instability bred instability. Changing sides became a regular pastime amongst the lesser rulers. For example, the Jat leader Churaman in carving out the foundations of the Jat state from the ruins of the Empire, was first a rebel against the Emperor Aurungzeb, then a supporter of one of his successors, which did not stop him looting the camps of both contending armies as they fought for the succession. Then Churaman became an Imperial officer with responsibility to collect tolls on the road between Delhi and the river Chambal, then again a rebel, looting another Imperial camp to the tune of six million rupees. His forces do not seem to have exceeded 10,000 men in total but in one expedition alone he went to Delhi with 4,000 cavalry at his back.[2] This is only a single example of the kind of politico-military chicanery that was the everyday currency of the waning Empire. At one point in 1752 the Emperor was actually at war with his own *wazir* (or prime minister) and the Imperial garrison of Delhi was 36 months in arrears of pay.[3]

Let us now look at the various traditional components of Mughal, and Mughal style successor state, armies.

Cavalry

Traditional Mughal armies consisted of four main troop categories; cavalry, elephants, artillery and infantry. The military tradition was similar to that of the Ottoman Turks in that cavalry were the senior arm, as well as being usually the most numerous in any army. Under Akbar the Great and his immediate successors the majority of Mughal cavalry had been the traditional Asian heavy horse. Armoured men on often armoured horses carrying lance and bow, with assorted maces, axes and swords as secondary weapons. By the mid-eighteenth century pistols – though rare and only for wealthier men or officers – were not unknown.

By the second half of the eighteenth century Mughal and successor state cavalry had, to a significant extent, lost the bow and horse armour, though they had not completely disappeared. Firearms were more in evidence,

---

1 K. Natwar-Singh, *Maharaja Suraj Mal* (London: George Allan & Unwin, 1981), Appendix 6.
2 Natwar-Singh, *Maharaja Suraj Mal*, pp.14–17.
3 Natwar-Singh, *Maharaja Suraj Mal*, pp.41–44.

especially amongst lighter cavalry. Mounted firearm cavalry had been in existence since the later seventeenth century, and these mounted matchlock men had become a major feature of local warfare by the middle of the eighteenth century. The dexterity needed to manage horse and musket must have been considerable. Yet these mounted firearm skirmishers were present in significant numbers.[4] Main weapons amongst the heavy, still largely mail clad 'battle' cavalry remained lance, sword, and mace or axe. Tactics were limited to the charge and discipline was often lacking, though individual weapon handling could be of an extremely high order. When required, the cavalry could and did dismount to fight, though this became less likely as the century progressed except when such cavalry were part of a fortress garrison under attack. Unit and sub-unit sizes were in theory decimal in organisation (the smallest sub-unit being 10 men then multiples of 10 on upwards) like their Mongol forebears but graft and corruption, even in Akbar's time, often reduced units to half their paper strength.[5] Nevertheless, the Imperial rank structure was still used. Officers – called *Mansabdars* – still led their troops. Such officers could be *Mansabdars* of 20, then ascending in increments of 10 to 60, then 80 and 100, then in hundreds up to 1,000, then up to several thousand; in theory they were expected to bring this number into the field. Officers of lower rank and therefore smaller numbers attached themselves to men of higher rank who in theory commanded larger numbers. However, abuses were common and many *mansabdars* did not keep up the supposed numbers of their commands. Apparently one Lutfullah Khan Sidi, although he held the *mansabdar* rank of 7,000, 'never entertained even seven asses much less horses or riders on horses'.[6] This is an extreme example and officers engaged in actual operations would have numbers somewhat closer to those that they were supposed to have, but even in times of relative peace falsifying the muster by borrowing men from other units, or even mounting bazar idlers on any horse that could be found for the day to make up the numbers for the inspection, were tricks of the trade. The once efficient administration of the army under Akbar the Great had by the mid-eighteenth century become a very poor shadow of its former self, riddled with theft and usurpation of the available funds.

Leadership was almost entirely personal, and payment became the province of the unit commander who would be awarded a *jaghir* – a holding of land or access to land revenue to pay his troops. These *jaghirs* were not hereditary but under a weak Emperor frequently became so, especially if the holder was strong enough to fight off any rivals. Thus, the armies became to a large extent feudal in composition. The soldiers' wages were always in arrears, with commanders using the arrears as an incentive to keep the soldiers in their following and to stop desertion. Needless to say, this did not always work. Units and groupings were often of different nationalities. Mughals, Persian, Turks, Afghans and Rohillas (Pathan tribesmen who had

---

4 Natwar-Singh, *Maharaja Suraj Mal*, p.35.
5 David Nicolle, *Mughul India* (Oxford: Osprey, 1993) p.18.
6 William Irvine, *The Army of the Indian Moghuls, it's Organisation and Administration* (London: Luzac & Co, 1909), p.22.

settled in northern India) all fought both for and against the Empire. In the past there had been recognized proportions of different races, tribes, or castes allowable within a command but this gradually fell into disuse as the Empire disintegrated.[7] The Hindu Rajputs were something of an exception to this, and being very caste sensitive served in their own units and were less likely to be in units of mixed tribes or castes, though even this was by no means a hard and fast rule.

As for the provision of horses and equipment, in the past the Emperor had provided all of this, but by the eighteenth century this was no longer the case. While wealthy unit commanders might provide horse, armour and weapons to some of his most loyal followers – and as such, these followers would be termed the *barghirs* of their leader – it was equally likely that the individual trooper would provide his own equipment and most especially his own horse or horses. This was known as *silladar* – the term variously referring to both the soldier and the system – and became the most popular way of raising cavalry. It was even possible for a *silladar* to bring members of his own family into the unit. If this man provided horses and equipment for his family members they would be his *bargirs* rather than those of the unit commander, the elastic meanings of the terms can become confusing. This of course meant that there was little or no standardisation of arms or equipment in all but those under the command of the wealthiest. It also tended to mean that the cavalry were often unwilling to fight in case they lost their livelihood, in the form of their horse. At best is made a *silladar* cavalry unit's morale a little brittle, at worst it made them useful for nothing more than pillaging.

Nevertheless, numbers of cavalry in Mughal forces could still be considerable and cavalry usually outnumbered infantry in these traditional armies. The same can be said up to a point for many of the Mughal successor states such as Hyderabad, Bengal and the Carnatic. All of these had similar institutions for, and methods of, raising troops and in all of them cavalry was considered the primary arm.

Elephants

Elephants commanded great respect in Mughal and successor state armies. For instance, in the Imperial service all elephants were given names and each animal had its own stable and set of personnel to see to its welfare.[8] In former centuries elephants had often been used on the battlefield but this was fraught with risk. Elephants are sensible and sensitive beasts who find the hurly-burly of battle frightening and unpleasant.

By the eighteenth century elephants were not often used in such numbers though Downing says one Rustum Ali Khan had '30 Elephants of War' with his army in 1722 or 1723 when Downing was in that general's service as his chief of artillery.[9] Orme gives an account of Clive's encounter with elephants during the siege of Arcot in 1751: 'The parties who attacked the gates, drove

---

7   Irvine, *The Army of the Indian Moghuls*, p.36.
8   Irvine, *The Army of the Indian Moghuls*, p.179.
9   Clement Downing, W. Foster (ed.), *History of the Indian Wars* (Oxford: Oxford University Press, 1924), p.135.

'THEIR INFANTRY AND GUNS WILL ASTONISH YOU'

Elephants carrying Mughal standards. Elephants were frequently used to carry standards in parades. The Maratha *juri-pakta* of the Peshwa was often carried on an Elephant. (Public Domain)

before them several elephants, who, with large plates of iron fixed to their foreheads were intended to break them down; but the elephants wounded by the musketry, soon turned and trampled those who escorted them.'[10]

However, elephants were still used by generals and commanders as it enabled them to see over the heads of their troops and, far more importantly, to be seen by the troops. This being considered vital in armies where the death or even temporary disappearance of a leader could cause the disintegration of that army. They were also used to move artillery and to act as baggage animals. However, one does get the impression that an elephant's main use was simply to lend magnificence to Mughal generals and statesmen. This 'lending of magnificence' would certainly continue under the British into the nineteenth century and beyond.

Artillery

Gunpowder artillery had been known in India since the second half of the fifteenth century.[11] The pre-Mughal Lodi dynasty had some primitive cannon, as did the Sultan of Gujerat. Thus, the Mughal invasion of 1526 did

---

10 Orme, *Military Transactions*, p.198.
11 Dr Sayed Zafar Haider, *Islamic Arms and Armour of Muslim India* (Lahore: Bahadur Publishers, 1991), p.249.

not introduce gunpowder artillery to India but under the Mughal Emperors artillery became far more important in the conduct of war. Until the end of Akbar the Great's reign in 1605, Mughal artillery almost kept pace in development with its European counterpart but from then on until the mid-eighteenth century development and innovation seemed to stagnate, despite the importance given to artillery in the various armies of the subcontinent.

The Mughals set great store by their guns. However, they were slow to load and incapable of battlefield movement, by the mid-eighteenth century many Mughal guns had not progressed beyond those of the European battlefields of the Thirty Years War, or even the Italian Wars of the sixteenth century. Indeed, some of the monstrous 'bombards' much favoured by some rulers would have seemed too cumbersome for Henry V or other medieval European Kings. Yet despite these obvious shortcomings, guns were plentiful in Mughal armies. The prominence given to this unwieldy artillery tended to mean that battles were somewhat similar; one side or another would dig in behind earthworks or a fortified camp and defy the other to drive them from their ground. Horse drawn artillery on the European model was unknown until the very late eighteenth century. Guns were moved, usually with tortuous slowness, by oxen or elephant. Even the traversing of some of these huge guns on the field of battle or at a siege was next to impossible, and some were on four-wheeled carriages and lacked trunnions – so even elevating or depressing the barrel was not possible without moving the whole cannon. As Syed Zafar Haider states:

> The heavy guns were called Top-i-khalan [Big guns] and in spite of their enormous size and weight they were not considered very effective by later observers, though a great deal of confidence was imposed in them by their users. They could not be fired for more than a few times in the day for fear of bursting the barrel and killing those operating them.[12]

By the early eighteenth century lighter guns, on two wheeled field carriages, called *top-i-khurd* were more in evidence – yet compared to equivalent European artillery pieces they were still slow and heavy for the weight of shot they fired. Pulled by two or four oxen, battlefield manoeuvrability was still severely limited.[13] Some larger guns also had two wheeled field carriages and trunnions by this time. The huge gun 'Zanzamah', supposedly used in the field by the Afghans at the Battle of Panipat in 1761, had a bronze barrel of 14.5 feet (4.42 meters) and a bore of 9.5 inches (241 mm) was such a gun on a recognizably European style carriage.[14]

Artillery drills in the European style also seems to have been unknown before the mid-eighteenth century, and even after that time its adoption by Indian forces was patchy to say the least, so in the more traditional armies rates of fire were slow and accuracy low. Yet guns appeared in considerable numbers in battles between the various successor states and in Indian armies

---

12 Haider, *Islamic Arms and Armour*, p.255.
13 Natwar-Singh, *Maharaja Suraj Mal*, pp.14–17.
14 Haider, *Islamic Arms and Armour*, p.256.

facing European led forces. At the battle of Plassey in June 1757 Suraj-ud-Dualah fielded 50 guns in an army perhaps 50,000 strong. Only four of these, being light field guns with French crews, caused Clive any problems.[15] Clive himself had only nine guns.

Both armies at the Battle of Panipat in 1761 had significant artillery trains. The Afghans had around 70 guns and the Marathas possibly as many as 200. These were not only of larger field guns but also, lighter *zambereks*, similar to a European wall gun, as used in fortresses. These light pieces were often in use especially in the more northern parts of the subcontinent. Essentially such weapons were long, heavy, large-bore, matchlock muskets, frequently transported and even fired from the backs of camels when the poor animal was in a kneeling position. Tactically they were often used in support of cavalry and fired shot of around half a kilogram in weight. They outranged infantry muskets but were significantly slower to load, especially as they seem to have used loose powder rather than prepared cartridges. However, they were capable of long-range harassment and proved to be something of a nuisance to the British whenever they encountered them.[16] In Mughal armies these weapons were usually classed as part of the artillery as with all the other guns under the generic term *topkhana*.

There remains one other peculiarly Indian weapon to examine as part of the artillery, the war-rocket. Gunpowder had been used in India for fireworks before it was used in war and these war rockets were a development of fireworks rather than of artillery. Basically, the Indian rocket was simply a larger version of those fired today on 5 November in Britain (or indeed 4 July in the USA). They had a bamboo pole approximately 2 meters long, and the cylinder head could contain either explosive, as well as the propellant, or have a sword blade strapped to the pole. Such weapons were either laid on the ground to launch or rather more dangerously thrown into the air immediately after ignition, rather like a javelin. These war-rockets could be used in significant numbers. Mahabat Jang, governor of Bengal, apparently had 2,000 rocket men in 1742. They had been used in Mughal armies since at least the mid-seventeenth century if not considerably earlier.[17] Such rockets were used by almost all Indian armies; Mughals, the various successor states, Marathas and Rajputs all had bands of rocket men. Indeed, those of Tipu Sultan the 'Tiger of Mysore' even incommoded one Colonel Arthur Wellesley (the future Duke of Wellington) and his 33rd Foot in a mismanaged skirmish near Seringpatam on 5 April 1799.[18] They provided a sometimes spectacular, but unreliable, alternative to an often unavailable mobile artillery arm in the Indian military arsenal.

---

15 J.W. Fortescue, *History of the British Army* (London: Macmillan, 1899), Vol.II, p.419.
16 M.R. Kantak, *The First Anglo-Maratha War 1774–1783* (Bombay: Popular Prakashan, 1993) pp.74–82.
17 Irvine, *The Army of the Indian Moghuls*, pp.147–148.
18 Jac Weller, *Wellington in India* (London: Greenhill, 1993), pp.62–65.

MUGHALS, MARATHAS AND MERCENARIES

Infantry

Of the various arms in the Imperial and successor state forces infantry was frequently the most neglected and very definitely of the least status. In the primarily cavalry armies of the Mughals infantry were most often used as camp guards or to support the artillery. They had no drill and were mostly incapable of manoeuvre. Often recruited by tribe, almost any weapon could be found within their ranks. Matchlock muskets, bows, spears, and swords were all used as primary weapons. In former times the Emperor Akbar had disposed of as many as 12,000 matchlockmen all paid by the Imperial treasury.[19] However by the eighteenth century this was no longer so.

In southern India infantry: '… consisted of a multitude of people assembled together without regard to rank or file, some with swords and targets who could never stand the shock of a body of horse, some bearing matchlocks which in the best of order can produce but a very uncertain fire.'[20]

Much of this lacklustre infantry were little better than a half-armed mob. There were exceptions, such as the Rohilla matchlockmen. Originally Pathan tribesmen who had settled in northern India. The Rohillas had carved out a nascent state of their own but often fought as mercenaries both for and against the Mughal Empire and were very much in demand. These troops were especially prized for the defence of fortresses and were doughty defensive fighters, using their long matchlock muskets known as *jezzails* to good effect. Equally they were capable of mounting a fierce charge, sword in hand, at need. However, they were fickle and might just as easily be bought off or might abandon a fortress they were supposed to be defending, especially if their pay was in longer arrears than normal. The Rohillas also had cavalry of their own, both mounted matchlockmen and smaller numbers of the traditional Muslim style armoured cavalry, but they do not seem to have used horse archery at all in the eighteenth century probably because their Pathan ancestors had no tradition of such.

William Henry Tone, brother of Wolfe Tone the Irish revolutionary, was an eyewitness to the Maratha military as he served as a mercenary to several Maratha *sardars*, including the *Peshwa*, describes the Rohillas he saw in somewhat disparaging terms: 'The Rohillas are all Mussulmans and generally are fellows of the most vile and dissolute characters; they are however, men of tried courage, and always reserved for storming or some such desperate

Mughal matchlockman. Such troops as these were common in most Northern Indian armies, sometimes called *nujeebs* or *najibs*. Those in the Army of Hindustan would be more uniform in appearance and unlike most of the irregulars would be capable of drill and manoeuvre. The 'ragamuffin battalions' mentioned by Smith in the service of other Maratha leaders would look similar though they would exchange the matchlock for a flintlock musket and bayonet. (Public Domain)

---

19 Irvine, *The Army of the Indian Moghuls*, p.168.
20 Orme, *Historical Fragments* as quoted in Irvine, *The Army of the Indian Moghuls*, p.161.

service; they do no other duty whatever, and have not even the shadow of discipline among them.'[21]

Other infantry of a more or less semi-regular nature were also armed with matchlock muskets, usually lighter and longer and of smaller bore than its European counterpart, with sword and shield as secondary weapons. Often called *najibs* or *nujeebs* by the eighteenth century they were the mainstay of such infantry as were available in the northern half of India.

Tone describes those he saw during his service with the Marathas: 'The Nujeebs are matchlock men, and according to their different castes are called Allegoles or Rohillas; they are indifferently formed of high caste Hindus or Mussulmans armed with the country musket… They also carry a target and sword and are men of great intrepidity.'[22]

Like the Rohillas these troops could also mount a charge with sword in hand. Soldiers such as these were the best of the traditional style infantry of the Mughal and successor armies. Yet they could not really manoeuvre and had little concept of drill in the western manner. Their fire was rather irregular as loading was by loose powder from powder horns or charge containers (like European seventeenth century 'apostles') rather than by ready-made paper cartridges in the European manner. Equally the bore of these matchlock muskets was not standardised, so each man was responsible for his own ammunition.

Tone is referring to those Rohillas and Najibs specifically in Maratha service, but his remarks could just as easily refer to those in the service of the Mughal Empire or indeed any of the successor states who hired such mercenaries.

Other infantry were of less account. There were even 'jungle tribes' who still used the bamboo bows that Alexander the Great's Macedonians had faced. In their own territory they could fight well but such tribes cannot be considered as part of 'regular' Mughal warfare; the so called *jang-i-sultan* or war of kings. The majority of infantry were, as Orme suggests, little more than a half-armed mob.

Supply and Logistics

It seems perhaps a little odd to be using the term logistics when discussing what are essentially medieval armies. Yet all Indian armies amassed huge supply trains. Often the numbers of non-combatants and their animals would outnumber the actual troops by two or three to one, or even more. All armies of any size at all would be accompanied by a bazar to supply the soldiers with food and entertainment. Elephants, gun-bullocks, and camels carrying supplies and luxuries, including troupes of dancing girls and boys to be sold to or to entertain the troops, all slowed down the movement of Indian armies, often to little more than a crawl. Each cavalry trooper would have at least one servant, his *syce* to cut grass as fodder for his horse, as well as possibly a groom. Often this same trooper would have several other servants

---

21 William Henry Tone, *Illustrations of Some Institutions of the Maratha People* (Calcutta: Times Press, 1818), p.48.
22 Tone, *Illustrations*, p.47.

as well, each with carefully delineated duties and often their families would also be present. An Indian army on the move was more like a tribal migration than a military movement. Such a mob of unorganised non-combatants was horribly vulnerable to raiders or bandits. We have already seen how the Jat leader Charuman looted six million rupees from the camp of an Imperial army. This kind of foray against an enemy camp was a recognised part of Indian warfare. This was something that even the British would have to learn and, despite repeated attempts, they were mostly unable to cut down the huge 'administrative tail' of camp followers, in their armies when they campaigned in India.

Successor States

Most of the Mughal successor states were of course the Empire writ small. Their organisations and institutions were initially copies of those of the Empire they had broken away from. Many, even after de-facto independence, still paid lip-service to the Empire and, when pressed, might even remit some of the tribute they owed to that Empire as its feudatories. The armies were mostly of the same types of troops raised in the same way, though there was some variation. The Army of Hindustan fought several campaigns against the Rajput states so a somewhat more detailed look at their slightly different armies is in order.

The Rajputs
The various Rajput states such as Jaipur, Jhodpur, Marwar and Bikaneer were technically subject to the Mughal Emperor in Delhi but, despite sometimes paying the appropriate tribute and often declaring loyalty to the Empire, they were essentially independent states. In this way they were often found to be allies of the Empire principally because of their dislike of the Maratha expansion under Madhaji Scindia.

The Hindu Rajput forces were, if anything, even more traditional than Mughal armies. Their often suicidally brave, feudal-style noble cavalry did not use the bow or firearms to any significant extent but simply charged with lance and sword until the enemy were routed or destroyed or they – the Rajputs – were dead. Major James Baillie-Fraser, translator and editor of James Skinner's memoirs, wrote: 'The Raja [of Jodpur] is chief of the Rhattores who are the bravest and best troops of all the Rajepoot tribes. The Rhattore horse are celebrated over all Hindustan for their indomitable courage…'[23]

Formations and tactics were of the crudest. Unit drill was almost unknown though individual weapon exercise was regularly practised and troopers were expected to be physically fit. The only formation was the *ghol* essentially a mob of cavalry – the bravest and best armed and armoured at the front, each warrior following his feudal chieftain. Such a headlong 'charge by mob' was almost their only tactic. Against similar but less fanatical cavalry

---

23 Major James Baillie-Fraser, *The Military Memoir of Lieut.-Col. James Skinner, C.B* (London: Smith Elder & Co., 1851), Vol.1, p.27.

it often worked, and against the poorly armed and undrilled infantry of the Mughals it was almost a guaranteed success. These noble cavalry were by far the best troops the Rajput states could put into the field and, along with an artillery arm that was similar in development to that of the Mughals, were the only troops of any serious consequence.

The Rajputs made considerable use of camels for transport, and for their rocket armed troops and their *zamberek* camel-mounted guns. This was especially true in the desert regions of Bikaneer. Camels were also used for a speedy messenger service in these dry desert regions.

However, by the mid-eighteenth century the rest of their artillery was seriously out of date. As was usual in India heavier guns were pulled by bullocks or oxen, and the battlefield manoeuvrability of these heavy guns was effectively nil. Once positioned, and often placed behind protective earthworks, that was where they stayed.

Infantry were of even lower status than in Mughal armies and were used mainly as camp guards and porters, though sometimes as skirmishers. Like most Mughal infantry they were undrilled and variously armed with spears, bows, and matchlock muskets. The musket does not seem to have been a really popular weapon until the mid-eighteenth century. As historian Rajendra Kumar Saxena wrote:

Zambureks. These light camel mounted guns were used by most northern Indian armies. The British found their long-range harassing fire a nuisance. (Public Domain)

> When the forces of Shahpura were proceeding towards Ujjain in 1769 a number of Rajputs joined the forces as mere auxiliaries. They sometimes joined the campaign just to maintain themselves. Bringing their own arms. Generally bows, arrows, spears and cheap swords were used by them until the third quarter of the eighteenth century when musketeers or Banduqchis became part of it.[24]

Infantry were used primarily to garrison forts, especially as musketeers became more popular. Some of these were not native Rajputs but mercenaries; Pathans, Rohillas or Sikhs. Nevertheless, Rajput garrisons would often put up stern resistance to any attacks and by the late eighteenth century bands of Rajput mercenaries were not infrequently used as garrison troops.

The Jats of Bhurtpore

Like other successor states that of the Jats, centred upon their fortress city of Bhurtpore, gained de facto independence in the first half of the eighteenth century. Initially their struggle for independence had been tribe, village and clan based, and led by small landowners and tradesmen rather than local Mughal nobles making a bid for personal power. To start with their guerrilla forces consisted of bands of well-armed peasants, but soon improved and increased so that Maharaja Suraj Mal fielded 6,000 cavalry for one engagement on New Year's Day 1750. The Jat tactics were somewhat innovative: '… their mounted matchlockmen closed in small bodies and discharged volleys upon the confused Muslim troopers without dismounting. Such a mobile force as Suraj Mal's mounted matchlockmen could hardly be brought to grapple in the darkness of night.'[25]

It seems unlikely that the Mughal cavalry were using the bow to any significant extent here, or they could have made a useful reply. Jat infantry also had more importance than in Mughal armies, probably because of the small farmer and small landowner heritage of the Jat people. Their great fortress city of Bhurtpore was garrisoned by infantry and guns, in the Mughal style.

At the siege of another of their fortress towns, Kumher, in 1754 the Jat infantry and labourers actually increased the size of their defences during the siege at the expense of the Mughal attackers.[26] The garrison of this place – whence many of the Jat clans had repaired under Mughal pressure – may have been as large as 50,000 men, but this probably includes non-combatants as well as the general population. What is clear is that most of the garrison were infantry.

Expeditionary forces, such as those against the Rohillas in late 1750 and again in 1751 in temporary alliance with both Mughals and Marathas, seem to have consisted largely of the aforementioned mounted musketeers. However, in response to the Afghan invasion Maharaja Suraj Mal gathered

---

24   R. K. Saxena, *The Army of the Rajputs – A Study of 18th Century Rajputana* (Udaipur: Saroj Prakashan, 1989), pp.215–216.
25   Natwar-Singh, *Suraj Mal*, p.35.
26   Natwar-Singh, *Suraj Mal*, p.51.

a force of 30,000 of all arms.[27] Suraj Mal's successors as *Maharaja* were often allied with the Marathas, seemingly as a counterpoint to the Rajputs. The Jats would provide many recruits for the new mercenary battalions.

The Marathas

Traditionally in the usual Anglo-centric view, Maratha armies consisted of swarms of light cavalry armed with lances or matchlock muskets and swords. They mostly lacked armour and their small 'country-bred' ponies, while hardy and able to travel long distance, were not of sufficient size or weight for the line of battle. Like many traditional views this is only partly true.

The first Maratha forces under Shivaji the Great in the late seventeenth century actually had more infantry than cavalry. This is hardly surprising as the first campaigns against the Mughals were in mountainous areas where large numbers of ponderous Mughal cavalry could not operate effectively. Some of Shivaji's early forces were quite small by the usual Indian standards. In 1668, for a proposed expedition against Portuguese Goa, Shivaji commanded a force of 2,000 horse and 8–10,000 foot. In 1673 another army was a mere 2,000 horse and 4,000 foot. In 1675 for the siege of Phonda the army numbered 2,000 horse and 7,000 foot. Even into the eighteenth century after Shivali's death infantry could still dominate. In 1707 Dhanaji Jadhav, one of Shivaji's generals, had an army of 25,000 foot but a mere 5,000 horse.[28] For these earlier campaign all the troops were mostly if not all native Marathas.

As Maratha controlled territory expanded these ratios were to change dramatically and the numbers of Maratha cavalry increased at the expense of the infantry forces. By the mid-eighteenth century Maratha expeditions or raids to collect their *chauth,* or tribute, were almost entirely cavalry. Infantry remained to garrison forts and towns but cavalry were the main striking force. These raiding parties could be several thousand strong and penetrated as far north-east as Bengal, and east and south into the Deccan. Indeed, in the decades before the fateful battle of Panipat in 1761 Maratha expansion was both extensive and rapid, with much of the subcontinent at least partially under their sway. They collided with the successor state of Hyderabad under its *nizam* and caused that ruler to give up significant portions of his territory. For a short time they even controlled, after a fashion, the Emperor in Delhi and as far north-west as Lahore in the Punjab.

However, much of this cavalry was not 'battle' cavalry in the Mughal style but rather raiders and skirmishing light horse. In 1787 the Portuguese reported that the Marathas could field 80–100,000 horse 40–50 guns but only 10,000 foot.[29] This decline in infantry was common in the Marathas forces for much of the eighteenth century. Many of the remaining infantry were

---

27 James Grant Duff, *A History of the Mahrattas* (New Delhi: Associated Publishing House, 1982), Vol.1, p.400.
28 Surendra Nath Sen, *The Military System of the Marathas* (Delhi: K.P. Biacchi & Co, 1979), p.64.
29 Sen, *Military System*, p.62.

non-Marathas. Tone commented: 'I shall now offer some observations on the state of Marathas armies as far as respects their foot establishments. In the various Marathas services there are very little more than a bare majority who are Marathas by caste; and very few instances occur of their ever entering the infantry at all.'[30]

So, the Marathas became famous for their fast moving and rapacious cavalry. Guerrilla warfare was their forte, the *gamini kawa* (or light foray tactics) were the favourite tactical method of many of the Maratha *sardars*. Yet for all their skill at raiding and extortion they could be a very fickle and unreliable battlefield cavalry, many lacking armour and ready to flee when under pressure. Yet again this was not the whole story. In theory the Maratha cavalry was divided into four distinct classes. The first, the *kala-paga*, were the picked cavalry of the *Peshwa*, paid by the state. Their numbers were always small. Of the 55,000 Maratha cavalry at the Battle of Panipat only 11,000 were of this class, but they were the elite of the Maratha horse and capable battlefield cavalry, armoured, and carrying lance and sword. Every major Maratha ruler would also have his own band of *kala-paga* horse of varying strength, depending upon his finances. Next in quality and importance came the *sillhadars* who were under contract to the state for the period of the campaign. These could also be reasonably capable though, being *sillhadar* cavalry and owning their own horse and equipment, they might be somewhat more fragile on the battlefield. Their performance would often depend heavily on the quality of their immediate commander and his ability to equip his men. Third in importance were the individual volunteers who also supplied their own horse and weapons, and consequently were similarly loath to risk these in battle. These too were, in theory, paid for the duration of the campaign. Finally, there were the *pindaris* – unpaid and only joining for loot and plunder. As battlefield cavalry they were usually useless; being the first to flee. This last grouping became more numerous in the latter part of the century. Indeed, in the Second Anglo-Maratha war of 1803–1805 Jaswant Rao Holkar's forces contained many thousands of these mounted bandits. In addition, Holkar's Muslim general Amir Khan commanded several thousand Pathan mercenaries, mostly horse but including some Pathan and Rohilla matchlock armed infantry.

A Maratha Soldier. A view of a dismounted cavalry trooper. Probably a volunteer, or even a *pindari*. (Public Domain)

---

30 Tone, *Illustrations*, p.44.

Most of the first three classes of Maratha cavalry would of course be native Marathas, though as the eighteenth century progressed the numbers of actual Marathas would fall. The fourth class, the *pindaris*, was always open to any plunderer with a horse and a sword.

In addition to the Rohilla and Pathan mercenaries Arabs were also found in Maratha armies. They were used as garrisons of fortresses and were mostly infantry, but there were some Arab cavalry. These Arabs were undisciplined and frequently savage fighters and plunderers. Even so, the infantry were paid, at least in theory, 15–16 rupees per month though, as usual, their pay was in arrears.[31]

Yet despite their skill at, and propensity for, raiding and guerrilla warfare the very expansion of Maratha controlled territory caused the Maratha high command to change its methods. The *Peshwa* and many of the higher nobles adopted the Mughal way of making war. For these men this meant attaching to themselves large camp equipages with all the pomp and paraphernalia of an Imperial court on the move. So, while smaller raiding parties could still move with fearsome speed the larger armies of the *Peshwa* and some of his generals would crawl along at the same snail's pace of any other Indian army. This was to have some serious and fatal consequences.

Military Developments of the Second Half of the Eighteenth Century: The Coming of the Mercenaries

Mercenary soldiers had been a feature of Indian warfare since at least the time of Tamerlane, if not before. In the Mughal period Persians, Turks and Afghans were all in the service of the Emperor and his various *satraps*. Even European mercenaries had been present since the later sixteenth century, usually serving as gunners or technicians. At first these were mostly Portuguese but even as early as the 1650s English and French gunners were to be found in Mughal and successor state armies.[32] Numbers were usually small, Clement Downing – in the service of Mughal General Rustram Ali Khan in 1722 – is one of three English artillery 'captains' with this army and like most of his contemporaries, and indeed predecessors, was an ex-sailor; in his case temporarily on the run for some unknown misdemeanour, possibly desertion.[33]

The appearance of the European trained infantry on Indian battlefields was to significantly change the mercenary scene from the middle of the eighteenth century onwards. The idea that these 'trained brigades' were battle winners would, without doubt, become a major feature of Indian warfare in the latter half of the century. Yet the first of these trained brigades was not raised by a European at all but by a 'Decani Moslem' by the name of Ibrahim Khan and his kinsman Muzaffar Khan. Both men had seen service under the French in the Carnatic and had risen to command French trained

---

31 Sen, *Military System*, p.66.
32 Irvine, *The Army of the Indian Moghuls*, pp.152–154.
33 Foster, *Indian Wars*, pp.141–145.

sepoy units. Muzaffar deserted the French service and took service with the Maratha *Peshwa*, Balaji Baj Rao, as early as 1752 and raised a corps of Sepoys which he commanded.[34] These men were non-Marathas and trained in the French manner. This corps had some success, but Muzaffar was eventually executed for a failed plot against his employers in 1759. Ibrahim Khan also had his own corps and for a while the two 'brigades' seem to have existed side by side, but by 1759 they were united under Ibrahim Khan at 10,000 infantry and artillerymen with their own guns organised as 10 battalions with European flintlocks and bayonets. They became known as *gardis* as the word had already attached itself to Ibrahim Khan as he had apparently been one of the French commander the Marquis de Bussy's guard company so that he comes down to us as Ibrahim Khan Gardi. As was usual in Indian warfare the guns were moved by oxen and this of course slowed down these new *gardis* to the speed of their ponderous artillery train, even though the guns were on European style carriages. However, in battle these guns may have been moved by men known as *kelsais* (sometimes spelled clashies by European writers) to differentiate them from the actual gunners, or *goladauz*. Somewhat later as we shall see General Benoit De Boigne's guns were certainly moved on the battlefield this way and there is no reason to suppose that Ibrahim Khan did not use this method. This may have enabled his guns to keep pace with his infantry. Nevertheless, on the march artillery was still moved at the speed of oxen. This slow movement of a large and cumbersome army burdened with artillery and other impedimenta went entirely against the customary style of Maratha fast moving cavalry-raiding warfare. This difference in the two modes of fighting was to cost Ibrahim Khan Gardi his life, and the Marathas upwards of 30,000 casualties.

Yet at first all seemed well with these new troops Sen makes the point that the Mahratta victory at Udgir in 1760 over the forces of the *Nizam* of Hyderabad was due in large part to 5,000 of these new *gardis*.[35] Yet Grant Duff tells us that, despite the Mahratta victory over the outnumbered enemy and the European style efficiency of Ibrahim Khan's artillery, the *gardis* lost 11 colours in the battle and were severely handled by 'a desperate charge' of cavalry.[36] Despite this, Ibrahim Khan's corps remained in being and when the Maratha's Deccan forces marched north for the Panipat campaign they were noted as 10,000 strong with 20,000 Maratha horse accompanying them.

The campaign and battle of Panipat of January 1761 hangs over eighteenth century Indian history like a pall. There is no escaping the bare facts of it happening, and of victory and defeat, but its longer-term results are another matter. It was a large battle with the Marathas calling in troops from all over their territories to repel the Afghan invaders led by Ahmed Shah Abdali (who would shortly change his name to Ahmed Shah Dourani, they are in fact one and the same). So, for the campaign the Marathas could count on a considerable army: 'The Marathas have been reckoned at 55,000 horse and 15,000 foot with 200 pieces of cannon with rockets and shuternals [camel guns

---

34 Grant Duff, *History of the Marathas*, Vol.1, p.364.
35 Sen, *Military System*, p.114.
36 Grant Duff, *History of the Marathas*, Vol.1, p.390.

or *zambureks*] without number besides their 15,000 Pindarees and followers of whom there are supposed to have been upwards of 200,000 souls.'[37]

As we have seen 10,000 or so of the infantry were the *gardis* of Ibrahim Khan the remainder being more traditional, but still largely non-Maratha, irregular infantry bands of varied and sometimes dubious quality.

By a series of strategic errors compounded by internecine squabbles the Maratha forces managed to get themselves into the unenviable tactical position of being stuck in a fortified camp, based around the town of Panipat roughly 60 kilometres north-east of Delhi. The original Maratha plan seems to have been to re-occupy Delhi, which was easily done, and then to move toward the town of Panipat and force the Afghans to fight simply by entrenching themselves there and cutting off the Afghan supplies. However, Maratha overconfidence led to the reverse being the case.[38] This came about as the Afghan cavalry were at least as mobile as that of the Marathas and significantly less likely to avoid a fight. After a couple of months in the same location the Maratha forces were slowly starving to death because they had 'eaten up' the surrounding territory and no more provisions could be had. They were blockaded by the Afghan forces and despite the Marathas launching several successful raids on their enemy's equally fortified camp in November 1760 they had not been able to score a truly decisive success. They had also managed to alienate the local population by their depredations and even one-time allies – such as the *Maharaja* Suraj Mal of the Jats –had removed their contingents from the army because no common strategy could be agreed.

The two sides of the tactical and strategic argument ran thus. Suraj Mal, the Jat *maharaja* and some of the Maratha leadership, most notably Mulhar Rao Holkar, were in favour of the continued use of the guerrilla style of cavalry raiding warfare against the Muslim supply lines and detachments. This mode of warfare, traditional to the Marathas, had already had some success against the Afghan invaders and their local Muslim allies. However, the Maratha commander Sewdasheo Rao Bhao (also known as the Bhao Sahib), wished to remain in his heavily fortified camp for a number of reasons. Partly because of his personal enmity to Holkar, but also because of the huge baggage train his army had with it, including many ladies of noble birth and the almost innumerable mass of camp followers. Couple this with the insistence – complete with threats of violence – from Ibrahim Khan that his *gardis* could win the day and, perhaps most tellingly, a letter to the Bhao Sahib from the *Peshwa* which said: 'You must destroy the enemy finally and hold all the Territory up to the Indus. On no account should you make friends with Abdali.'[39] In effect this gave the Marathas little option except to fight, especially as the *Peshwa* was, it was believed, collecting more forces to come to the Bhao Sahib's relief.

---

37 Grant Duff, *History of the Marathas*, Vol.1, p.402.
38 Sen, *Military System*, pp.148–149.
39 H.G. Rawlinson, *An Account of the Last Battle of Panipat and the Events Leading up to it. Written in Persian by Casi Raja Pundit who was present at the battle.* (Oxford: Oxford University Press, 1926), p.18.

For these reasons then Sewdasheo Rao Bhao despised the guerrilla strategy, with the upshot that Suraj Mal withdrew his 30,000 men from the Hindu host and returned to his own territory around Bhurtpore. Since the Rajputs had also withdrawn their troops (leaving only around 2,000 in Delhi with some 6,000 Maratha horse as a garrison) because of their distrust of Maratha intentions, the upcoming battle would be a fight between the Afghan Muslim invaders with their local allies and a Hindu Maratha army with its body of non-Maratha mercenary European style infantry led by a Muslim commander.

The Afghan army was formidable by the contemporary standards of the military art of the northern half of the Indian subcontinent. It comprised of 41,800 horse and 38,000 foot with roughly 70–80 guns.[40] Many of the cavalry were of the heavy type, mail armoured 'battle' cavalry, and a significant number of the foot were Afghan and Rohilla matchlockmen but also included chosen bodies of Persian musketeers. The Afghan forces had been joined by those of the *Nawab* of Oudh and several Rohilla chieftains. This Allied host also comprised of around 2,000 *zamburek* camel guns and the same number of rocketmen. Many of the latter being Rohillas. How many of these impressive numbers were actually combat troops is impossible to ascertain but the combined Muslim armies were certainly formidable and unlike the, by now, increasingly desperate Marathas, able to draw on local food supplies to feed their host.

Indeed as 1760 became 1761 the Marathas realised their stark choice; fight or starve. Therefore, on 14 January 1761 the Marathas marched out of their camp in battle array to confront the Afghan army. There seems to have been an air of desperation in the Maratha camp. In the evening before they marched forth the Maratha leaders distributed the very last of their food so that their men might have a final meal before the battle.[41] The battlefield for the upcoming engagement was a wide, flat, featureless sandy plain. As the Maratha army advanced the Afghan forces came out of their camp in response. Each army was formed in several distinct divisions in a single line. Eight divisions for the Marathas and nine for the Afghans and their allies. The Afghans however had a tenth division around Ahmed Shah's tent consisting of his bodyguard cavalry.

Both armies deployed in traditional fashion with artillery to the fore and massed bodies of troops behind the guns, though the Afghans seem to have had *zambereks* and Persian sharpshooters interspersed with their gun line, in advance of their main line of battle.[42] On the Maratha left the drilled battalions of the *gardis* imposed an almost European notion of order to the array but otherwise this was to be an encounter between more or less traditional Indian armies with personal and almost heroic medieval styles of leadership. As was traditional the battle opened with a mutual cannonade, including rockets and camel mounted *zambureks*. Then Ibrahim Khan advanced his division which, on the day of battle, consisted of 9,000 infantry

---

40 Grant Duff, *History of the Marathas*, Vol.1, p.402.
41 Grant Duff, *History of the Marathas*, Vol.1, p.404.
42 Rawlinson, *Last Battle of Panipat*, pp.34–35.

in nine battalions with 'firelocks and bayonets', and 40 guns with 2,000 cavalry all 'disciplined after the European manner.'[43] These troops advanced against their opposite numbers with seven of his battalions, leaving the remaining two to guard his outermost flank. The opposition being the Rohilla divisions of Dhoondy Khan and Hafiz Ramut Khan. In a hard three hour fight the *gardis* caused some 8,000 Rohilla casualties at the cost of almost half of their own men, pushing back the Rohillas so that 'few of the people remained with their Chiefs.'[44]

In the centre of the Maratha line the Bhow Sahib's division – consisting of the *kala-paga* household troops backed up by 7,000 of his brother-in-law's cavalry – launched a furious charge against the division of Ahmed Shah's Grand Vizier, Shah Vulli Khan, dispersing much of it back to the Durrani camp and past the tent of Ahmed Shah Durrani who had set up his command post with his bodyguards behind the main Afghan line. At this point the Marathas were on the verge of a great victory. Kasi Raj, a *mutasaddi* (secretary) in the service of Shuja-ud-daulah, *Nawab* of Oudh, wrote that his master:

> … could not see what was going om, on account of the dust, but finding sound of men and horses in the quarter suddenly diminish, he sent me to examine the cause. I found the Grand Vizier in an agony of rage and despair reproaching his men for quitting him. 'Our country is far off my friends, wither do you fly.'[45]

The Afghan line was looking distinctly shaky despite the efforts of the Afghan and Rohilla troops on the left of their line who had managed to hold off the Maratha cavalry using quickly dug temporary earthworks and by the firing of volleys of rockets, apparently up to 2,000 at a time, which disordered the approaching Maratha horse as well as causing significant casualties.

At this point, early in the afternoon, the battle was possibly the Maratha's to win, but Ahmed Shah was the better soldier and now he proved it. Gathering his bodyguard of heavy armoured cavalry about him he sent a detachment to scour his own camp for fugitives and skulkers to get them back into the fight or be executed where they stood, and with the rest of his bodyguard and other troops from the reserve around his tent he ordered a charge at the tired and disorganised Maratha centre. This charge was supported by the left wing who took the Bhow's division in the flank and smashed it into flying remnants.

The pursuit was relentless and bloody. The prisoners, contemporary accounts say upwards of 40,000 were killed including Ibrahim Khan Gardi who, badly wounded, fell into Afghan hands.[46] The Maratha high command was almost wiped out. The coded message to the *Peshwa* telling of the cataclysmic defeat read: 'Two pearls have been dissolved twenty-seven Gold Mohurs have been lost, and of the silver and copper the total cannot be cast

---

43   Rawlinson, *Last Battle of Panipat*, p.19.
44   Rawlinson, *Last Battle of Panipat*, p.36.
45   Rawlinson, *Last Battle of Panipat*, p.37.
46   Rawlinson, *Last Battle of Panipat*, p.40.

up.'⁴⁷ Indicating the huge losses not only amongst the high command – the two pearls and 27 Gold Mohurs – but also of the lesser officers and soldiers, the silver and copper.

The results of the battle are somewhat harder to ascertain. At the very least the Marathas lost their hold on northern India, but Hindustan did not fall into the hands of the Afghans. By late March 1761 the victorious allies had broken up their forces to take their considerable loot home. Ahmed Shah Durrani would not come to Hindustan again. The main result of the battle was, in effect, to create a temporary power vacuum. In Delhi the Emperor continued to sit on his shaky throne and the various successor states such as the those of Oudh and the Rohilla lands, and even the slowly rising power of the Sikhs in the Punjab far to the west, had nothing to fear from the currently prostrate Marathas who had been sent tumbling back south of the River Nerbudda. Indeed, so disconcerted was he by the terrible news that the reigning *Peshwa* returned to his city of Poona and expired there at the end of June 1761.

The lack of strong leadership in the north of India also meant that organised resistance to the encroaching British power was somewhat patchy to say the least. In the decade after Panipat, the British succeeded in destroying the French and further extending their own territorial holdings, especially in Bengal, where by 1770 they were in complete control.

In the longer term however, the battle was merely a bump in the Maratha road to power (albeit a serious one). While many of the Maratha leaders had been killed Madhaji Scindia, although wounded, had survived. If Panipat did anything it cleared Madhaji's way to power for the house of Scindia. Never again would the *Peshwas* be as powerful as they had been before the battle. Panipat also had the result of splintering the always fragile Maratha show of unity. The rivalry between the houses of Holkar and Scindia would increase and eventually flare into open warfare later in the century. Both sides in this internecine conflict would use European trained brigades. Almost as serious a rivalry would erupt between Madhaji and Nana Phadnis another survivor of Panipat. This man would exert his considerable political skill in controlling the now almost puppet *Peshwas* with himself as effective prime minister and constant intriguer against the rising power of Madhaji Scindia.

In the next decade Scindia used all his considerable political and military skill to rebuild his power. Even the rather scrappy and indecisive First Anglo-Maratha war with the British from 1775 to 1782 did not do more than slow this rebuilding, though it may have added to his determination to have a military force more reliable (and loyal) than the flighty Maratha cavalry. Captain William Popham's astonishing coup de main against Scindia's 'impregnable' fortress of Gwalior, where, on 3 August 1780, he led 1,200 *sepoys* up the cliffs and over the walls, thereby capturing the fortress and garrison without firing a shot or losing a man, could not fail to impress a ruler who had already seen British trained infantry scatter Maratha horse as well as seeing the 'almost success' of Ibrahim Khan Gardi at Panipat. What could he not do with troops trained in this manner who were loyal to the House of Scindia?

---

47 Grant Duff, *History of the Marathas*, Vol.1, p.409.

3

The Man from Savoy: The Making of a Military Entrepreneur

While this is not the place for a complete biography of the future commander of the Army of Hindustan, a sketch of the life and career of Benoit De Boigne prior to his entering mercenary service in India shows how an Italian middle class merchant's son came to a position where he was able to command a well trained and equipped army which would eventually be 30,000 strong.

The soldier of fortune who would become the greatest military entrepreneur of late eighteenth century India was not born to a military family. Born in Chambery, Savoy, on 8 March 1751 Benoit La Borgne was the son of a hide merchant and furrier of considerable success.[1] This success gave young Benoit a reasonable education at the Royal College in Chambery where he seems to have stayed longer than other boys of his bourgeois origin. His father having died when he was 14, his mother wished him to become a lawyer. This was not the career he sought. He was a high-spirited youth – being once charged with assaulting the watch – and soldiering seems to have caught his imagination early on, and whilst a commission in the army of Charles Emmanuel of Savoy was denied him due to his parentage, a similar post in the Irish Brigade of the Royal French Army was not and he duly entered that service in 1770 as an ensign at the age of 18 or 19. It was at this time that Signor La Borgne became Monsieur De Boigne, so from now on he was Benoit De Boigne.

He served for three years in Regiment Clare of the Irish Brigade, one of the famous 'Wild Geese' regiments of the eighteenth century French army. By the 1770s this brigade was no longer exclusively Irish in composition, but it was still an elite formation within the Army. De Boigne had a sojourn in Mauritius with his regiment but saw no active service and despite learning the basics of soldiering, peacetime service was not for him, so he resigned his commission to take up a captaincy in the Russian forces then fighting

---

1   Young, *Fountain of the Elephants*, pp.17–22.

THE MAN FROM SAVOY

the Ottoman Empire in the Mediterranean. De Boigne became an officer in a battalion of Greek levies being raised by the Russian Admiral Orlov. This kind of multi-national force was by no means as unusual in the eighteenth century as it seems to us today. Mere nationality was not seen as quite so important as loyalty and ability – loyalty being to one's paymaster rather than to a cause or country. However, De Boigne was to come seriously unstuck in his first action being captured by the Turkish garrison of the island of Tenedos during a botched raid on that island by his unit. Carried off as a prisoner to the Turkish held Greek island of Chios, De Boigne had a small stroke of luck. It was here he made the acquaintance of Lord Algernon Percy, brother of the Duke of Northumberland, who was, like many English gentlemen of the period, making the Grand Tour of Europe for his education. Percy was to render De Boigne an 'essential service' by organising his release and just perhaps paying any ransom demanded by the Turks.[2]

General Benoit de Boigne. This image shows the General after he returned to Europe. (Public Domain)

At any event De Boigne was released towards the end of 1774 and for three years nothing much is heard of him. That he travelled in the Middle East is possible, and that he may have gone to the court of Catherine the Great to propose a project to reconnoitre and survey an overland route to India is propounded by Young on some circumstantial evidence.[3] What is certain is that he next appears as a victim of shipwreck in Egypt and is assisted by George Baldwin, sometime British consul-general in Cairo and an employee of the East India Company, to journey on to Madras where he arrives, almost penniless, in January 1778.[4]

Madras in the late eighteenth century was a town 'on the make', money and the acquisition of money was its *raison d'etre*. It was the oldest of the East India Company presidencies (first fortified in 1642) but had recently lost its past supremacy to Bengal where the new governor general, Warren Hastings, now resided. Nevertheless, Madras was a thriving commercial centre run as a sort of closed shop by the East India Company. Landing a couple of years later, actually in March 1780, Lieutenant Innes Munro of the British 71st Regiment of Foot had a mixed impression of the place:

---

2   Young, *Fountain of the Elephants*, p.29. There was a story, current in De Boigne's later life in Savoy, that he was a slave of the Turks and was ransomed by his parents, and that he then travelled to St Petersburg. See Charles Raikes, *Notes on the North-Western Provinces of India* (London: Chapman & Hall, 1852).
3   Young, *Fountain of the Elephants*, pp.31–35.
4   Bidwell, *Swords for Hire*, p.19.

> The Town is regularly built and capable of lodging eight thousand men in time of siege, though the present garrison seldom exceeds two hundred Europeans and two battalions of Sepoys. It is an inconvenient place for strangers there being no taverns or any decent place of public accommodation. Nor can the hospitality of the inhabitants be much boasted of: though they gain greatly upon acquaintance. I think it would be commendable in the Company to establish a good Tavern or Lodging House in Madras, if it were only for the housing of their own Cadets upon their arrival in this country. Being destitute of friends and acquaintances, many are obliged to take up their residences in the Black Town which are little better than the 'spunging house' in London, where they must mix with all kinds of low company, a circumstance from which quarrels and fatal consequences often ensure.[5]

For a foreign adventurer with little money this was a daunting prospect, especially as some thought him a French, or even possibly a Russian spy. Doubtless De Boigne spent the first period of his life in Madras in the low company disparaged by Munro as, for a time, he was forced to make a precarious living as a fencing master; teaching swordsmanship to the young clerks and junior officers of the Company. However, after a few months, letters of introduction, provided by Baldwin bore fruit and De Boigne once again found a place in the profession of arms. In July 1778 he was commissioned as an ensign in the 6th Madras Native Infantry.

Each of the East India Company's three Presidencies maintained its own armed force. Over the preceding century or so these had grown from little more than a force of armed watchmen to three fully fledged armies each with both European and native regiments, armed and disciplined in the prevailing style of European armies of the eighteenth century. In the Madras presidency the first formal 'Battalions of Sepoys' were formed in 1758 (previously there had been individual companies) with European weapons and drill under European and native officers. When De Boigne joined the Madras army there were at least 18 of these battalions, mostly uniformed in red coats with blue turbans and different coloured facings – much like European troops of the time. Munro's description of the Madras *sepoys* in 1780 shows the kind of soldiers De Boigne was commanding at this time in the 6th Madras Native Infantry:

> Their uniforms have a very military appearance, consisting of a red Light Infantry jacket, a white waistcoat and a blue turban placed in a soldier like manner upon the head, edged round with a tape of the same colour as the facings and having a tassel at the lower corner. The Sepoy has a long blue sash, lightly girded round his loins with the edge passing between his legs and fastening behind. He wears a pair of white drawers, tightly fitted, coming half way down his thigh and being coloured at the lower end with a blue dye appears to be scalloped all round. A pair of sandals on his feet, white crossbelts, a firelock and bayonet complete the Sepoy's dress.[6]

---

5   Arthur Haley, *The Munro Letters* (Liverpool: Bullfinch Publications, 1992), pp.25–26.
6   Haley, *Munro Letters*, p.28.

Each of the Madras infantry battalions consisted of 10 companies, of which two were designated grenadiers. Unlike European infantry at this time, these native battalions had no light infantry companies. Despite De Boigne's relatively lowly rank of ensign, which was, of course, the lowest commissioned rank in most European armies of the period, his responsibilities as part of a native infantry battalion were somewhat different to the equivalent rank in a similar formation in the French or British armies in Europe. In the 6th De Boigne was one of only 11 European commissioned officers who along with 10 European sergeants made up the non-Indian portion of each native battalion. This of course assumes that the European complement was up to strength which was often not the case. There being, at least in 1777, a distinct shortage of junior officers in some battalions.[7] This of course meant that De Boigne's responsibilities were significantly greater than those of an officer of the same rank in a European battalion of the same period.

De Boigne remained with the 6th for almost four years but saw no action despite the war against Haidar Ali of Mysore in which his battalion was actively engaged. At the time of his unit's severest trial, he was on detached duty commanding the escort to a grain convoy.

By 1782 service with the Madras army had lost its lustre, if indeed it ever had any, and De Boigne was ready to resign. There seems to have been some scandal over 'taking undue liberties with the wife of a brother officer' but he was acquitted of these charges by court martial.[8] Nevertheless, he had decided to return to the Russian service by making an overland journey first to Delhi, then on to Lahore and through Afghanistan. In this he had the backing of the governor of Madras, Lord Macartney, a gentleman he had met during his Russian service, who supplied him with a letter of introduction to the great Warren Hastings in Calcutta:

> This letter will be delivered to you by Mr De Boigne an Officer formerly in the Russian Service, to which he is now returning. He has been in ours for some time past but seeing little prospect of rising has desired leave some months since to resign. His intention is to proceed to Delhi and Lahore and endeavour to get into Russia by a new Route, You will please to furnish him with any Passports which you may imagine will be of use to him in this undertaking.[9]

In May 1782 De Boigne resigned his commission and set off for Calcutta on what he believed to be the first stage of a journey to Russia.

However, events were about to take a somewhat strange turn. On arrival in Calcutta, De Boigne presented Macartney's letter to Warren Hastings, the governor general. According to Young they seem to have hit it off rather quickly, despite De Boigne being a relatively obscure former ensign. The evidence is circumstantial but De Boigne's Russian experience and the project to travel overland to Russia seems to have caught Hastings imagination.

---

7   Lt. Col. W.J. Wilson, *History of the Madras Army* (Madras: Government Press, 1888), Vol.1, p.364.
8   Young, *Fountain of the Elephants*, pp.41–42.
9   Young, *Fountain of the Elephants*, pp.43–44.

Young goes further and maintains that to all intents and purposes De Boigne became a British agent. De Boigne's sponsor in this affair, Lord Macartney, had significant experience of the Russian court, having previously been British ambassador there. Was the 'Russian Project' some early attempt at what Victorians would call 'The Great Game'? We cannot know, but the idea is tantalising.

At any event Hastings sped De Boigne forward with various passports and letters of introduction to both British representatives and local princes. De Boigne first travelled to Lucknow, capital of Oudh where he spent five months leaning Persian and Urdu – two languages which would be of value in his onward travels. It was here he encountered the Frenchman, Claud Martine, a man who was to become his lifelong friend and sometime business partner, Martine held the post of chief artificer to the *Nawab-Wazir* of Oudh, which effectively meant that he ran all the supplies for the *Nawab's* mostly unpaid and not infrequently mutinous army, and indeed much of the commercial life of the *Nawab's* court. Martine was an astute man of business and was in the process of amassing a considerable fortune. He would become an important part of De Boigne's life. De Boigne was also presented to the *Nawab-Wazir* who, on the recommendation of the British resident there, presented De Boigne with a *khilat*, or robe of honour, and letters of credit worth 12,000 rupees. The *khilat* was sold to provide another 4,000 rupees in ready cash. Thus fortified De Boigne continued his journey on towards Delhi but was 'delayed by the jealousy of the Emperor's ministers.'[10] In the company, therefore of David Anderson – the British resident – he proceeded to the camp of Madhaji Scindia, who was then besieging Gwalior. At this point he was robbed of his baggage by Madhaji's men and although all was restored at the insistence of Anderson, the letters of credit simply disappeared. Further progress on the journey to Russia was thus impossible.

Once again, De Boigne had only his sword to sell in order to make a living. However, this time he was not exactly friendless and after some abortive negotiations with the *Rana* of Gohad, from whom Scindia was trying to wrest Gwalior, and also with the Rajput *Rajah* of Jaipur (but this project was disapproved of by Hastings),[11] in late 1784 De Boigne accepted a contract from Madhaji Scindia to raise and command a force of two battalions of European trained infantry with appropriate artillery. There was a stipulation in the contract that these troops should not be used against the British. De Boigne was soldiering once again, this time as a mercenary.

---

10 Sir Evan Cotton, 'Benoit De Boigne' in *Proceedings of the Indian Historical Records Commission* (Calcutta: Government of India Central Publication Branch, 1927), Vol.IX, pp.14.

11 Cotton, 'De Boigne', p.14.

4

Building an Army from the Ground Up: De Boigne's First Campaign

Now that he had secured his first mercenary contract De Boigne faced a formidable task. Although the initial contract was for a mere two battalions and supporting artillery these units had to be raised, clothed, armed, and trained. Mercenary soldiering was not new, any more than European 'trained brigades' were new so De Boigne would be working in an environment that was already familiar to his employers. By the 1780s 'trained brigades' had become rather common in Indian armies, though their quality was decidedly variable. Ibrahim Khan's *gardis*, despite their defeat and destruction at Panipat, had left their mark in the minds of Indian statesmen and generals as had the operations of the European trained and disciplined Sepoys of both the British East India Company and the French *Compagnie Française pour le commerce des Indes orientales*. In the continuing political turmoil of the disintegrating Mughal Empire local rulers sought to increase and widen their military options. Trained and disciplined infantry therefore, seemed the best way of doing this in the changeable environment of late eighteenth century India. Also, it was somewhat fortuitous that the end of the Seven Years War left a significant number of former French soldiers scattered about India looking for a living to make so that, hopefully, one day, they could go home.

The effect that trained infantry had on the minds of Indian generals can be shown by a conversation between Lal Mohammed Khan and his master, the Maratha commander or *sardar* Appa Khande Rao, the same general who would be De Boigne's first army commander:

> You have raised an army as numerous as ants and locusts but these men are utterly useless without a stiffening of disciplined musketeers. A single British trained

and led *sepoy* battalion, when properly trained and handled, can drive away your 40,000 horse and foot like so many crows and kites.[1]

The demand for European officers to raise and train these troops was therefore considerable. However, it would be remiss if we did not also take into consideration those Indian commanders who also raised bodies of trained troops in imitation of Ibrahim Khan Gardi. One Jahangir Khan, amongst others, commanded a force of three battalions in Ranjit Singh Jat's service in 1788.[2] He later deserted to Ismael Beg. This same Ismael Beg had a commander known as Ramru who had four battalions and 16 guns. He also would change his allegiance – deserting to the Marathas at a critical time.

The blueprint for all of these 'trained brigades' was broadly similar; a group of European trained and disciplined infantry battalions with a varying number of guns. The guns, also European in style and with drilled crews in the European manner, were usually the main offensive power of these brigades. The artillery pieces themselves being lighter and more manoeuvrable than normal Indian artillery. The drilled and disciplined crews could, once trained, fire two or three times faster than the usual badly served guns of the Mughals or the local successor states. The infantry, whilst capable of offensive action were, therefore, frequently used in a supporting role to the guns, often to protect the gun line from the swarms of cavalry that the brigades would usually face on the battlefield. However, the infantry battalions were, of course, essential for the storming of the numerous forts and fortified towns which were such a feature of the warfare of the time.

The first full brigade sized force in northern India was raised by Walter Reinhart – alias 'Sombre' or more usually 'Somru.' He arrived in India as a sailor in the French navy, from which service he deserted and was then a multiple deserter from the forces of both the French and British companies. Apparently born in the village of Silbertal in Austria around 1720 he was in India by 1750, serving in the French forces in the Carnatic from which he deserted. He then moved north to Bengal, where he was for a short time in the British service before deserting again to join the French at Chandernagore, who gave him the rank of sergeant, but from whom he again deserted to sell his services to the various Indian princely states. Such was the desire to acquire European military expertise that many of the rulers and princes were not too choosy, and almost any European could find a job with one of the armies if they wanted one.[3]

In the service of Gurgan Khan, minister to the *Nawab* of Bengal, Somru, as he now called himself, raised a force of two battalions, trained in the French manner. By 1768 his force had grown to four battalions of infantry, a small cavalry regiment, and a strong complement of guns. However, his

---

1 Quoted in Sir Jadurnath Sarkar, 'De Boigne in India', in *The Proceedings of the Indian Historical Records Commission* (Calcutta: Government of India Central Publication Branch, 1938), Vol.XV, p.11.
2 Grant Duff, *History of the Marathas*, Vol.2, p.145.
3 Jorran Klassens, *European Mercenaries in the armies of Post-Mughal successor states 1775–1849: The Case of Acculturation,* Master's Thesis, Leiden University, 2018, p.36.

participation in the Patna massacre of that year, when he and his troops slaughtered British prisoners, meant that he had to keep well away from British territory. Not the least of Somru's skills was that of knowing exactly when to depart for pastures new. In the next few years Somru's brigade was in and out of the service of several Indian states including Oudh and Jaipur until finally it entered the service of Najaf Khan who was *Wazir* (or prime minister) to the Mughal Emperor Shah Alam II in Delhi. For his services he was paid a fee of 65,000 rupees a month which of course included the pay of his troops, as well as his own salary. He remained in Mughal service until he died in May 1778.

However, comparative wealth did not raise the quality of his battalions who were always in arrears for their pay. In extremis the unpaid soldiers would mutiny, sometimes, in desperation, setting a trouser-less Somru, astride a hot cannon barrel until he disgorged some of the money he owed them. This kind of behaviour did not make for military efficiency. With one observer noting: 'Sombre's party had never been conspicuous for their military achievements, nor famed for their military trophies: they never lost a gun nor ever gained one … but they were remarked for their excellent retreats.'[4]

In fact, Somru's brigade was defeated more than once, most notably when in the service of Nawal Singh the Jat *Maharaja* at the Battle of Barsana in 1773, during a war between the Mughals and the Jats of Bhurtpur, but was never actually destroyed and he was always able to recruit anew and rebuild his forces. Rene Medoc's brigade was also present at this battle in the service of the Mughal *Wazir* Najaf Khan, so the two mercenary brigades fought each other.[5]

After his death Somru's brigade survived under the titular command of his Indian wife Farzana, the *Begum* Somru, who employed various European officers to command the troops in action. She would eventually be known as the Princess of Sardhana, a territory granted to her husband when in Mughal service as a means of paying his troops, which in the chaos of the time this clever and intelligent, one-time dancing girl, hung on to and turned into a small independent principality which even the British did not remove from her. She even increased the size of the brigade so that by September 1803 it consisted of 4,000 infantry in six battalions, 200 cavalry and 30–40 guns.

Raised only a few years later the similar 'brigade' led by the French mercenary Rene Medoc or Madec was of comparable composition being of five battalions, 20 guns and 500 cavalry. Like Somru's brigade each battalion had a European commander and one or two European junior officers. Also, in theory, there were European NCOs in charge of each gun crew but many of these in the parlance of the time were 'country born', or in other words of mixed heritage. The brigade suffered at least one disaster when in 1776 it

---

4   Lewis Ferdinand Smith, *A Sketch of the Rise, Progress and Termination of the Regular Corps formed and Commanded by Europeans in the Service of the Native Princes of India* (Calcutta: Greenway, 1805), p.5.
5   Lester Hutchinson, *European Freebooters in Moghul India* (London: Asia Publishing House, 1964), p.23.

was ambushed by 1,500 Rohillas in a ravine during a rainstorm, losing 12 of its European officers killed or wounded and all of its guns.[6] Medoc himself narrowly escaped, eventually reaching the city of Agra where he raised and trained a second somewhat smaller force which he sold lock, stock and barrel to a Jat chieftain, the *Rana* of Gohad in 1782. He then retired to France with the proceeds. This new unit was then commanded by Major George Sangster, a Scot, and a man of considerable technical skill who was to be of significant importance to the Army of Hindustan.

There were other mercenary trained forces available in the mercenary market. The Maharaja of Bhurtpur had a force of three battalions, commanded by a Monsieur Lestineau composed of tough Jat infantry along with another six or so battalions commanded by Muslim mercenaries in imitation of Ibrahim Khan's famous *gardis*. These also would be of some importance in De Boigne's early career.

So as the preceding paragraphs indicate, De Boigne was doing nothing revolutionary. However, he would take the accepted system and make it work efficiently and well. The troops he would eventually raise and train would become the best armed, organised, equipped and most importantly, paid, army outside the British territories and would enable Madhaji Scindia to become de facto ruler of the remains of the Mughal Empire, as well as the strongest member of the often squabbling Maratha Confederacy.

But first De Boigne had to raise and train the two battalions and the appropriate artillery for his current first contract:

> The Commission he received from Madhaji was to raise two battalions of disciplined infantry with a suitable complement of artillery. He was to receive 8 rupees a month for each soldier in the force and his own pay was fixed at Rs 1000 per mensem. The Battalions were to consist of 850 men each and be formed as nearly as possible upon the lines of those in the Companies service with similar accoutrements, arms, and discipline…[7]

Only in one particular was De Boigne unmoveable. Under no circumstance would he or his troops fight the British.

Recruits were the easy part. Soldiering was an honourable profession in India and in such disordered times *sepoys* and *golandauz* (gunners) were easy to find, as were the *kelasis* who would manhandle and move the guns on the battlefield. Doubtless some had seen service with other brigades or were former East India Company *sepoys*, but we cannot know for sure. What is certain is that none of these infantry or gunners were Marathas. Infantry recruits came from the area around the city of Agra and from Oudh, the nursery of *sepoys* for the Bengal army in later years. In the troublesome times of the last quarter of the eighteenth century even the prospect of regular pay was a significant inducement for recruitment.

---

6   Smith, *Regular Corps*, p.6, and Hebert Compton, *A Particular Account of the European Military Adventurers of Hindustan* (London: Fisher Unwin, 1893) p.371.
7   Compton, *Particular Account*, p.31.

As for the European officers, these were somewhat harder to find, especially for a new formation such as De Boigne's. Nevertheless, the Scot Sangster came in and because of his technical skill as a cannon founder and small arms maker was installed as foundry master and arms manufacturer. This enterprise alone was to grow significantly until Sangster oversaw a major arms manufactory capable of turning out cannon and flintlock muskets as well as other arms in sufficient quantities for the whole of the army. However, we are jumping ahead somewhat as in 1784 much of this was still in the future. The initial two battalions each needed a European commander and possibly a couple of junior officers as well. The later, somewhat smaller, battalions had a European commander and a European second in command ranked as captain and lieutenant respectively. Earlier brigades had a similar structure, to judge by Medoc's casualties when his brigade was ambushed by the Rohillas. His five Battalions suffered a total of 12 European officer casualties.

It would therefore seem unlikely that De Boigne or his paymaster departed far from this known structure. The first commanders of these two battalions were Jan, or John, Hessing a Dutch officer, and one Monsieur Fremont a French mercenary. Both were men who had previous experience; Hessing had been in the subcontinent since the 1760s serving various Princes and Fremont had been a junior Officer in the French garrison of Chandernagore.[8] Both of these men would be with De Boigne for a considerable time.

Even so De Boigne spent a little over six months putting together these first two battalions and their associated artillery.[9] We do not have a detailed table of organisation for these early units, but a few clues may enable us to reconstruct some details of these first battalions.

As we have seen De Boigne's contract called for the battalions to be like those of the East India Company. De Boigne had served with the Madras army of the EIC therefore it seems logical that these two battalions would have a similar organisation to those units he was familiar with. This logic would therefore give each battalion 10 companies of which two were grenadier companies with a somewhat higher status and a little higher pay than that of the other eight line or centre companies. This conjecture is supported by the fact that the later battalions definitely had grenadier companies, who were paid at a slightly higher rate than the others in their respective battalions. The 10 companies were entirely under the direction of, and commanded by, native officers. Each company was commanded by a *jemadar* (lieutenants) with *havildars* (sergeants) and *naigues* or *naiks* (corporals) as NCOs. The administrative and technical staffs of the battalion such as armourers (to maintain the weapons), pay masters and secretaries were all, of course, locally recruited. De Boignes later battalions actually had only eight companies so it is entirely possible that these first two units also had only eight companies each, but we cannot be certain.

---

8   Though Young says Fremont did not join De Boigne until 1790. If this is so then, so far, the identity of the other battalion commander is obscure, though there is a chance that at this early date it may have been Sangster.
9   Young, *Fountain of the Elephants*, p.81.

The artillery component of the formation was organised somewhat differently. In De Boigne's later brigades each battalion had its own artillery element of four cannons and a howitzer, with appropriate crews and ammunition waggons, or tumbrils. The earlier brigades of Somru and Medoc averaged four or five guns per infantry battalion so we might conjecture that at this point in 1785 De Boigne's new formation also had four or five guns per battalion.

After six months training these two battalions with their artillery and transport were a compact trained – but untried – force of around 2,000 men and were ready to take the field for the first time sometime in 1785. Bidwell makes much of De Boigne's supposed use of Dundas' *Principles of Military Movements* as his drill book and training aid.[10] This is, however, simply not possible as Dundas' work would not be published in England until 1788. Since his pattern was, as his contract tells us, the Madras Army then it is far more likely that he used the same system of drill as in that force. This would be similar to the British regulations of April 1756 or their 'entirely corrected and enlarged' edition of 1758.[11] These regulations emphasised the use of close-range fire both by subunits within the battalion and also, at need, by volley fire of two of the battalions with three ranks firing at once. In the British service infantry fire was usually delivered at very close range; 50 metres or less being the optimum. Blasts of close-range fire in this manner had emptied many a saddle on the battlefields of Europe and three rounds a minute meant that the rate of fire was significantly higher than anything De Boigne was likely to meet on an Indian battlefield.

What was astonishing here was that, at least to begin with, De Boigne had to do all of the training and administration himself. This entailed an immense amount of work. Young wrote:

> De Boigne had to start from scratch to form two battalions 'as nearly as possible on the plan of those in the English service and armed, disciplined and clothed in that manner.' His reflection that 'the labour which this imposed on an individual may be easily conceived by any person acquainted with military affairs" will not be challenged.[12]

Not the easiest task of the many that confronted De Boigne was that of extracting the money needed to pay and equip this new force with its muskets of English manufacture and red uniforms made with cloth from Calcutta, from his Maratha paymasters. Financial practice in the Maratha confederacy was convoluted to say the least. The various generals and chieftains, like any government, were always loth to part with ready money. De Boigne's immediate commander, once his force was actually in the field, the Maratha general Appa Khande Rao, was no exception. De Boigne's first campaign was

---

10　Col. David Dundas, *Principles of Military Movements* (London: Cadell, 1788).
11　David Blackmore, *Destructive and Formidable: British Infantry Firepower 1642–1765* (London: Frontline, 2014), p128.
12　Young, *Fountain of the Elephants*, p.80. Young's quotations are from the few surviving letters of De Boigne's which he had access to.

more a kind of live firing exercise than a major campaign, being, in fact, a punitive expedition against various minor *rajas* and landowners who were refusing to pay their *chauth* to their Maratha overlords. This kind of expedition was the small change of Maratha military life, but it would give De Boigne time to shake down his new command. Despite the contempt in which the Maratha cavalry held De Boigne's new infantry force, his two battalions' baptism of fire at the taking of the fort of Kalinjar drew forth a paean of praise from Appa Khande Rao. Unfortunately, it drew little else. In a letter marked 'In camp near Kalinjar July 3rd 1786' De Boigne writes:

> For some months past I was in very good hope of our marching before the rainy weather towards you. But as the Devil will have it no appearance is now to be entertained as the rivers are everywhere immensely swelled and the mamlats [tribute money] not finished with any of the Rajas. It appears their panic has now left them, having has time enough to make themselves perfectly well acquainted with the Generalship and abilities as well as the courage of my great chief Apa of whom the troops are very much tired as no pay is to be got from him.[13]

The problem of regular pay bedevilled many of the trained brigades. Indian rulers simply could not or would not pay their men on time, or even at all, if they could get away with it. Arrears of pay for all troops of any type was the norm as we have already seen in the traditional armies.[14] The troops often had no redress but mutiny, which in fact was more often a withdrawal of labour, or strike, than it was any other form of rebellion.

De Boigne continues:

> The few lakhs [of rupees] which have already been paid on account have been packed up … and the troops are starving. Mr. Taylor's troops have been for eight or ten days very mutinous for their pay; however a little money has pacified them for the present but I am much afraid that many other mutinies will soon take place. For my part as long as I shall be able to keep my troops from doing any such thing I will do it and exert all my power, and I shall not leave myself with a penny as several times I have done already to prevent mutiny, wishing to leave Apa with honour and satisfaction which I beg to be soon as nothing but danger, loss, empty words is to be expected from him.[15]

However, the ever-changing political scene in Hindustan at this time meant that Madhaji had need of De Boigne's battalions. So it was that in July 1787 De Boigne found himself and his battalions on the plain of Lalsot, as part of an allied Maratha and Imperial Mughal army sent to chastise the Rajput *Rajas* of Jaipur and Jodhpur for withholding of tribute, nominally due to the Emperor in Delhi, but of course mostly intended by the Maratha leader Madhaji Scindia for his own coffers, and also for use in furthering his political ambitions.

---

13 Young, *Fountain of the Elephants*, p.82.
14 See Chapter 2.
15 Young, *Fountain of the Elephants*, p.82. The quotations are again from De Boigne's own letters. Mr Taylor appears to be an otherwise unknown mercenary in Appa Khande Rao's service.

'THEIR INFANTRY AND GUNS WILL ASTONISH YOU'

Madhaji Scindia. The greatest of the Maratha leaders after Shivaji. The Army of Hindustan was raised at his behest. (Public Domain)

Madhaji wanted no less than de facto rule of the rump of the Mughal Empire. Unfortunately, at this point in his career Madhaji overreached himself. The Rajput forces may have numbered as many of 40,000 men including 15,000 Rathor cavalry and 5,000 Naga musketeers as well as other infantry and some rather outdated guns. Two of the main commanders of Scindia's Imperial allies switched sides and joined the Rajputs with most of the Imperial cavalry. This kind of treachery was by no means unusual in warfare on the subcontinent, and still less so in the kaleidoscopic and chaotic conditions of eighteenth century Hindustan. Yet neither of the deserters were dishonourable men. They simply did not wish the Mughal Empire – or what was left of it – to fall under the sway of the Marathas. Once they had changed sides the two leaders, Mohammed Beg Hamadani and his nephew Ismael Beg, drew up their troops opposite the Maratha cavalry with the Rajput cavalry facing De Boigne.

The Battle of Tunga, or Lalsot, fought on 28 July 1787 is important in the story of the Army of Hindustan as it was De Boigne's first set piece battle. Indeed, it was almost his first time under fire. Yet we know comparatively little about De Boigne's precise role in it. De Boigne had not yet reached his later fame. Here he was merely commanding two new battalions of trained *sepoys*, simply another European mercenary, similar to those that had gone before him and those others scattered about in various parts of Hindustan. He was not even the only European commander in the Maratha forces as brigades commanded by Le Vassoult and Lestineau were also present.[16] Each of these formations was larger than De Boigne's new *campoo*. Lestineau having three battalions and Le Vassoult perhaps four, each with their own artillery contingents.

In basic terms De Boigne's two battalions and their accompanying artillery were deployed on the left of the Maratha front line, with the rest of the European led troops to his right forming a front line of trained battalions with perhaps as many of 40 or 50 guns. There were other troops in this front line; a band of Rohilla mercenaries under Murtazi Khan Barech and Ghazi Jhan, as well as some unenthusiastic Naga musketeers and even some Rajput levies.[17] Maratha cavalry were on the flanks and the remaining Imperial troops were in the centre of a second line, along with other Maratha infantry and rocket troops. As was normal in battles of this era the fighting began with a long artillery duel and the Marathas scored an early

---

16 Sir Jadurnath Sarkar, *The Fall of the Moghul Empire* (Hyderabad: Orient Blackswan Publishing, 2019), 4th Edition, Vol.3. p.225.
17 Sarkar, *The Fall of the Moghul Empire*, Vol.3. p.225.

BUILDING AN ARMY FROM THE GROUND UP

This slightly fanciful Victorian image does however give a reasonable impression of the better classes of Maratha cavalry. These could even pass for the *kala-paga* of a middle ranking sardar. (Public Domain)

success when Mohammed Beg was killed by a cannon shot and his troops began to waver. At this point Ismael Beg showed himself a soldier of some talent by rallying the wavering Moghul horse and launching a ferocious charge upon the Maratha right wing. After a short fight the Maratha horse were sent flying with Ismael and his troopers in hot pursuit. In the centre the remaining Imperial troops sat upon their hands and did nothing to retrieve the situation. They had obviously been suborned and seemingly had no intention of involving themselves in the unpleasant proceedings occurring around them. Yet other Maratha troops stood fast and continued to cannonade the Rajput line. These troops included the trained battalions under Lestineau and Le Vassoult.[18] Compton does not place either of these men at the battle though Lestineau certainly worked with De Boigne in the following year and the Persian news writers certainly place both men at the battle. Later battles would see the Marathas forming the mercenary brigades as their first line with Maratha cavalry on their flanks. There is no evidence to suggest that this was any different with De Boigne's two new battalions forming the left of this first line.

---

18 Dr G.R. Parihar, *Marwar and the Marathas 1724–1843* (Jodhpur: Hindi Sahitya Mandir, 1968), p.114. Parihar gives the Maratha forces a total of six trained battalions plus artillery. However, the total was more likely nine. This being two of De Boigne's, three of Lestineau's and four of Le Vassoult's. There also seem to have been some battalions of Rohillas and Najibs.

Opposite De Boigne's new and comparatively untried battalions the Rajput horse, Rathor nobles and gentry, perhaps as many as 10,000 strong but probably nearer 4,000 began to advance against the two trained battalions, themselves not more than 2,000 strong including their gunners.[19] Possibly as few as 1,300 men were actually carrying musket and bayonet. Their commander had formed his men into a single hollow square with the front face masking his guns. Of course, in order to accommodate his guns within the square it was actually shaped as a rather shallow rectangle. Each side made up of infantry three ranks deep. Precise details of De Boigne's square are lacking, but according to the British 1764 regulations a company containing perhaps 75 muskets in three ranks would occupy a frontage of just over 16 metres, or somewhat over 17 yards. With a possible six, or less likely eight, company frontage the square would have had a total frontage of something over 100 metres (with another 30 metres or so if an eight company frontage). This would allow the deployment of eight 6-pounder or 3-pounder guns within the square masked from the approaching Rajput cavalry by the front face infantry. Smoothbore artillery of the type De Boigne had with his battalions could fire roughly one round every 20 seconds, or perhaps for short periods as many as four rounds a minute, approximately the same rate of fire as well-trained infantry, or even as Bidwell has it somewhat faster.

The approaching cavalry had no knowledge of this. They were used to the rather leisurely pace and inaccuracy of the old-fashioned Mughal style artillery. Add to this the natural contempt of high-caste noble and gentlemen cavalry for mere infantry and there seemed to be no reason why these impudent red-coated foot soldiers should not be crushed under the hooves of the massed chivalry of Jaipur and Jodhpur. The force approaching the small square of inconvenient infantry were not an army in the European sense at all. Certainly, they were brave. Brave almost beyond reason, and they possessed significant individual skill at arms. But organisationally they were medieval. Each chieftain led his warriors personally from the front. Of drill, discipline, and unit manoeuvre they knew nothing.

As the Rajput horse continued its advance the front face of the square retired slightly, unmasking the guns. We cannot know the range at which they opened fire but, assuming 6-pounders then around 1,200 metres or less is not unreasonable. Major General B.P. Hughes in his book *Firepower* cites tests done in the early nineteenth century which show that British gunners would be expected to fire 11 rounds at an attacking cavalry target starting at a distance of 1,500 yards before contact was made, of which the last few rounds would be the deadly canister (where each gun would spread its deadly 85 or so slightly larger than musket ball sized shot in a single blast, like a huge shotgun).[20] Even assuming a somewhat less polished performance by these new gunners something like 50–60 rounds of artillery fire – roundshot, grape and canister – would be flung at the charging Rathor horsemen. Despite

---

19 Compton, *Particular Account*, p.35.
20 Maj.Gen. B.P. Hughes, *Firepower: Weapons Effectiveness on the Battlefield 1630–1850* (Staplehurst: Spellmount, 1997), p.34.

this the cavalry managed to contact the square and set about cutting down the gunners as well as flowing around the immovable infantry who began musketry at close range.

While it is easy with the safety of time to overestimate the actual casualties caused by this storm of shot, what is clear is that the Rathor cavalry broke away after a few mad minutes allowing De Boigne to reform his men. What happened next is unclear. Compton has De Boigne shaking out his square formation into line and advancing upon the disordered Rajput horse as they rallied but cites no source. This is unlikely as another account states:

> Four thousand Rathors charged the post of Ambaji at about four o'clock. The Maratha batteries on the left under Khandoji Appa ploughed through their dense rank but heedless to it they swept the Marathas guns sabred the gunners. And still advancing fell upon the supporting Maratha infantry. Even De Boigne's Sepoys after firing a few volleys were forced back in confusion. However the Rathor retreat was forced back by the artillery of Rane Khan bringing their casualties to 20 chieftains of note and 400 or 500 killed and wounded … The remaining Rathors tried again to break through the Maratha defences four or five times towards the evening but the artillery blocked their way.[21]

These differing accounts are by no means irreconcilable. That the Rajput horse charged De Boigne's men is undeniable, and that his two battalions beat them off equally so even if 'forced back in confusion' they were not routed or destroyed. The question is, how much support from other Maratha forces did De Boigne have? Clearly there was some, the idea that two battalions alone were left facing upwards of 15,000 Rathor horse plus other troops is simply untenable and as we have seen there were other European led battalions present. Yet Maratha artillery, including De Boigne's guns clearly had a major effect and successive attacks simply could not break the Maratha line despite battalions being 'forced back in confusion'. Tactically Tunga is a drawn battle but strategically it is a Rajput victory, especially after the remaining Mughal troops joined Ismael Beg and the Rajputs a day or so after the battle. The Maratha army had no choice but to retreat a few days later, with the trained battalions seemingly doing most of the rear guard work. Once Ismael Beg realised the Marathas had gone, he gave chase with such of his Mughal horse as he could rally to the task.

De Boigne's battalions had survived their first major battle somewhat battered perhaps, but still intact. These two battalions would campaign on for two more hard years fighting two more major actions (see Chapter 6) but by 1789 Madhaji had come to realise that a mere random collection of battalions would not serve his needs and so asked De Boigne to increase the size of his force. These new troops were not to be a mere couple of battalions but a full-sized brigade. Indeed, by the standards of the time 'Mr De Boigne's party' – as British reports often referred to this formation – was to be a small division of all arms, horse, foot and guns, all under De Boigne's personal command.

---

21 Dr G.R. Parihar, *Marwar and the Marathas* (Jodhpur: Hindi Sahitya Mandir, 1968), pp.114–115.

Dressed, organised, and drilled in the British manner and most importantly of all, paid regularly. This last was, of course, the most difficult part of the operation. Yet without an assured regularity of pay the troops would be more likely to become the mutinous near rabble to which other trained brigades had descended when the financial pressure was at its most acute. During the Lalsot campaign for example both Lestinea and Le Vassoult complained to Scindia that they had been forced to sell their personal possessions in order to pay their hungry soldiers something on account.[22]

To facilitate the regular payment of this enlarged force Madhaji Scindia allowed De Boigne the income from large tracts of land around the cities of Agra and Gwalior. These land grants were set aside specifically for the payment of the troops. As such they were known as *jaidad* to somewhat distinguish them from a *jaghir* which frequently did the same job but was attached to the person of the commander rather than the specific task. As De Boigne's force grew so did the land grants and the accompanying civil administration. All of this was under the general's own hand. In order to put some kind of check upon the then customary percolation of funds De Boigne adopted the expedient of keeping two sets of accounts (and therefore one assumes two sets of accountants). One set was kept in French and the other in Persian, each keeping a check upon the other. This kept theft to a controllable minimum. De Boigne's own salary as general was set at Rs 4000 per month and as his civil administrative tasks grew in proportion to the land grants for the army, he was also allowed a two per cent 'rake off' of the land revenue collected. This, plus his private trading ventures with his friend Claude Martine in Lucknow, would make him a wealthy man.

However, in the meantime the new general had to raise, arm and train this new army. Another formidable task which perforce saw him working 12–15 hours a day. This time he did not quite have to start from scratch. The nucleus of this the First Brigade was, of course founded upon his first two battalions. To these he added those remaining from Lestineau's corps now that its erstwhile leader had returned to France (decamping at speed with the back pay of his men along with the loot acquired after the Battle of Agra).[23] This gave him possibly five or perhaps even six battalions who already had some training and battle experience. Other recruits would have come from the unpaid and almost mutinous ranks of those 'brigades' commanded by native officers such as Jahangir Khan. Indeed, although this is nowhere mentioned in the sources, it is hard in retrospect to escape the conclusion that, having found a man he could trust, who had proved himself in the field, Madhaji was, in a sense, putting all his eggs in one reliable basket and allowing De Boigne to unify the disparate collection of mercenaries already present into one well organised and trained command.

---

22 Dr P. M. Joshi (ed.) and Jadunath Sarkar (trans.), *Persian Records of Maratha History* (Bombay: Published by the Director of Archives, Government of Bombay,1953), Vol.2, pp.2–3.
23 For more details on this entertaining rogue see Chapter 6 and Compton, *Particular Account*, pp.368–369.

The new brigade, or *compoo* as the various trained forces were often termed, was off to a fine start. This was because his new formation was to have a total of 10 battalions, these were to be *telingas* that is to say regular *sepoys* trained and uniformed as before in the manner of the EIC's Madras army but with the important addition of an artillery company crewing four guns and a howitzer to each of these battalions. These new *sepoy* units were somewhat smaller than the original two battalions having only 416 privates per battalion, excluding the artillery company, plus officers, NCOs, and staff. A total of 516 men – including two Europeans as the battalion commander, ranked as a captain, and his deputy, ranked as a lieutenant – who could be classed as combatants in each of these battalions of *telingas*. Civilian staff included the all-important accountant and his two secretaries as well as a surgeon. As with the Madras Infantry which were De Boigne's model there was no light company but there was at least one or possibly two grenadier companies per battalion.

The artillery company was commanded by a European sergeant major with five European gunners under him. In action these five men would each command a gun crew. Guns were bullock drawn and comprised four 4 or 6-pounders and a howitzer per company. In action the guns would be man-handled by the *kelasis* or 'clashies'. At full strength each gun crew would be around 15 men including the European gunner and the vital 'clashies' to move the gun. In total, including a detachment of *beldars* (sappers to build earthworks), blacksmiths, carpenters, and bullock drivers the full strength artillery company numbered 140 men.

There were initially seven *telinga* battalions organised in this manner in the First Brigade rather than the 10 stipulated. They were named after their areas of recruitment. Thus, there were Delhi, Agra and Gwalior battalions.[24] The remaining three battalions were composed of Pathan and Rohilla mercenaries known as *najibs*. There were irregular troops armed with matchlock muskets, sword and shield, and had a fearsome reputation. Initially they were allowed to fight in their own way and were chiefly used as garrison troops or for assaults on forts, and do not initially seem to have had integrated artillery companies. However, as the brigades became more settled these *najibs* became similar to the *telingas*, for example losing their shields and gaining bayonets for their muskets, and later gaining artillery companies of their own.

In addition to the infantry the brigade had a small cavalry component varying between 300 and 500 men. Again, these were commanded by a European officer and drilled in a more or less European style. They were armed with sword and pistol, with some at least having matchlocks or carbines. Sometime later each *rissalah*, or squadron, would receive a light 2-pounder galloper gun pulled, unusually for Indian armies, by two horses. These guns were of course an early form of horse artillery introduced to give some extra mobile fire power.

---

24 Bidwell, *Swords for Hire*, p.57.

In order to deal with the almost continuous number of petty *rajas* – each holed up in his fort and refusing to pay his tribute – the brigade had its own siege train of heavier guns in addition to those field pieces that were part of each *telinga* battalion. This heavy artillery consisted of eight 'battering guns' (most likely 18-pounders), as well as heavier howitzers and two mortars. The shells fired by the howitzers and mortars were of stone. In addition to this formidable armament the brigade also had around 500 Mewati irregulars to do duty as camp guards.[25] Thus taking the onerous duties of the camp away from the frontline troops.

All of this De Boigne accomplished in around five months, despite some of the new uniforms being temporarily lost somewhere between Calcutta and Lucknow. William Palmer, British agent at Scindia's camp, wrote in January 1790, whilst the Brigade was still training: 'The corps consists of near 5000 *sepoys*, chiefly clothed, armed and disciplined in the manner of ours, eighty pieces of artillery served by European gunners and 350 Hindustani Horse.'[26]

His officers for this brigade were something of a mixed bag. Palmer writes again.

> A number of European Officers are attached to this Corps and several who have gained experience and reputation in the country service; these are all foreigners. But I am sorry to observe that several British subjects have found their way into it, some of whom are worthy of better service and some who would be a disgrace to any service.[27]

Palmer of course was somewhat biased and, despite being a personal friend of De Boigne, might be expected to write what his masters in Calcutta expected to hear, and in fact most of De Boignes officers knew their jobs. Indeed, another later opinion states:

> The officers of this body were principally Europeans of all nations, many of them British and men very respectable by birth, education and character; and all lent their General their willing aid in his arduous duty of bringing under and preserving discipline of these new levies.[28]

Most would remain in the Maratha service until death or retirement. There is no doubt that they were, however, a mixed bag. Initially the majority were French with British running them a close second (and later being in the majority of junior posts) but John Hessing, the Dutch soldier, was still there and a countryman of De Boigne, another Savoyard, one Drugeon, also appears at this time. George Sangster has control of the armament manufactory and Robert Sutherland, another Scot and a former regular British Army officer,

---

25 Details of the organisation of De Boignes first brigade come from Smith, *Regular Corps*, p.51, and Compton, *Particular Account*, pp.64–66.
26 Young, *Fountain of the Elephants*, p.113.
27 Young, *Fountain of the Elephants*, p.109.
28 Baillie-Fraser, *Military Memoir*, Vol.1, p.60.

cashiered for some misdemeanour, later joins the brigade and will eventually command it.[29] Pierre Cuillier, alias Perron, a French citizen who had served as a junior officer in Lestineau's corps was given command of one of the new battalions. He would eventually become De Boigne's successor as commander of the Army of Hindustan.

By the end of March 1790 this new formation, the First Brigade, was ready to take the field.

---

29 An Ensign Sutherland, no first name given, was commissioned 9 December 1782 into the 2nd Battalion 42nd Foot, which was the battalion sent to India and which then formed the 73rd. (TNA: WO 65/36). Then in the 1787 Army List (TNA: WO 65/37) his name is just crossed out with no reason given. While this evidence is only circumstantial and by no means certain it does lend colour to Sutherland's supposed cashiering. I am indebted to Rob Griffith for this fascinating snippet of information.

5

The Army of Hindustan: Organisation, Weapons and Uniforms

Almost as soon as the First Brigade had taken the field for the campaigning season of 1790 it was clear that the still rising House of Madhaji Scindia would need more trained troops. Indeed, Persian newsletters coming from Madhaji's camp to Delhi in early in 1790 imply that the Second Brigade began to be raised while the First was still completing:

> Scindia had organised a Campoo [Brigade] of paltans [battalions] through De Boigne so that De Boigne, equipping his paltans with arms and standards brought them to Mathura. Madhaji Scindia reviewed the campoo twice and was highly pleased, he told the Firengi to take from his topkhana [artillery park] as many guns as he needed, saying that he wished to form another Campoo of that sort.[1]

The continuing war between Scindia's forces and the Rajput states with their Mughal ally, Ismael Beg, demanded both Madhaji's and De Boigne's immediate attention, so it was not until 1791 that the Second Brigade took the field followed by a Third Brigade in 1793.

All three of these Brigades were to be of the same pattern. Each was in effect a self-contained division of all arms with its own supply arrangements and siege train. Rates of pay were standardised, and such was the relationship between Madhaji and De Boigne that as the army grew so did the lands needed to finance that army. De Boigne and his mercenaries had made Madhaji the effective ruler not only of the house of Scindia's ancestral lands around his capital of Ujjain but also of the rump of the Mughal Empire, its last real province, that area of northern India known as Hindustan. This part of the sub-continent provided the majority of the recruits. Indeed, Hindustan was the nursery of these trained brigades.

---

[1] Joshi and Sarkar, *Persian Records*, Vol.2, p.34.

Despite serving Scindia's nascent Maratha state none of the men in De Boigne's force were actual Marathas. Regular infantry service was simply not in their nature. The locally recruited junior officers, NCOs, and rank and file were of various tribes and castes and of both the Hindu and Muslim faiths. Many were Jats from around Bhurtpur and Agra, but others were from Oudh and the Doab. The *Maharaja* of Bhurtpur was one of Madhaji's most steadfast allies. His Hindu peasantry made fine infantry as the behaviour of Lestineau's battalions at the battles of Tunga and Agra had shown. De Boigne's recruiting parties took all the Jats they could get. Others were Rajput or Muslim farmers. Most of the cavalry were Rohillas or Pathans, as were a majority of the *najib* irregular infantry. De Boigne's personal cavalry bodyguard were mostly Persians, mounted on horses of De Boigne's choice and ownership. In local terms these cavalry were De Boigne's *bargirs* or paid men.

The European officers were of various nationalities. Those of the First Brigade had an audience with Madhaji as reported by the Persian news writer: '7th Jan 1790 De Boigne visits Madhaji Scindia and presents nuzzurs [ritual offerings] on behalf of the campoo. Perron, Hunter, Drugeon, La Fontaine and eight other sahibs totalling 12 sahibs were with him, and also seven Indian commandants of the campo.[2]

This note indicates that not all of the commandants were in fact European. Certainly, the Rohilla battalion was normally commanded by a chief of its own but this implies that other commanding officers – commandants – were also Indian for at least some of the Army of Hindustan's existence. It is possible that these were junior officers, *subedars* and *jemadars*, but there is no reason to suppose that, given the numbers of *gardis* and *telinga* battalions commanded by Indian Officers in service with other rulers that some could not have gravitated to Scindia's service.

Each of De Boigne's three brigades required at least 20–25 European officers, plus the European sergeant major and five gun captains for each of the Telinga battalion's gun companies, this number would be increased if the *najib* battalions had gun companies which is uncertain, at least in the beginning, although Skinner states that the *najib* battalion which he commanded had its own guns, though this was a little later and after De Boigne had retired.[3] Nevertheless at the Battle of Patan in 1790 the First Brigade fielded 50 guns, so it is more than possible that all the battalions had gun companies from the outset. Potentially then each brigade would need approximately 75 'Europeans' though of course many of these, especially the junior posts were, 'country-born' men of European fathers and Indian mothers. The three Brigades would need over 200 Europeans, and, after De Boigne retired to Europe, General Perron, his successor as commander, would raise two more brigades and the 'Hindustani Horse' this last perhaps as many as 5,000 strong. All these formations would also need European officers. In addition, there were other Brigades in Maratha service commanded by Europeans, so the demand for officers was both strong and consistent.

---

2   Joshi and Sarkar, *Persian Records*, Vol.2, p.31.
3   Baillie-Fraser, *Military Memoir*, Vol.1, p.174.

The British Resident at Scindia's camp on 7 April 1802 – when Perron was fully in command wrote to the Governor-General in Calcutta concerning the Army of Hindustan as it then was:

> General Perron Commands four Brigades of native infantry, each consisting of ten battalions of Sepoys; the complement of a battalion is seven hundred and sixteen firelocks and every corps is commanded by two or three European officers. There are also four field pieces and a howitzer attached to each battalion with a liberal proportion of golandaz, Lascars, carriage etc.
>
> Exclusive of the battalion field pieces every brigade has a park consisting of 16 guns of a large calibre; and also a risala of regular cavalry with gallopers. General Perron has likewise in his own pay a body of four thousand cavalry, the horse of which are his exclusive property. This corps is nearly on the same establishment with the Hindustani regiment received from General De Boigne into our service.[4]

So even several years after De Boigne's retirement the basic organisation of each brigade remained the same. The European officers would come from a variety of sources and nations some with military backgrounds some not. Speaking of his own service in the Second Brigade in 1798 Skinner says: 'As for the officers of our regular infantry, we had them of all nations – French, English, Germans, Portuguese and country born of English fathers'.[5]

James and Robert Skinner were both 'country-born' and so went into the Maratha service rather than the East India Company's. James of course, and to a lesser extent his younger brother Robert, both attained rank in the British service subsequent to their service with the Marathas. Other officers came from various previous careers. Colonel Robert Sutherland, for instance, had been an officer in the British Army but was cashiered and during his service with Scindia's forces at various times commanded the First, Second and indeed Third Brigades.[6] At one point it looked as if he would succeed De Boigne as commander of the whole of the Army of Hindustan, but he appears to have been out manoeuvred by Perron. Keene quoting letters he had sight of between De Boigne and Sutherland heavily implies that Sutherland was the General's preferred candidate.[7] Skinner served under him in the Second Brigade but did not like him. Captain George Carnegie who would also serve under him somewhat later has a different opinion as Sutherland's daughter was sent to live with Carnegie's young sisters at their family home in Scotland.[8]

---

4   Maharaj Ragubhir Sinh, G. S Sardesai, & J Sarkar. (eds.) *English Records of Maratha History: Poona Residency Correspondence* (Bombay: Governm.ental Central Press, 1943) Vol.9, letter 50, p.98.
5   Baillie-Fraser, *Military Memoir*, Vol.1, p.142.
6   Major William Palmer, the British resident refers to Sutherland as 'a volunteer in the 73rd.' see Sardesai, & Sarkar, *Poona Residency Correspondence*, Vol.8, letter 27; Smith, *Regular Corps* p.52; and Compton *Particular Account* p.411. Only Compton mentions Sutherland in command of the Third Brigade. Skinner gives the Third Brigade to Col. Pedron as does Smith.
7   H.G. Keene, *Hindustan under Free Lances, 1770–1820* (Shannon: Irish University Press, 1972), p.197.
8   A.A. Cormack, *The Maratha Wars: Letters from the Front by Three Brothers* (Banff: Privately Published, 1971), p.39.

Sutherland was a competent soldier and commanded the Second Brigade from 1795 to 1799, ranked as major, before being promoted to colonel and taking over the veteran First Brigade in 1799, before being sent back to the Second Brigade by Perron in 1802.[9] Captain George Carnegie served with Sutherland from early 1800 when he entered Scindia's service as an ensign, moving with Sutherland when he changed brigades back to the second in 1802. When Sutherland moved to the First Brigade, the Second Brigade was taken over by the Hanoverian, Major Pohlmann another competent officer with whom Skinner, at least, preferred to serve.

Under De Boigne, and to an extent Perron, the command structure was rather fluid. Trusted officers being detached to undertake specific tasks with a given force. The almost continual low-level warfare of the time meant that there were always tasks to undertake. These most often entailed bringing refractory minor *rajas* and *zemindars* to heel to make them disgorge the taxes that the Marathas thought they owed to the state, but that these same *rajas* and *zemindars* frequently declined to pay without forceful persuasion: 'Without an armed force it is dangerous to make Collections and a body of troops must always accompany the Chief, appointed by the Prince, as the Jemadar of a district.'[10]

However, there were no subordinate formations within each brigade. Task forces could be a single battalion upwards, depending upon the job in hand. This meant that experienced European officers capable of commanding such detachments, were always in demand. There were never quite enough to go around especially as turnover – casualties from battle and disease – was fairly high. George Carnegie's younger brother Thomas, given a commission as ensign with Sutherland in 1802, died of fever soon after reaching Scindia's capital of Ujjain in February of that year without actually doing any duty with the brigade.[11] Colonel George Hessing's independent brigade, previously commanded by his father John Hessing, had 16 European officers or gunners killed in a single lost battle outside Ujjain against Scindia's deadliest Maratha rival Jaswant Rao Holkar in July 1799: 'In this sad affair sixteen country-born officers who were all my school fellows were killed at their guns. They had all entered the service within a month of each other'.[12]

In the same July 1802 letter to his mother in Scotland noted earlier George Carnegie writes: 'The first brigade has lost since I joined it 2 European Officers killed and 5 wounded and between eight and nine hundred men Killed and wounded.'[13] One is forced to wonder why so many men both European and Indian volunteered for such hazardous service? Individual officers, of course had their own reasons, and money was obviously one of them. For James Skinner it was because he hated being an apprentice printer and preferred the life of a soldier.[14]

---

9 Smith, *Regular Corps*, p.52.
10 Cormack, *The Maratha Wars*, George Carnegie to his mother July 1802, p.42.
11 Cormack, *The Maratha Wars*, p.107.
12 Baillie-Fraser, *Military Memoir*, Vol.1, pp.170–171.
13 Cormack, *The Maratha Wars*, George Carnegie to his mother July 1802, p.42.
14 Baillie-Fraser, *Military Memoir*, Vol.1, p.107–108.

For George Carnegie his reasons were purely financial:

> Meantime we are not without our advantages. Our pay is better and promotion quicker than in the King's or Company's service. We lead an active and a sober life (having frequently nothing to drink will account for that), no temptation to spend half a crown out of sixpence a day. Being deprived the Society of our Country women, we are also excused the expenses of Balls, Plays, Fruit and Glove shops, which ruin one third of the Company's Officers.[15]

In terms of promotion Carnegie had a point. In his Maratha service Carnegie rose from ensign to lieutenant then to captain lieutenant in 1801 and was captain the following year.[16] He commanded the cavalry regiment of Sutherland's brigade. Each step up meant an increase in pay. By comparison De Boigne remained an ensign for all of his almost four years' service in the East India Company's Madras Army. Carnegie achieved the rank of captain effectively 'learning on the job' as he had no prior military experience. Within the brigades promotion seems to have been by a mixture of merit, patronage and purchase. Carnegie seems to have reached captain entirely through the patronage of Sutherland, yet Compton has Pedron, a French officer, purchasing his majority, so the system seems to have been somewhat fluid to say the least.[17]

Monthly rates of pay for European officers in Maratha service in Hindustan during De Boigne's time were as follows.[18] Colonels, lieutenant colonels and sometimes majors usually commanded brigades – so there were very few of these ranks at any one time. Captains commanded individual battalions with usually a lieutenant as second in command.

Table 1

Colonel	Rs3000
Lieutenant Colonel	Rs2000
Major	Rs1200
Captain	Rs400
Captain Lieutenant	Rs300
Lieutenant	Rs200
Ensign	Rs150

These rates of pay compare very favourably with those of the East India Company, in whose service the pay of an ensign was a miserable 95 rupees a month. Nevertheless, Carnegie found cause to complain: 'An Officer cannot save anything considerable from his pay, while under the rank of Major; for constantly marching, we are obliged to keep a large establishment of Animals. I have never less than five camels for my Baggage and tent besides three or four Horses as commanding the Cavalry.'[19]

---

15 Cormack, *The Maratha Wars*, p.44.
16 In this context captain lieutenant was the senior lieutenant. Next in line for a captaincy.
17 Compton, *Particular Account*, p.378.
18 Smith, *Regular Corps*, p.51.
19 Cormack, *The Maratha Wars*, p.36.

William Henry Tone puts it a little differently, serving as he was at the time in the rather more relaxed forces of the *Peshwa* in Poona:

> The pay of subalterns in the Native service were from two to five hundred rupees monthly; this pay, though not regular, was always certain, and the duty very trifling. Service is, however, very precarious, and the expenses very great as it is almost a constant campaign, which obliges an officer always to keep up a field establishment of servants and animals both of which occasion very serious deductions from his pay.[20]

However, there were always chances to pick up the odd bonus or two. De Boigne made significant sums in private trade with his friend and business partner Claude Martine (even possibly taking a cut from supplying the red cloth for his men's uniforms) and high-ranking officers would often acquire extra allowances as 'table-money' to keep themselves and their staff in provisions from the bazar which always accompanied any sizable force on the march. For more junior officer and the men there was always a chance of loot from the taking of a city or a victorious field action.

After one major Maratha victory against the Jaipur Rajputs Skinner entered their abandoned camp with the cavalry regiment of Pohlmann's Brigade:

> I marched into the encampment; it was the largest and best I had ever seen. Here were most beautiful tents and large Bazars filled with everything imaginable, but not a man to be seen. My three hundred sowars dispersed and went to plunder, I myself, with two of them, went on and reached the Rajah's wooden bungalow, the most beautiful thing I ever saw– all covered with embroidery and crimson velvet. I entered and saw nothing but gold and silver … I found two golden idols, with diamond eyes which I immediately secured in my bosom for fear they should be discovered. I found also several other trinkets which I likewise took.[21]

He later mentions that the assorted 'trinkets' were valued at Rs2000. Doubtless the sowars of the cavalry regiment he was with also had a profitable time.

Rates of pay for the lower ranks were also standardised and paid with far more regularity than was usual in the armies of the various 'Country Powers'. It was this regularity of pay as much as the quality of training which gave the Army of Hindustan its decided edge over the other 'Trained Brigades' of Scindia's rivals for power.

The following is a breakdown of the numbers of men and rates of pay for infantry, cavalry, artillery, civilian staff and the technical branches. Payment was by the month.

---

20 Tone, *Some Institutions*, p.66.
21 Baillie-Fraser, *Military Memoir*, Vol.1, p.152.

Infantry battalion

Commanded by a European captain and a European lieutenant. The currency is the Rupee the lesser being the Anna of which there are 16 to the Rupee thus Rs12.8 is 12½ Rupees.[22]

Table 2

8 *subedars* – each commanding a company	Rs35 each
16 *jemadars* - 2 per company each commanding a platoon	Rs20 each
1 *havildar major*. Equivalent to a regimental sergeant major.	Rs12.8 each
32 *havildars* (sergeants) of which eight are senior, 1 per company as CSM	Rs10.8 each
32 *naiks* (corporals)	Rs8.8 each
2 colour bearers	Rs12 each
10 drummers and 10 fifers	Rs12 each
104 grenadiers in two companies	Rs6 each
312 centre company sepoys in 6 companies	Rs5.8 each

The Artillery Company

One artillery company permanently part of each infantry battalion and the main firepower of the battalion. Commanded by a European sergeant major with five European gunners as gun-captains for each of the unit's four 6-pounder guns and one howitzer. Though Skinner notes that all the guns in his battalion were 6-pounders.

Table 3

1 European sergeant major	Rs60
5 European gunners	Rs40 each
1 *jemadar*	Rs30
1 *havildar*	Rs15
5 *naiks*	Rs9 each
35 *golandauz* (gunners) 7 per gun.	Rs 6, 7 or 8 each
35 *kelasais* for manhandling the guns on the battlefield. Again 7 per gun.	Rs4.8 and 5 each.

Gun crews appear quite generous. Including a *naik* and the European gunner there would be a maximum of 16 men per gun on the battlefield, assuming all were present and correct.

Technical, Transport and Battalion Staff

In Smith's table some of these, such as the pioneers and blacksmiths are, administratively speaking part of the artillery company but by more modern standards they would be 'rear echelon' and not directly combat troops. Blacksmiths, armourers and carpenters were of course responsible for the

---

22   The following tables are taken from Smith, *Regular Corps*, p.51 and Compton, *Particular Account*, p.64.

maintenance of the battalion equipment. *Beldars*, or pioneers, would dig gun emplacements and be invaluable in sieges. The various bullock masters and bullock drivers looked after the numerous cattle used to pull the guns and ammunition waggons of the battalion's integral transport. Some of the administrative staff were not soldiers but rather civilian employees. Once again pay rates are monthly.

Table 4

1 *pandit* (accountant)	Rs60
2 *matasaddis* (writers or secretaries)	Rs20 each
20 *beldars* (pioneers)	Rs4 each
24 *garewans* (bullock drivers)	Rs4 each
5 *sarangs* (bullock sergeants) NCO's in charge of the animal transport	Rs9 each
5 *tindals* (park sergeants) NCOs in charge of the maintenance of the waggons, guns and of the pioneers	Rs6.8 each
4 blacksmiths	Rs6 each
4 carpenters	Rs6 each
11 *bhistis* (water carriers) essential when campaigning in the hot season. Doubtless, like Kipling's Gunga Din, these men often braved fire to get water to the troops in the battle line	Rs4
7 Armourers to repair and maintain the weapons of the battalion. Especially the small arms.	Rs7 each
2 *hiccarrahs* (message carriers)	Rs5 each
1 surgeon for the Indians rather than the Europeans	Rs10
4 *gurreealas* (time keepers) for marching	Rs5 each
1 *masalchi* (torch-bearer) doubtless essential for nightly officers' rounds when the battalion was in camp or cantonment	Rs5

Note that the battalion accountant is paid more than a *subhedar* commanding a company, as much as the European sergeant major commanding the artillery company. Obviously, this was to keep him honest! The last thing any commander needs is a corrupt accountant.

Carnegie, writing in 1801, makes the point regarding the importance of the financial administration:

> De Boigne was a man of strong natural talents well acquainted with the language and manners of the people he had to deal with. He secured from the late Madhaji Scindia a tract of Country adequate to the pay of the Brigades so that the troops do not depend on the bounty of the Prince for their pay. The General, whoever he is, takes care of the Collections and furnishes each Colonel with a sum necessary for the pay of the Brigades they command, and the General accounts to the Prince for the whole amount of Collections and expenses. You may think it very possible for the General as well as Colonels of Brigades to make an improper use of the revenues of the Jaoads [Jaidads land revenue grants for military use]. However I can assure you that it can not be done as the accounts of every battalion are kept with the utmost exactness and inspected very frequently by the Servants of Government.[23]

---

23 Cormack, *The Maratha Wars*, p.35.

Smith also makes the point regarding secure finances: 'A Jaidad producing 16 lakhs of rupees [1.6 million] per annum was granted for the expense of the army , which still continues appropriated to that purpose, and as long as this is the case the army will be well paid, well regulated , powerful and victorious.[24] From the security of finance all else followed.

In addition to the fighting troops each battalion had its own integral transport. This aspect, very unusual for the time and place, made the organisation of De Boignes brigades somewhat ahead of the British, and very much ahead of the other local rulers armies.

The battalion transport consisted of:

120 bullocks
18 camels used to carry the men's baggage, one per platoon, so two per company plus a couple extra.[25]
2 bullock carts
5 tumbrils, the contemporary name for ammunition waggons, in this case each pulled by 12 bullocks. The five guns were each pulled by 8 bullocks.

Ammunition scales for the guns were generous.

300 roundshot per gun
100 rounds of grapeshot
50 stone shells for the howitzer
50 rounds of grape for the howitzer.

We can multiply this by 10 for a complete brigade to which must be added the personnel and equipment for the brigade's siege train. This siege train with its heavy guns and mortars would require roughly twice the bullocks, waggons, and tumbrils of the lighter artillery of the infantry battalions.

Now we come to the cavalry of the brigades. These were always of secondary importance to the infantry and guns, simply because the Marathas could produce thousands of light cavalry almost at the drop of a hat. However, each brigade needed reliable cavalry drilled in the European manner and under discipline to support the infantry. Equally such integral cavalry would provide escort and reconnaissance detachments which the irregular Maratha cavalry could not, or would not, always undertake. These cavalry would also at need provide a steadier mounted element than the sometimes rather flighty and unsteady masses of irregular horse which were the mainstay of the Maratha cavalry.

In theory each brigade disposed of a single regiment of cavalry divided into varying numbers of *rissalahs* or troops each under an Indian *rissaldar* (equivalent to a *subedar* in an infantry battalion). Each *rissalah* including its officers was about 75 strong. Compton gives a strength of 800 men for the regiment but this is far too high, especially as two contemporary sources both give strengths of 250–300 and 300 respectively for the cavalry unit of

---

24 Smith, *Regular Corps*, p.76.
25 Bidwell, *Swords for Hire*, p.56.

their different brigades.²⁶ The lower figure would, however equate to the four *rissalahs* which Compton states as the strength of De Boigne's own bodyguard. None of the men in these cavalry units were Marathas. As a general rule most were Pathans or Rohillas and of the Muslim faith, though there were also some Hindu Rajputs. They were armed with sword and pistols with some *rissalahs* also having carbines or matchlocks too. They operated similarly to European style light cavalry, upon which their drill was modelled. However, despite this drill they were still somewhat more irregular than European cavalry of the same period. At least some of these cavalry were raised upon the time honoured *silladar* system, where the trooper brought his own horse, which was his own property. Unlike many other similar but more irregular bands the *silladar* cavalry in the Army of Hindustan were assured of restitution for any losses of horseflesh. This of course made them significantly more reliable in combat than was the norm.

As one would expect pay of the cavalry was significantly higher than that of the infantry, simply because the cavalry trooper was responsible for the care and feeding of his horse as well as himself. This would almost certainly entail paying a groom, and possibly a *syce* or grass cutter, to provide forage for the animal. Neither of these men would be combatants but like many other people both male and female, part of the very considerable number of camp followers, usually significantly out numbering the combat troops that accompanied any army in the field in any Indian campaign.

The rates of pay of *silladar* cavalry were as follows, again per month.²⁷

Table 5

Rissaldar	Rs80
Jemadar	Rs40
Daffadar (NCO equivalent to *havildar*)	Rs30
Kettledrummer	Rs24
Trooper	Rs24

De Boigne's own cavalry bodyguard regiment was somewhat different. The men were mostly Persians and De Boigne selected all the horses himself, which were his property. By the standards of the time therefore the men were his *bargirs* or, in European terms, retainers, as he provided for all their military needs, supplying horses and weapons to the whole regiment. When De Boigne retired in 1795 he brought this unit into British territory and sold the whole lot, bag and baggage, to the Begal Army in February 1796. At that time the regiment consisted of: 'a corps of 600 chosen cavaliers of Persian nationality, superbly armed, equipped and mounted and attended by 100 camel riders and four light field pieces.'²⁸

---

26 See Compton, *Particular Account*, pp.65–66, Cormack, *The Maratha Wars*, p.43, and Baillie-Fraser, *Military Memoir*, Vol.1, p.152.
27 Compton *Particular Account*, p.66.
28 W. Y. Carman. *Indian Army Uniforms under the British, Cavalry* (London: Leonard Hill, 1961), p.32, and also Grant Duff, *History of the Marathas*, Vol.2, p.174.

As De Boigne's dependents and therefore not having to pay for the upkeep of their own horses, these men were paid significantly less than the *silladar* cavalry of the brigades.

Table 6

Rissaldar (commander)	Rs40
Naib risaldar (second in command)	Rs30
Jemadar (lieutenant)	Rs18
Daffadar (NCO)	Rs12
Trooper	Rs8
Gunner	Rs8
Kettledrummer	Rs7

Compton's total of four *rissalahs* for 600 men is far too low unless each of these bodyguard *rissalahs* were double strength. This is by no means impossible but in this case mere conjecture based upon the fact that one each of the four field pieces was assigned with its gunners, to each *rissalah*. Unusually for Indian artillery at this period these light guns were horse drawn in the so-called galloper style by two horses in tandem the rear or wheel horse being between the shafts of the gun carriage which also formed the trail of the gun when in action. Such galloper guns had been known in Europe since at least the mid-seventeenth century but only appear in India in the late eighteenth century.

All of the above assumes that the brigades were always up to strength. Of course, this was not always the case. Carnegie notes the campaign wastage in his time above. To sum up we can do no better than quote Lewis Ferdinand Smith – who served with the brigades – writing in January 1797 from Agra to a Calcutta newspaper under the pen name of Longinus. Of De Boigne's forces at that time he says:

> He now commands an army of fourteen battalions of Sepoys and ten of najibs four thousand Sebundies, twelve hundred regular cavalry and a large train of one hundred and fifty pieces of cannon, His Sepoys are armed, accoutred and disciplined in the English manner and commanded by European Officers. The najibs are armed with matchlocks with bayonets, commanded mostly by Europeans and disciplined nearly the same as the Sepoys; only the words of command are delivered in Persian.[29]

Sebundie is another term used for irregular matchlock armed infantry, often used to collect revenue.

---

29 Smith, *Regular Corps*, p.74.

Uniforms and Equipment

When the French first began to train their *sepoys* in the European manner they were not uniformed, but wore their normal, largely white, clothing with European style equipment. A little later by the 1750s, some companies were wearing uniforms but by no means all.[30]

Uniform details for the early mercenary brigades have, so far, been impossible to locate, even assuming such exist. Due to the often temporary nature of many of the early units it is unlikely that there was ever time to provide them with uniforms, especially as many of their employers were unable or unwilling to disgorge a single rupee more than they had to for the upkeep of their troops.

The British, had equally, at least to begin with, left their 'rabble of peons' without uniforms.[31] This continued even when the decision was taken to organise more permanent companies drilled in the manner of the British Army. Indeed, it was not until April 1756 that British East India Company *sepoys* were officially uniformed: 'The President acquaints the Board that there being a great number of Sepoys in the Company's pay, that it had occurred to him that if they could be prevailed on to wear an uniform of Europe cloth it would serve at once to give them a more martial appearance and take off a considerable quantity of woollen goods.'[32]

One is forced to wonder which was more important in the minds of the EIC merchants, martial appearance or moving otherwise unsaleable woollen cloth. Nevertheless, from this point the majority of the Company's native army would wear British red coats. It was this army that De Boigne joined 20 or so years later and from which the pattern for his brigades of the Army of Hindustan would come.

Once again, De Boigne showed himself significantly different from the usual run of European mercenary officers in the northern half of the subcontinent. His troops were not to be the 'ragamuffin battalions' of some of the other mercenary corps.[33] So the *telinga* battalions, the regular *sepoys* if you will, were to be clothed in red, the same as the Madras or Bengal armies. Initially the red cloth came from Calcutta forwarded to De Boigne's business partner Claude Martine in Lucknow and then on to De Boigne's headquarters in the city of Koil, or later at nearby fortress of Aligarh. Martine was an invaluable asset as he dealt with all the non-military business along with their agents in Calcutta the Scottish company of Hamilton and Aberdeen.[34] This company seems to have had several fingers in the mercenary pie. Colonel Robert Sutherland certainly dealt with them spending £4,000 on two shares of a merchant ship, the *Nonsuch*, in 1802.[35] Indeed, Captain George Carnegie

---

30 For more details on early French *sepoy* units see Peter Abbot, *Rivals to the Raj* (Nottingham: Foundry Books, 2010) pp.76–82.
31 Philip Mason, *A Matter of Honour. An account of the Indian Army. Its Officers and Men* (London: Cape, 1974), p.29.
32 Col. W.J. Wilson, *History of the Madras Army* (Madras: Government Press, 1888), Vol.1, p.126.
33 Smith, *Regular Corps*, p.46, referring to six battalions of Ambaji Angria's forces in 1802.
34 Young, *Fountain of the Elephants*, pp.109–110.
35 Cormack, *The Maratha Wars*, p.42.

initially came out to India from Scotland to be employed by the company and only joined Scindia's service because: 'Both Nicholas [George's elder brother] and Mr Alexander Aberdein have given me broad hints that in the present state of affairs there is more to be expected from the Sword than from the Quill.'[36]

The company seems to have been quite deep in the material side of the mercenary trade. Hamilton and Aberdeen were to go bankrupt in 1804.[37] Susan Carnegie, Captain George's mother, referred to Alexander Aberdeen as an 'abominable unprincipled scoundrel' amongst other terms of disapprobation, due to his various financial mismanagements which had had a deleterious effect upon the Carnegie family's finances.[38] Captain George alone losing some Rs15,000. One is forced to wonder how badly the company suffered because of the Maratha War and the destruction of the mercenary brigades.

However, at the time of the raising and organisation of De Boigne's brigades all that was far in the future. In 1790 Hamilton and Aberdeen appeared as a solid commercial company used as agents by several of the mercenaries for their private trading ventures and also to purchase the goods they needed from British territory that they could not otherwise acquire. In the case of De Boigne's First Brigade this included one Mr. Shippard, a band master, and Mr Leander, a musician, as well as several musical instruments including French horns.[39] The plan seems to have been to train a regimental band for the First Brigade. In 1802 Charles Metcalfe the assistant to the British resident saw them: 'The band which was in full tune as they marched by my little camp played nothing but English tunes, perfectly in the European style.'[40] The known uniform details are outlined below.[41]

Telingas
Red coats of European cut, white underclothes in the local style with *jahangir* style short drawers. Black crossbelts and ammunition pouch. Blue turbans 'with a coxcomb.' Arms; firelock (flintlock musket) and bayonet. The different battalions were given the names of the cities where they were raised so one might conjecture that, like the Madras forces upon which they were modelled, the different battalions in a given brigade had different coloured facings on cuffs, lapels and collars but there is no hard evidence to support this, however Charles Metcalfe saw some of Scindia's troops in 1802 'the uniforms of the Sepoys are the same as the Company's with the exception that they carry a sword as well as a bayonet and musket.'[42] The East India Company's Bengal Native Infantry regiments wore a blue turban with an upright false front which has given them the name of 'sundial turbans' in some sources,

---

36 Cormack, *The Maratha Wars*, p.23.
37 Cormack, *The Maratha Wars*, p.58.
38 Cormack, *The Maratha Wars*, p.61.
39 Young, *Fountain of the Elephants*, p.110.
40 Channa Wickremesekera, *Best Black Troops in the World, British Perceptions and the making of the Sepoy 1746–1805* (Delhi: Manohar, 2002), footnote 121, p.71.
41 Compton, *Particular Account*, p.65.
42 Wickremesekera, *Best Black Troops in the World*, p.71.

equally this upright piece of cloth might be referred to as a coxcomb.[43] Yet it is equally possible that the blue turbans were tied individually depending upon the traditional style of the caste or religion of the wearer.

Najibs

Locally produced blue quilted Persian style coats. These would be long coats reaching to mid-calf or thereabouts. Otherwise dressed in the local north Indian Muslim style with sashes and turbans. Arms, initially matchlock muskets of local make. Together with sword and buckler. Later matchlocks produced by Sangster's factory at Agra had bayonets. Although to begin with these *najib* battalions were more irregular in style than the *telignas* by the time of Skinner and Smith's service with the Army of Hindustan they had become more regular, even having their own artillery: 'The Telingas composed mostly of Hindus from Oudh were disciplined according to the old English exercise of 1780 and the Najibs who were mostly Mussulmen (Muslims) were exercised in nearly the same manner.'[44]

This would give the *telinga/sepoy* battalions a very similar appearance to the contemporary British units of the East India Company's army. The only obvious difference being the black crossbelts of De Boigne's *sepoys* and the swords they carried. The obviously Indian style dress of the *najib* battalions would make them look more distinctly different.

Weapons for the *telinga* battalions were flintlock musket and bayonet, the standard arms of eighteenth century European Infantry. De Boigne's first battalions may have sourced their muskets initially from Calcutta, but it is equally likely that they were locally made. Certainly, the weapons of the three brigades that De Boigne eventually raised and commanded were manufactured in local arsenals under the supervision of the Scottish adventurer Major George Sangster, who had been with De Boigne since his earliest days as a mercenary.[45] The arsenals and foundries based around Agra and later Gwalior would provide small arms (with muskets at Rs10 each) and cannon for the whole of the Army of Hindustan.

A contemporary European witness makes a vital point regarding the production of arms locally:

> The late regulations of the Company, respecting the return to Europe of all unserviceable arms, may for a time prevent the increase of infantry corps, but then it will drive them to the expedient of making their own firelocks as Scindia has done, and his are very excellent ones, far superior to the ordinary Europe arms to be met with in the Bazars.[46]

---

43 Boris Mollo, *The Indian Army* (Poole: Blandford, 1981), p.42, plate 25 shows Bengal Native Infantry of the period.
44 Smith, *Regular Corps*, pp.50–51.
45 Young, *Fountain of the Elephants*, p.80.
46 Tone, *Some Institutions*, p.54.

Sangster and his artisans were certainly getting something right. By the end of the century Sangster and his staff were overseeing and running a considerable arms industry.

Cavalry

The regular cavalry of the brigades were uniformed in green *kurtas*, the usual knee length coat of northern Indian cavalry, with red sashes and turbans. De Boigne's bodyguard having the same uniform but with silver wire in their turbans and sashes to emphasise their superior status as the general's personal troops: 'His cavalry cut a good appearance being dressed in a uniform of green jackets with red turbans the folds of which were intermixed with silver wire. They seemed to be very well disciplined and each horseman was armed with a pair of pistols, a gun and a sword.'[47] Other senior officers also had their bodyguards. Colonel Pohlmann is described as: 'Attended by a guard of Mughals all dressed alike in purple robes and marching in file in the same way as a British cavalry regiment.'[48]

European officers seem to have been allowed a wide latitude in their dress. A portrait of De Boigne as an old man – full of riches and honour – shows him in a red coat with dark blue collar and cuffs, but this is the style of the 1820s rather than the 1790s when he was in India. However red was certainly the colour used by many of his infantry so there is no reason to assume that some officers at least dressed in red coats of a cut similar to the European officers of the British East India company. However, Colonel Pedron, the French mercenary who commanded the Third Brigade for a time was, when captured by the British, 'clad in a green jacket with gold lace and epaulettes,'[49] so one perhaps wonders if his Third Brigade wore green, at least under his command which continued after De Boigne retired. The small *sepoy* contingent of the French garrison of their trading station at Pondicheri also wore green, with red facings, so one might conjecture that some at least of the post De Boigne era troops may have worn green.[50] Also found when Alighur was captured by the British were thousands of 'regimental uniforms, chiefly blue jackets with red facings, made after the French manner', so it is also possible that the newer brigades wore these blue uniforms.[51] It is equally possible that they were never actually issued as there simply was not time due to the political and military turmoil.

However, there is evidence to suggest that some officers also chose to wear the local dress rather than that of the European colonists. Skinner speaks of wearing armour in one cavalry skirmish: 'We repulsed this attack also but my mare was wounded by a sabre cut, and I received two or three sword blows on the body from which I was only saved by my armour.'[52]

---

47 Compton, *Particular Account*, p.92.
48 Compton, *Particular Account*, p.382.
49 Compton, *Particular Account*, p.379.
50 Rene Chartrand, *Napoleon's Overseas Army* (London: Osprey, 1989) p.39.
51 Thorn, as quoted in Compton, *Particular Account*, p.304.
52 Baillie-Fraser, *Military Memoir*, Vol.1, p.127.

Other mercenaries such as Sombre and George Thomas also wore Indian clothing. Personal weapons also seem to have been a matter of choice. Skinner carried a shield during one assault on a fort.[53] It is nevertheless true that the few surviving images of the mercenaries, made for western consumption show them in western dress, in the case of George Thomas this is also true of surviving rupee coins he had minted which show his head in profile with a western style military coat.[54] Once in British service both of the Skinner brothers, James and Robert, wore a light dragoon style uniform complete with Tarleton helmet and braided jacket almost identical to that worn by British light dragoon units in the Peninsular War. At the same time the Indian officers and troopers of his famous cavalry regiment, Skinners Horse, wore the usual long coat of Indian cavalry; in the case of Skinner's regiment in yellow. Other irregular cavalry units in British service around this time also wore Indian style coats: Lieutenant Colonel William Gardner's (another former mercenary) regiment wore green, with red turbans; Lieutenant Colonel Bruces's Independent Regiment of Cavalry of 1796 wore a light blue grey coat, again with red turbans and crimson sashes. These were the men that had previously been De Boigne's bodyguard regiment which De Boigne sold to the East India Company when he retired.[55]

Consequently, a degree of conjecture is inevitable about the uniform or otherwise of the European mercenaries in Mahratta service. It seems that for senior officers almost any kind of costume was allowable as long as it did not interfere with their duties. Personal taste was everything. For the lower ranks – European NCO gun captains and the like – a version of the infantry uniform is far more likely, perhaps with European style breeches and a wide brimmed hat to keep off the sun. Certainly, many Europeans preferred where possible to keep their own forms of dress even if these were locally made in lighter local fabrics.

Lest it be thought that uniforms amongst Indian forces was a European invention, we can note that the Mughal palace guards were clothed in red well into the seventeenth century and that even some of the Maratha's *gardis* which existed before De Boigne's brigades had uniforms: 'Their coats are of red serge with blue collar and cuffs cut in the country taste to lap over before and tied with strings.'[56] This all too brief description implies that these *gardis* wore the standard long coat, turban and sash of the *najibs* but in red rather than the blue of De Boigne's *najib* battalions. Being *gardis*, and therefore a sort of regular infantry, they would not be Marathas by caste or tribe, but more likely Muslims from further north as were De Boigne's *najibs* a few years later.

---

53 Baillie-Fraser, *Military Memoir*, Vol.1, p.135.
54 Captain William Franklin, *Military Memoirs of George Thomas* (Tunbridge: Pallas Armata, 1996), frontispiece.
55 W.Y. Carman, *Indian Army Uniforms under the British: Cavalry* (London: Leonard Hill, 1961) p.32.
56 Lt. E. Moor, *A Narrative of the Operations of Captain Little's Detachment* (London: Privately Published, 1792), p.83.

Colours and Standards

Each of the *telinga* battalions of De Boigne's brigades had on the books two colour bearers, who were paid 12 Rupees per month. Only marginally less than the *havildars* or sergeants, so a post with considerable responsibility. It is therefore logical to assume that each battalion had two colours or flags.

James Todd that worthy (and wordy) historian of the Rajputs conversed with De Boigne during his retirement in Chambery and states that at the Battle of Merta in 1790 De Boigne fought under the white cross of Savoy.[57] This would of course be a white cross and a red field. Raikes says: 'Wherever the White cross of Savoy flashed across the battlefield victory followed in its train.' And that 'these were the colours of De Boigne.'[58] So it is not too great a stretch to postulate the flags of his regular battalions being based upon the flag of his native Savoy. However precise details are lacking.

In Indian armies flags and standards were plentiful and colourful. As well as the traditional white yak-tail standards of their Mongol ancestors, the Mughals used both flags and metallic standards not unlike Napoleonic French eagles. Other metallic standards included an upraised hand, a dragon's head, a golden ball, and a golden jewel-encrusted fish. Often the more important and symbolic standards were carried on an elephant.[59] The metallic standards especially were the insignia of particular offices or honours, conferred by the Emperor upon a subject. Flags were often triangular and bore devices such as lions and snakes, swords, crescent moons, stars and even fish.[60]

As for the Marathas the national colour of the Mahratta people from the time of Shivaji was yellow, or yellow ochre, or saffron. Before the Battle of Panipat many of the Marathas covered their faces with turmeric powder (yellow ochre in colour) as a sign that they were prepared to die.

Kadam mentions the *bhagvan jhenda*, the flag of the Marathas, as an ochre or saffron coloured flag.[61] This was apparently in use before the time of Shivaji. Traditionally this flag was swallow tailed and of a single colour, variously described as orange, yellow ochre or saffron. Shivaji's own flag in 1666 was described as 'orange and vermillion coloured with golden decorations stamped upon it.'[62] This flag became known as the *jaripakta* and was initially only flown by the *Peshwa* or his nominated commander. However, in practice over the years assorted versions of this flag were flown by many commanders, often on elephants and not infrequently with kettledrums also on the elephants.

Two descriptions of different *jaripakta* are as follows: 'Jari Patka – The Banner "Zari Patta" which was always carried before Ragobah was small and

---

57   Lt. Col. J. Todd, *Annals and Antiquities of Rajasthan* (Delhi: Motilal Banarsidass, 1987), Vol.2, p.881.
58   Charles Raikes, *Notes on the North Western Provinces of India* (London: Chapman and Hall, 1852), p.177.
59   Irvine, *Indian Moghuls*, pp.32–33.
60   Sayed Zafar Haidar, *Arms and Armour*, pp.283–285.
61   V.S. Kadam, *Maratha Confederacy – A Study in its Origin and Development* (Delhi: Munshiram Manoharlal 1993), p.128.
62   Kadam, *Maratha Confederacy*, p128.

swallow tailed of crimson and gold tissue with gold fringes and tassels'[63] and; 'The jerry-put is a small standard made of cloth of gold or as it is called "Farre", It is cut swallow tailed and does not exceed the size of a common pocket handkerchief'.[64]

In practice the various Maratha *sardars* and generals would each have their own version of the *jaripatka*, despite strictures against such pretentions.[65] This proliferation would continue and become especially noticeable as the laws against such transgressions were no longer enforced. Another eyewitness description of Maratha flags appears in the diary of Captain John Pester who served as a quarter master of brigade in Lakes army and saw several actions. Here he writes of the troops he saw on the walls of Agra in October 1803: 'Scindia's colours were also plainly visible flying over the Delhi gate of the fortress and along the walls. They appeared very superb at the principle flagstaff. It was a red silk ground with a white snake diagonally.'[66]

One remaining interesting piece of conjecture remains. In Wise and Rosignoli's *Military Flags of the World* illustration no. 193 is identified as a French Infantry colour 'taken in the first Maratha War' where no French troops fought, thought they did fight further south in Mysore.[67] This is in standard pre-Revolution French style; a white cross dividing the four quarters of the flag which are in this case the upper hoist quarter red with the other three quarters blue. Nothing unusual except that in the upper hoist quarter, the red one, there is a snake stretching from the middle of the quarter to well into the white cross. The snake is not a French motif but is an Indian, and indeed a Maratha one, as witnessed by Pester. One might speculate, therefore, that this flag is possibly from one of De Boigne's battalions as it uses motifs similar to those known to have been used by both De Boigne and his employer. However, without more information this must remain speculation.

---

63 Sen, *Military System*, p.25.
64 Tone, *Some Institutions*, p.24.
65 See Kadam, *Maratha Confederacy*, pp.128–131 for the use and abuse of the *jaripatka*.
66 John Pester, *War and Sport in India 1802–1806* (London: Heath, Cranton & Ouseley, 1912), p.190.
67 Terence Wise and Guido Rosignoli, *Military Flags of the World* (Poole: Blandford, 1977).

6

The Army of Hindustan at War: De Boigne's Campaigns

From the raising of De Boigne's initial force of two battalions in 1786 to the destruction of the Army of Hindustan in 1803 there was no time when part or all of the army was not at war. These campaigns could range from large complex campaigns against other rulers such as the *Rajas* of Jaipur and Johdpur which would result in battles similar in size to European battles of the Seven Years War, with tens of thousands of men engaged on each side, to smaller expeditions of just a couple of battalions to collect revenue, punish non-payment or put down a minor rebellion, of which there were many. These small rebellions and expeditions were the everyday work of De Boigne's brigades, though we have little information about most of them.

Lewis Ferdinand Smith, who participated in several such smaller expeditions, frequently in command, leaves us an impression of several of them:

> Other actions of less importance performed by De Boigne's Brigades were the storm of Ballahairee a hill fort … In 1792 by six battalions under Major Fremont where Captain Bulkeley was killed. The sieges of Suwalghur and Toree Futtephur two strong forts by eight battalions under Major Gardner and Major Sutherland in 1795 and 1796. The siege and storm of Calapoor near Poonah by five battalions under Captain Brownrigg where Lieutenant Remeau was killed, the storm of the town of Nurwur by four battalions under Major Sutherland in 1795; the action before Dutteah in 1794 where Major Fremont commanded eight battalions; the battle of Kutowlee in 1800 where three battalions defeated six of Sumbernaut's and took six guns; the capture of Sumbernaut's camp, baggage and twenty-four pieces of cannon, and the surrender of seven of his battalions, by six battalions commanded by Captain L.F. Smith; the defeat of above ten thousand Rohillas, collected by an Imposter called Sultaun Shaw in December 1799 by three battalions under Captain L.F. Smith: the defeat of two rebel battalions of Monsieur Le Marchand at Daillie [Delhi] in 1800 by one battalion under Captain E.F. Smith [Lewis Smith's brother, later killed in action] who took four guns; the

THE ARMY OF HINDUSTAN AT WAR

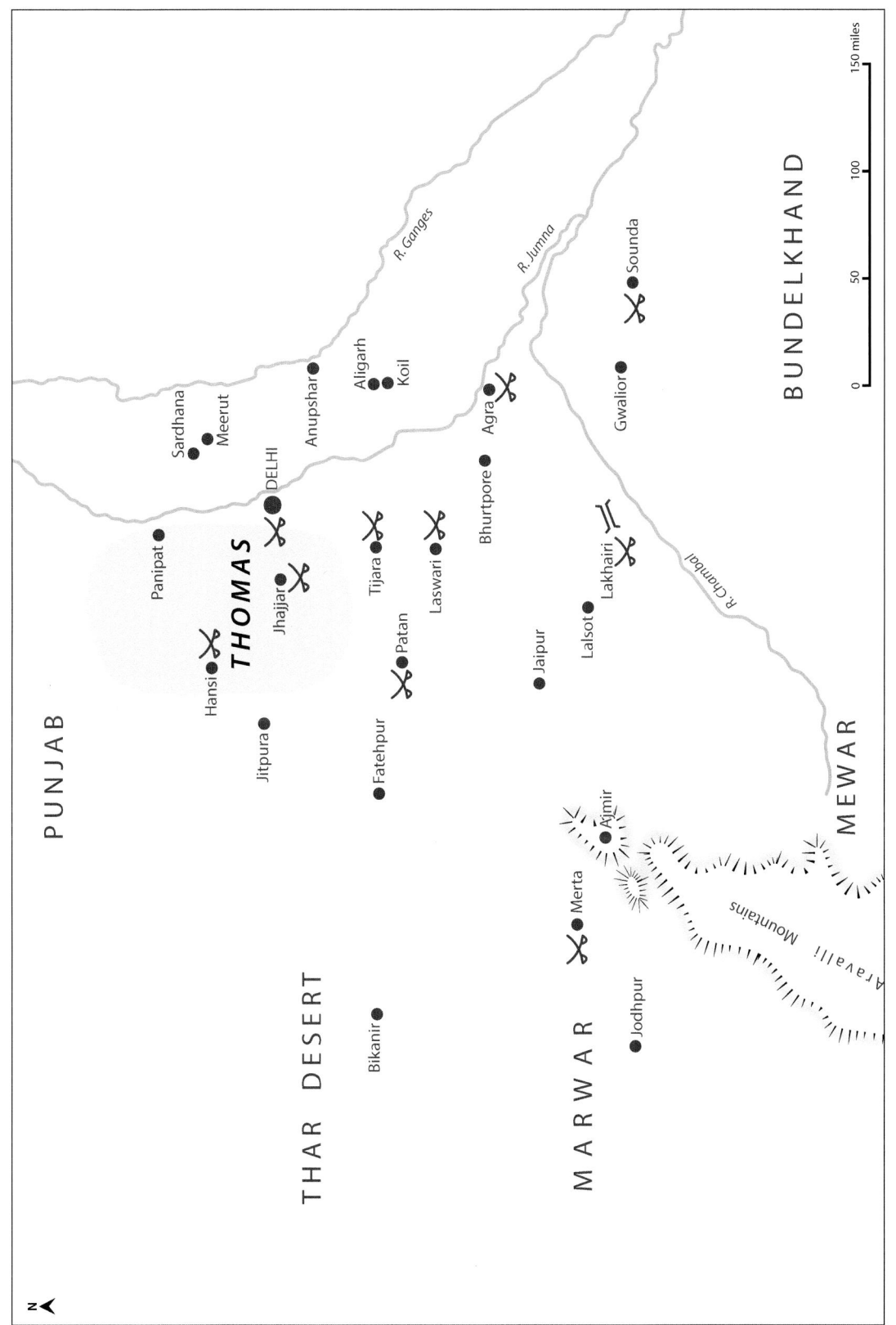

Hindustan and Rajastan. This was the arena for most of the campaigns of the Army of Hindustan.

defeat of the Bhopaul forces in 1798 by one battalion and one thousand horse under Lieutenant L.F.Smith…[1]

What is clear from this is that, aside from Smith's understandable pride in his, his brother's and his troop's achievements, there was always work for Scindia's regular troops to do. This was by no means an easy service, either for the European officers or for their much put-upon soldiers.

Of course, these smaller actions were in addition to the main campaigns. Right from the very first raising of the first two battalions by De Boigne in 1786, the brigades were used to further Madhaji Scindia's political ambitions. De Boigne and his army became Madhaji's strong right arm in the deadly game of northern Indian power politics. The following sections covering the battles involving De Boigne's forces is not by any means a list of all the major engagements in India during the latter part of the eighteenth century but covers only those involving the Army of Hindustan. De Boigne's first battle at Tunga, or Lalsot, is covered in Chapter 4 so this list begins with his second major engagement.

The War Against Ismael Beg and Ghulam Kadir

After the Battle of Tunga/Lalsot Madhaji was forced upon the strategic defensive, largely through lack of money. Those lands in Hindustan and around Delhi which his garrisons had controlled fell one by one to the forces of Ismael Beg, and to those Imperial officers who had resented the elevation of Madhaji to regent of the Empire. Madhaji had overreached himself and the fragility of his position in Hindustan was amply demonstrated by its speedy collapse. Yet his policy never wavered. Tunga and its aftermath was merely a setback. Of all the temporary conquests of 1786–1787 only Agra and Aligarh remained. Madhaji was forced to melt down his own silver plate into rupees to pay his remaining troops.[2] Nevertheless De Boigne's two battalions stayed with the army and as money came in and the plethora of minor rebellions, which resulted from Madhaji's perceived weakness, were put down the Maratha position slowly improved despite the fall of Agra city, but not it's immensely strong fort which remained in Maratha hands under its redoubtable *killadar* (governor) Lakwa Dada. There was considerable fighting around Agra in which De Boignes battalions were sometimes involved but the overall inferiority of Madhaji's forces meant that despite re-supplying Lakwa Dada's garrison on more than one occasion the Marathas could not completely drive away the besiegers. To all intents and purposes, the siege was a stalemate, with neither side strong enough to break the other.

---

1 Smith, *Regular Corps*, pp.17–18.
2 Sarkar, *Fall of the Moghul Empire*, Vol.3, p.241.

The Battle of Chaksana 24 April 1788

Learning of Scindia's discomfiture and seeking to profit thereby, the Rohilla leader Ghulam Kadir had captured Delhi, driving out its Mahratta garrison, then, quickly taking the fortress of Aligur, he formed an uneasy alliance with Ismael Beg, the almost-victor of the Battle of Tunga. Ismael Beg comes down to us as a competent but unlucky soldier, as well as an honourable man who fought consistently to preserve what was left of the Mughal Empire. By contrast Ghulam Kadir was simply a bandit and freebooter, and by today's standards quite possibly a dangerous psychopath. Although ferociously brave in battle, he was cruel and dangerous, and would later personally blind the Mughal Emperor Shah Alam II in his own throne room. However, at this point the two commanders were cooperating against the Marathas and their Jat allies.

Leaving a covering force to continue the siege of Agra fort, Ismael Beg and Ghulam Kadir seemingly decided to advance upon Bhurtpur to try to break the current impasse. The *raja* there, Ranjit Singh Jat, was Madhaji's firm ally. Their army supposedly consisted of 12,000 cavalry, 25,000 infantry of sorts, and perhaps 100 guns.[3] However, this seems rather high especially if the two commanders left a covering force in front of Agra fort. They were opposed by a Maratha-Jat army of roughly the same total strength but more numerous in light Maratha cavalry, and lacking heavy guns. Of regular drilled infantry the Marathas and Jats had at least four different mercenary units. De Boigne's two battalions stood on the left of the Maratha first line as part of the left wing of the Maratha-Jat forces. The French mercenary Lestineau, now in the service of the Jat *rajah*, commanded three battalions with the French mercenary Louis Borquien as one of his battalion commanders, and with Perron as a junior officer in another battalion while the rest of the Jat regular infantry, also in the first line, were commanded two Muslim officers, including one Jahangir Khan who led a force of three battalions and 10 guns.[4] The Maratha section of the combined army was led by Rana Khan, Madhaji's confidante and close friend but also a general of significant talent, especially in the normal Maratha guerrilla style. The Jats were commanded by Sew Singh Foujdar but the command of the Jat infantry seems to have devolved upon Lestineau. Having possibly the larger half of the Maratha-Jat forces the Jats took up the right and the Marathas therefore the left of the combined battle line. Overall deployment followed the traditional style with cavalry on each flank and in a second line – this second line being mostly the more irregular parts of the Maratha forces. The centre of the battle line therefore being composed of the regular infantry with their guns to the front.

As was customary in formal Indian battles this engagement opened with a cannonade, in this case from Ismael Beg's guns. Ghulam Kadir then advanced against the infantry of the Jat portion of the allied forces eventually putting them to flight along with much of the assorted cavalry in that part of the field. Lestineau's infantry however stood firm and, despite the treachery of

---
3   Sarkar, *Fall of the Moghul Empire*, Vol.3, p.248.
4   Sarkar, *Fall of the Moghul Empire*, Vol.3, p.249.

Jahangir Khan's mercenaries, who changed sides, held on. Over on the other flank it was a similar story. Ismael Beg quickly seeing off much of the Maratha cavalry but being unable to complete the victory because of the steadiness of De Boigne's two battalions and their guns. As night fell the surviving regular battalions of Lestineau and De Boigne formed an ordered rear guard and the Jats and Marathas retreated to Bhurtpore to lick their wounds. De Boigne's troops, along with the equally steady battalions of Lestineau, had once again proved their worth.

The Battle of Agra – 18 June 1788

Flushed with their victory Ismael Beg and Ghulam Kadir now captured the Jat fortress and arsenal of Kumher almost without firing a shot. They captured immense quantities of munitions and food enabling them to continue their campaign. However, the next move, against the fortress of Dig in mid-May 1788, which was also in Jat hands, proved a costly failure as Ismael's attempt at an escalade using dismounted cavalry turned into a bloody shambles despite the courage of his troopers.[5] The nearby Maratha cavalry under Rana Khan pursued Ismael Beg's shattered forces killing many. Yet once reunited with Ghulam Kadir, Ismael's forces were still able to encamp outside Agra fort again by the end of May.

In the meantime, Madhaji had received more men from the Deccan as well as at least some money to relieve his straitened finances. These new troops consisted of some 5,000 cavalry under Devji Gauli who were added to Rana Khans forces. This host then proceeded to cut off all supplies to the two Khans siege camp at Agra: 'The troops of the Jat Raja and Scindia hover at a distance of eight to 10 *kos* (roughly 20–25 kilometres) around the army of Ghulam Kadir and Ismael Beg. In whichever direction the two khans turn their faces, our men do not stay, but flee away being too afraid to stand a fight.'[6]

This kind of guerrilla warfare was no place for De Boigne's or Lestineau's trained infantry, but it was the *raison d'être* of the Maratha light horse. Rana Khan now proved his ability as a general again. Devji Gauli was sent on a long-range raid across the River Jumna into that tract of fertile country known as the Doab to stop supplies and reinforcements reaching the two Khans' siege camp at Agra. In these raids the Marathas captured nine guns and destroyed at least one battalion of *sepoys* belonging to Ghulam Kadir. The city of Koil, at that time belonging to Kadir, was pillaged mercilessly with food, horses and cattle being taken. Vital grain convoys to feed the army besieging Agra fort were captured and diverted to the Maratha forces.

Faced with this threat to his Jaghirs, and therefore his income, Kadir abandoned his ally and retired into the Doab to protect his territory. Ismael Beg was left with a much-diminished army, short of food and munitions, suffering daily desertions and plummeting morale amongst his now hungry and ragged forces. The situation became so bad that Ramru, one of Ismael's commanders, whose *compoo* consisted of four battalions of *telingas* with 16 guns negotiated secretly with Rana Khan to turn his coat in return for Rs

---

5   Sarkar, *Fall of the Moghul Empire*, Vol.3, p.249.
6   Sarkar, *Fall of the Moghul Empire*, Vol.3, p.250.

60,000 and a *jaghir* of his own. This offer was gratefully accepted, apparently on the eve of battle.

Rana Khan deployed his army on the open plain with all his European led battalions in the first line with, as normal, their guns in front of the infantry. There were at least five battalions; two of De Boignes and three of Lestineau's, numbering perhaps as many as 4,000 but probably a little less. There were also an unknown number of other infantry, survivors of the earlier actions, but it is unlikely that the Marathas had as many as 8,000 infantry of all types. On each flank there were large bodies of cavalry, with a third body of horse forming a second line behind the infantry centre. These last, assuming traditional deployment and command, would be under Rana Khan's own hand. The two flanking bodies of the first line being commanded by Appa Khande Rao and Devji Gauli. As usual cavalry outnumbered the infantry by some margin. Devji Gauli's 5,000, or at least their victorious survivors, had returned from their raiding and Rana Khan and Appa Khandi Rao also had their own followings present. It is therefore not too wide of the mark to estimate the Maratha cavalry at between 15,000 and 20,000, though at least some of these would be little more than *pindari* bandits who could by no means be relied on in battle.

Ismael Beg was in trouble, caught somewhat by surprise in his camp, expecting only the usual Maratha raids and skirmishing, his forces were not initially deployed for battle. Numbers are uncertain and it is possible that he was actually outnumbered. However, he got his guns into action and these, being heavier than those of De Boigne and Lestineau, at first caused some casualties on the advancing Maratha army. Ramru's four battalions of regular *telingas* with their guns refused to take part in the action, suborned as they had been, so Ismael, courageous as ever, personally led a series of neck or nothing cavalry charges with his Mughal and Pathan horse against the Maratha regulars in the centre. However, these regular *sepoys* were now veterans and were not discomfited by the bravery of Ismael's attacks. They beat off these reckless assaults with showers of grape and the steady platoon fire of muskets. As the Mughal assaults failed the Maratha horse from the wings outflanked Ismael Beg's tired troopers and put them to flight. A wounded Ismael fled to Agra city and, pausing only to place his favourite mistress upon an elephant to join him in his flight, crossed the Jumna and arrived at Ghulam Kadirs camp alone. The unfortunate mistress having drowned whilst crossing the rising river.[7]

De Boigne's trained infantry had once again proved their worth along with the equally steady battalions of Lestineau, but needing rest, payment, and refitting the Maratha forces waited for three months at Gwalior before approaching Delhi. Ismael Beg, having quarrelled with Ghulam Kadir, submitted to Madhaji and De Boigne's battalions were installed as part of the garrison of Delhi fort where finally the now blind old Emperor was freed

---

[7] The account of the Battles of Chaksana and Agra are drawn from the varying accounts in Compton, *Particular Account*, pp.38–44; Grant Duff, *History of the Marathas*, Vol.2, pp.144–146; and Sarkar, *Fall of the Moghul Empire*, Vol.3, pp.242–255, though Sarkar dates the Battle of Agra as 17 June.

from the lunacy of Ghulam Kadir's rages. Kadir was pursued by forces which included Lestineau who upon Kadirs capture seems to have acquired that man's saddlebags filled with the jewels he had looted from the Emperor's *zenana* and with which, together with the back pay of his battalions, he absconded to British territory and thence to France.[8] Lestineau's battalions would, of course, become part of De Boigne's veteran First Brigade.

The War Against the Rajput states

The next time De Boigne went to war he had a full brigade at his call. The complex politics of northern India need not detain us long. Suffice it to say that Ismael Beg, having renounced his temporary submission made after his defeat at Agra, was by 1790 once more in the field. This time he was in alliance with the Hindu *rajas* of the Rajput states of Jaipur and Jodhpur who had declared against Scindia, whose ambition they rightly feared. These two *rajas* had promised to pay the expenses of Ismael's new army but, as was normal, promises did not produce actual cash. Nevertheless Ismael Beg, Pratap Sigh of Jaipur and Bijay Singh of Jodhpur gathered a significant army of as many as 50,000, with perhaps 125 pieces of artillery, and encamped at the mouth of the pass to the city of Patan some 95 kilometres (60 miles) north of Jaipur. The allied forces then entrenched themselves, seemingly to await events during the hot weather and allow time for Ismael Beg to recover from a fever. The Maratha forces including De Boigne's new brigade came up by mid-May and encamped some 13 kilometres (eight miles) from the allied camp. Nothing of note took place for almost a month, other than skirmishing, the usual Maratha raiding, and attempts to interdict the Rajput and Mughal supplies which had some success. However, an attempt against the Rajput lines on 22 May was a failure with the fighting costing De Boigne around 200 casualties and Ismael Beg about the same.[9]

The Battle of Patan – 20 June 1790

All was not well in the allied camp. As usual Madhaji had sought to sow dissention amongst his enemies. In this endeavour he had some success. The Rajputs did not trust the Mughals or visa-versa. The two Rajput *rajas* could not put aside their own age-old rivalries, and even within the Mughal section of the combined forces there was serious tension. Abdul Matlab Khan who commanded five or six battalions of *sepoys* with 25 guns separated himself from the main Mughal force and encamped amongst the Rajput Rathor cavalry, so much did he fear for his personal safety. This was perhaps because he may have been induced to change sides for a bribe of one and a half lakhs of rupees (Rs 150,000).[10] The allied command was, therefore, far from unified. This disunity was to have serious consequences.

---

8   Compton, *Particular Account*, pp.368–369.
9   Sarkar, *Fall of the Moghul Empire*, Vol.4, p.16.
10 Sarkar, *Fall of the Moghul Empire*, Vol.4, p.18.

On the morning of 20 June, the Maratha commanders, stung by a letter from Madhaji urging action drew up for an assault on the Rajput-Mughal lines. The forces of the fragile alliance were encamped behind their earthworks with Ismael Beg's contingent forming the extreme right of the line, which was also the southern end of the position so, working northwards, next came a body of Rathor cavalry, then the possibly treacherous battalions of Abdul Matlab Khan. Next came the main body of Rajput and Rathor horse in the centre, and finally at the northern, or left wing extremity, came a body of Rajput infantry and artillery. As was customary the infantry was drawn up behind the dug in guns. There were around 100–125 guns, many slow firing and perhaps only those of the *sepoy* battalions – such as the 25 pieces under Abdul Matlab – could be even remotely compared with the guns of De Boigne's brigade.[11]

De Boigne gives the following strengths for the troops opposing him in a letter written four days after the battle and later published in the *Calcutta Gazette*:

> The enemy's force consisted of 12,000 Rathor cavalry, 6,000 from Jaipur. 5,000 Moghals under Ismael Beg, and 2,000 under Allyhar Beg Khan; of foot, they had 12,000 men and 100 pieces of artillery, and with Ismael Beg, 5,000 Telignas and matchlockmen with 21 pieces of artillery, 4,000 Rohillas, 5,000 Fakeers called Attyles and Brakys, and Rajput Sybundees with eight pieces of cannon, and 4,000 Menahs who were of great service to the enemy, as the battle was given at the foot of the hills.[12]

So, the forces that faced De Boigne were a polyglot mixture of the traditional and the almost new. Ismael Beg's *telingas* were commanded solely by Muslim officers and were, as has been previously noted, modelled on Ibrahim Khan Gardi's battalions, who were themselves raised in imitation of European troops Such brigades seem to have been quite common amongst those Indian warlords who could not, or would not, engage Europeans to train their infantry and artillery. However well trained these frequently unpaid soldiers were, their commanders were in it for the money and could be, and sometimes were, suborned by promises of bribes and *jaghirs*.

De Boignes brigade was in the centre flanked by two large bodies of Maratha horse with a third large body behind. The only artillery on the Maratha side were De Boigne's lighter pieces, but having European-style drilled crews these 50 or so guns had a far faster firing rate than the heavier metal of the Mughal-Rajput forces, certainly twice the speed and perhaps three times as fast for short periods. However, despite being drawn up for battle for six or seven hours nothing happened, other than a little skirmishing between rival cavalry outposts. As the sun began to set with action looking increasingly less likely some of the Rajput and Mughal soldiers began to prepare their evening meal. As their watchfulness decreased De Boigne saw

---

11 Sarkar, *Fall of the Moghul Empire*, Vol.4, p.18.
12 W.S. Seton-Karr, *Selections from the Calcutta Gazette* (Calcutta: O.T. Cutter, Military Orphan Press, 1865), Vol.II, p.269.

his chance. A petty cavalry skirmish began the action, but it soon escalated as some 2,000 Maratha horse – mainly *pindaris* – attacked the Mughal-Rajput gun bullocks as they were brought into camp for the night.[13]

The following account of the fighting is De Boigne's own, from the same letter published in the *Calcutta Gazette*:

> I have often tried to harass and surprise the enemy, but their natural, strong, and almost impregnable situation, added to their very great superiority in numbers both in troops and artillery, rendered all my exertions fruitless. At last, tired out with vexation, I determined to march from our ground in three columns, so as to form the line from the centre of each, with ease and celerity; in that way I advanced at a little more than gun-shot distance from the enemy, where I formed my little army consisting of two lines and a reserve, the Marhatta horse in the rear and on our flanks. After waiting the best part of the day with impatient hopes to see them marching against us, as they had threatened, at last about three o'clock, a few Marhatta horse began to skirmish with the enemy's right wing, consisting of horse, which shortly increased from five to six thousand; but they were soon beat off. I was now encouraged to try if something better could not be done by our side; and in order to induce them to come out from their stronghold, I ordered the line to advance, after a warm cannonade of about an hour from both sides; the enemy not appearing to come out, I still advanced till we came within reach of grape-shot; the halting, we gave and received from each gun nearly forty rounds of grape, which made it a warm business, we being in the plain, and they in the trenches. The evening was now far advanced, and seeing at the same time such numerous bodies of the enemy's cavalry in motion, and ready to fall on us if they could find an opening, I thought it prudent to move on rather quicker, which we did till the firing of platoons began; but we had already lost such numbers of people, principally clashies, that those remaining were unable to drag the guns any further; I therefore gave immediate orders to storm their lines sword in hand, which was as soon executed, upon which the enemy, not relishing at all this close fighting, gave way on all sides, infantry as well as cavalry, leaving us in possession of all their guns, baggage, bazar, elephants and everything else. The day being now closed, put an end to the slaughter of the enemy, which must have been very considerable if we had had an hours more day-light.[14]

The victory was gained by the superior discipline and training of De Boigne's brigade. The ability of his drilled gunners to fire at least twice as fast as the opposition (Sarkar calls De Boigne's guns 'quick firing') gave his lighter artillery, once in range, a decided edge. His mention of platoon fire also shows that his infantry, trained and disciplined in the British style, had an edge over even the trained *sepoys* of the enemy and a huge firepower advantage at close quarters over the miscellaneous matchlocks of the Rajput and Rohilla irregulars. However, the disunited command of the Mughal-Rajput forces did not help matters. According to Indian sources Ismael received more

---

13 Sarkar, *Fall of the Moghul Empire*, Vol.4, p.19.
14 Seton-Karr, *Selections from the Calcutta Gazette*, Vol.II, pp.268–269.

troops during the battle but these merely began to plunder his camp. He was therefore forced to divert troops to stop this:

> ... two battalions from the brigade of Hamraj Bakhshi which was confronting De Boigne. On seeing this untimely movement, De Boigne ascribed it to a panic among the enemy and made a sudden assault and routed the *paltans* seizing their twenty-five guns. ... Jiva Bakhshi with 20,000 cavalry delivered a charge and fell in a tumultuous body on the Mirza. The Rajputs came to the defence of Ismael and fought well but De Boigne showered so many shot that many of them were slain ... At last it came to hand to hand fighting. The chief sardar of the Rathors was slain and this in the end became the cause of the Rajput defeat.[15]

It is questionable if De Boigne could actually see such a movement during his advance, but seeing some kind of confusion in the enemy line is certainly a possibility and De Boigne's drilled troops would be capable of taking advantage of it. What is clear here is that the Maratha cavalry took a more serious part in the fighting than De Boigne's somewhat disparaging remarks imply, and that there was significant fighting between the Maratha cavalry protecting De Boigne's flanks and Mughal horse under Ismael Beg. This combat must have allowed De Boigne to make his assault unmolested.

A question arises over the much-vaunted bravery of the Rathor cavalry. That there was some fighting between these reckless cavaliers and the Marathas is indicated by Sarkar:

> Ghopal Rao sent some squadrons to skirmish against the Rathors in the centre. These Deccani masters of Parthian tactics after a little demonstration, pretended to give way. The Rathors followed in reckless pursuit at full gallop with loud cries of victory, leaving their sheltered position on the heights. As soon as they descended into the plain, and came within range, the artillery of De Boigne opened a deadly fire mowing down hundreds among the dense Rajput masses. The remnant fled back to the hills. De Boigne followed up this success by advancing at the head of his battalions and seizing the artillery of Abdul Matalb.[16]

Todd, in his *Annals and Antiquities of Rajasthan*, asserts that the Rathor cavalry once again 'charged up to the muzzles of De Boignes cannon' and further that the Rathors suffered 3,000 casualties.[17] De Boigne's letter makes no mention of this except to say: 'The Maratha cavalry stood on our flanks as spectators; they began the skirmish in which they had only six men killed and forty wounded. Had it not been for two battalions of mine which changed front when the enemy's cavalry were charging ours, the Marathas would have seen fine play.'[18]

Yet Todd also gives us a rather disparaging rhyme, still current when he wrote 30 or so years after the battle, which gives a little credence to the idea

---

15 As quoted in Sarkar, *Fall of the Moghul Empire*, Vol.4, p.19.
16 Sarkar, *Fall of the Moghul Empire*, Vol.4, p.20.
17 Todd, *Annals and Antiquities*, Vol.2, pp.876–877.
18 As quoted in Compton, *Particular Account*, p.53.

that the Rathors were not their usual do or die selves on that particular day. Freely translated, the rhyme runs:

> Five of the things of Marwar,
> Horse, Shoes, Turban,
> Manly moustache and Sword.
> Five signs of manhood,
> Left the Rathors at Patan.[19]

These apparently conflicting sources are somewhat irreconcilable. The current author's own interpretation of the battle based upon these disparate accounts runs as follows.

Once deployed, in two lines with a reserve, there was little De Boigne could do until an opening occurred. The opportunity came as the Marathas began the fight to acquire the Mughal and Rajput gun bullocks. Ismael Beg's reaction as usual was to attack and he led a charge which dispersed this Maratha incursion. This fracas caused De Boigne to begin his advance and at this point the action became general, with the Mughal-Rajput forces opening a cannonade. Ismael Beg was personally involved in the fighting so could not command his troops. This may have given rise to Dr Parihar's assertion that Ismael Beg 'deserted at the first shot', which on his past battlefield behaviour seems somewhat unlikely.[20] Indeed Grant Duff asserts precisely the opposite and that Ismael Beg 'fought with his usual bravery and a body of his Pathans thrice charged through the regular infantry of the Marathas.'[21]

Again, De Boigne's account makes no mention of such a charge so, even assuming it happened, it had no major effect on De Boigne's advance to the enemy trenches. Whatever the precise course of events the fractured command of the allies led to considerable confusion. One of Ismael Beg's two regular brigades had possibly been induced to treachery and, as has already been noted, was encamped amongst the Rathor horse some distance away from the rest of Ismael's troops. The Deccani Maratha cavalry under Ghopal Bhao faced the main mass of the Rathor horse and were charged by them in response to Maratha skirmishing and upon being charged fled. This may have been a feigned flight as suggested by Sarkar but the end result was the same and caused the only serious dislocation of De Boigne's advance.[22] He had two of his battalions change front to face the threat from the Rathors and to cover his now exposed flank. It must have been the fire from these two battalions that caused the Rathors to break and flee, and it would be this action that caused the majority of Rathor casualties. Once his flank was secure De Boigne could once more advance and enter the enemy works 'sword in hand' completing his victory.

De Boigne's own account continues:

---

19 Bidwell, *Swords for Hire*, p.64.
20 Parihar, *Marwar and the Marathas*, p.121.
21 Grant Duff, *History of the Marathas*, Vol.2, p.174.
22 Sarkar, *Fall of the Moghul Empire*, Vol.4, p.20.

Our victory is astonishing! A complete victory gained by a handful of men, over such a number in such a position. It may surprise you when I say that in less than three hours time 12,000 round and 1,500 grape shot were fired by us and by the enemy much more as they had two guns to our one.

During all the engagement I was on horseback encouraging my men. Thank God I have realised all the sanguine expectations of Scindia. My Officers, in general, behaved well; to them I am a great deal indebted for the fortunes of the day.

We have had 120 men killed and 472 wounded, the enemy not more perhaps not so much, as they were entrenched, but they have lost a vast number of cavalry.

I have taken 107 pieces of artillery, 6,000 stand of arms, 252 colours fifteen elephants (amongst them are Ismael Beg's five elephants) 200 camels 513 horses and above 3,000 oxen. I intend to send the whole to Scindia as soon as it may be practicable. All their camp was burnt or destroyed; they have absolutely saved nothing but their lives.[23]

While the huge expenditure of artillery ammunition may seem improbable there is no doubt that the Battle of Patan was won primarily by De Boigne's disciplined infantry and gunners. Traditional Indian armies were no match for these troops. The combination of drilled *sepoys* and more importantly drilled and mobile artillery had won the day against formidable odds.

Ismael Beg's army was no more, 10 of his battalions, doubtless those of the brigades of Abdul Matlab and Hamraj Bakhshi, surrendered when the town of Patan was taken three days later. One may conjecture that De Boigne recruited many of these mercenary *sepoys* to replace his casualties but also to become the core of the Second Brigade which would take the field in 1791.

The Battle of Merta – 10 September 1790

The war against the Rajput states was by no means over. Patan was a major defeat, the Rajput *rajas* of Jaipur and Jodhpur were down but not out. However, disunity prevailed and lack of money to pay the troops was, as usual, at the heart of this. In the months following the battle of Patan Ismael Beg remained in the field with a scratch force of around 10,000, mostly his own retainers, guarding the frontiers of Jaipur against a threatened Maratha invasion. However, Jaipur was as usual without funds to pay Ismael and, in the interim, the Marathas had by passed Jaipur and sat down in front of the Jhodpur fortress of Ajmer to take it by siege. Bijay Singh, Maharaja of Jodhpur therefore, promised to pay Ismael Beg sufficient money to keep his forces in the field, Ismael began to transfer his troops from Jaipur to Jodhpur but the Marathas were too quick for him and, leaving a covering force of 2,000 horse to blockade Ajmer, raised the siege and marched to the town of Merta where a Jodhpur army was gathering for the relief of the fortress. It was this army that Ismael Beg was supposed to reinforce. The Marathas however forestalled this by moving to attack the assembling Jodhpur forces before Ismael could join them. Bijay Singh made an effort to persuade De

---

23 As quoted in Compton, *Particular Account*, p.53.

Boigne to turn his coat offering him the fortress of Ajmer and its attendant lands, if he would change sides.[24] De Boigne, according to the *India Gazette*, rejected this offer in a letter to Bijay Singh: 'Scindia had already given him Jhodpur and Jaipur, and that he would not be so unreasonable, as to expect, that he would exchange them for Ajmir.'[25]

The Jodhpur forces gathering at Merta were, even more than usual, traditional in style. Merta was a traditional mustering site and had been fought over several times in its history. Bijay Singh called in all the clans and fighting families at his command. The Rajas of Bikaneer, Kishnagar and Rupnagar (all members of Bijar Singh's extended family) contributed troops, though the Bikaneer contingent withdrew before the battle.[26] The core of this army was, as would be expected, the Rathor and Rajput cavalry some 25,000–30,000 strong. A mere 10,000 infantry accompanied the horse. None of these infantry were regulars and only the Naga matchlockmen were of any use at all. The artillery was laughable, a collection of 25 'old guns' scraped together and 'put into repair' were all that Jodhpur could command.[27]

Yet Todd makes it clear that the Rajput cavaliers were prepared to fight manfully for their independence: 'The Prince ... issued his summons to every Rathor in his dominions to assemble under their Raja's banner, once more planted on the ensanguined plains of Merta. A fine army was embodied; not a Rathor who could wield a sword but brought it for service in the cause of his country.'[28]

For all the high-flown rhetoric Todd's words speak more of scraping the bottom of the barrel in desperation than of military efficiency. Even so, the coming campaign would be no matter of mere marching. De Boigne had his own problems. In crossing the sandy bed of the dried up River Luni several of his guns and tumbrils stuck fast, and precious time was lost digging them out. The Rajputs seem to have known of this yet declined to fall upon the mercenaries with their cavalry, preferring instead to remain in camp, their high command listless from the effects of opium and under orders from an absent *raja* and his idiotic minister to remain where they were. De Boigne therefore eventually managed to get his guns across the riverbed without molestation, doubtless heaving a sigh of relief, and continued his march, arriving before the Rajput camp at Merta on the morning of 9 September. De Boigne – despite the entreaties of the Maratha commander, the experienced and canny Lakwa Dada – insisted on resting his men and scouting the enemy position. The 9th, therefore, saw only a little cannonading from the Rajput camp.

Early on the morning of 10 September De Boigne drew up is brigade for the attack on the Rajput position. The Maratha forces consisted of roughly 25,000–30,000 horse plus De Boigne's brigade. The total number of guns is

---

24 Compton, *Particular Account*, p.55 cites a letter written on 1 September 1790 and published in Calcutta.
25 As quoted in George-Marie Raymond, *Mémoire sur la Carrière Militaire et Politique de M. le General Comte De Boigne* (Chambéry: Puthod, 1830), footnote p.89.
26 Todd, *Annals and Antiquities*, Vol.2, p.879.
27 Parihar, *Marwar and the Marathas*, p.124.
28 Todd, *Annals and Antiquities*, Vol.2, p.878.

THE ARMY OF HINDUSTAN AT WAR

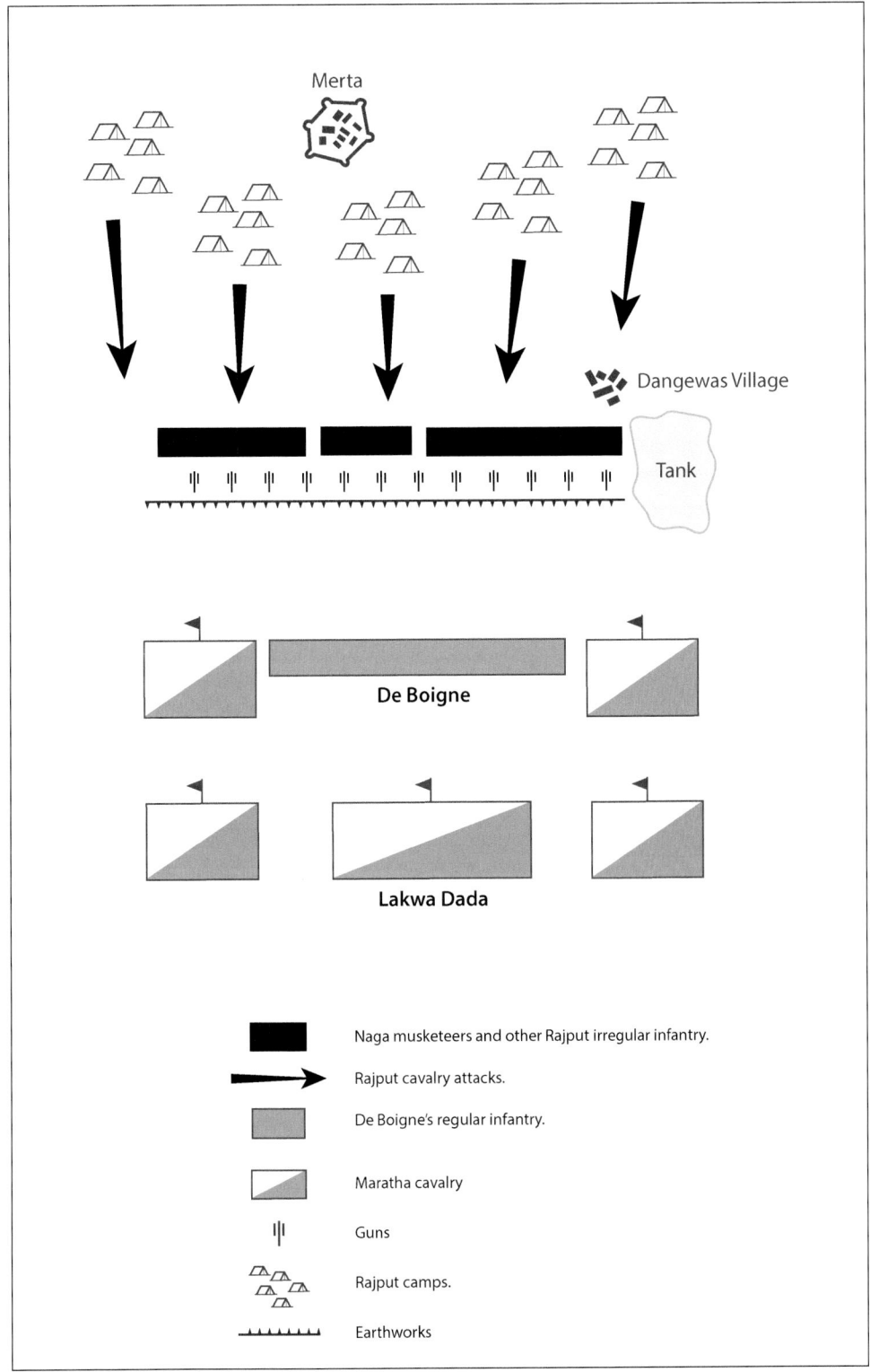

Sketch of the dispositions at the Battle of Merta (not to scale). The Maratha second line cavalry being somewhat further back than the plan suggests.

given as 80 which would probably indicate that other artillery, of the old style, was present as well as the 50 guns of the regular brigade.[29]

Deployment was in the usual style, identical to that used at Patan. De Boigne's battalions were in two lines, possibly with a reserve, guns to the front. Gun bullocks remaining in camp, guns and possibly tumbrils moved on the battlefield by *kelasis* as well as the gunners themselves. A full-strength brigade had, as we have seen, 10 battalions with each battalion having a five gun battery attached, either 3-pounders or 6-pounders. In theory one of the five guns was a howitzer but not all of the battalions seem to have had these. Skinners battalion, a little later, had five 6-pounder guns and no howitzer. In addition – again in theory – the brigade could have also deployed a small battering train of heavier pieces and mortars, but it is very unlikely these would be used in the field as moving these heavy pieces would prove problematic. Possibly their crews and *kelsais* were added to the field gun detachments, but this is pure speculation. So this leaves 50 guns to face the Rajput 25, with the infantry battalions behind as at Patan in two lines with a reserve.

The rest of the Maratha deployment is easily dealt with. As usual large bodies of Maratha horse were on each flank and to the rear of De Boigne's mercenaries. However, a mile to the rear was another body of Marathas horse. These were not Madhaji's troops but those of his rival Tukaji Holkar, present as allies but in reality there to stake a claim for the results of any Maratha victory. No love was ever lost between the houses of Scindia and Holkar and the presence of these 5,000 cavalry would in time cost both houses dear.

The Rajput deployment is a little more problematic. Their guns, supported by the Naga matchlock musketeers occupied a defensive position in front of the village of Dangewas with that village's tank, or reservoir, to their left, protecting their flank. As usual the guns were dug in the infantry posted behind. These Naga musketeers were irregulars rather than *telingas* and had little idea of drill or manoeuvre. The rest of the Jodhpur forces consisted of cavalry and these seem to have been spread out and encamped below the walls of the town of Merta in a somewhat haphazard manner.[30] There seems to have been no effective central command. Each clan chieftain led his own warriors into the fighting as they became aware of the Maratha approach. Certainly, they were not prepared for battle when De Boigne began his assault against the Rajput artillery and Naga infantry at dawn on 10 September. Indeed, many of the chieftains seem to have been in an opium induced haze as taking the drug seems to have been a major vice of the Rajput nobility.[31] Todd writes:

> About an hour before daybreak De Boigne led his brigade to the attack and completely surprised the unguarded Rajputs. They were awoke by showers of grape-shot which soon broke their position: all was confusion; the resistance was feeble. It was the camp of the irregular infantry and guns which broke and

---

29 Compton, *Particular Account*, p.60.
30 Parihar, *Marwar and the Marathas*, pp.124–125.
31 Compton, *Particular Account*, pp.57–58.

endeavoured to gain Merta, and the civil commanders took to flight. The alarm reached the more distant quarters of the brothers in arms the chiefs of Awa and Asop. The latter was famed for the immense quantity of opium he consumed, and with difficulty could his companion awake him with the appalling tidings.[32]

A contemporary letter to 'a Calcutta paper' takes up the story:

> On our side the same number of horse [30,000] 6,000 or 7,000 rank and file and 80 pieces of artillery. On the 10th, at break of dawn, we were ordered to advance on the enemy, the disposition of our troops being the same as at the memorable battle of Patan. A heavy cannonade soon commenced supported on both sides with great vigour. Our first line of 50 pieces of cannon shortly after began to fire with grape. And by means of our superiority of guns drove the enemy from their lines. But a French Officer of Scindia's, elated with success advanced without orders of the line of battle at the head of three battalions. The enemy soon took advantage of his imprudence and charged him so vigorously that it was not without great difficulty that he affected his retreat.[33]

The 'French Officer' was one Captain Rohan in command of the left wing of the mercenary brigade. These three battalions, presumably two from the first line and their second line supporting battalion, led by Rohan, advanced somewhat faster than the rest of the battle line and became isolated from the rest of the brigade. A body of Rathor cavalry, coming to the battle from their camp, had the good fortune to arrive at just the right place at just the right time to exploit this gap in the line and, without further ado, charged Rohan's unsupported battalions like a tsunami and rolled them up, putting many to the sword and effectively destroying them. While it is nowhere specifically stated this must have happened after the Rajput infantry had been dispersed, because the surprised Rajput cavalry arrived on the battlefield rather haphazardly as their leaders awoke from their drug induced slumbers. Seeing this disaster De Boigne put the other seven battalions of his command into a large hollow square, while the Rathors pursued the broken fugitives and ploughed exultantly into the Maratha cavalry of the second line of the army. This success brought more Rathors out of their various camps so that despite seeing off the Naga musketeers and other Rajput infantry, De Boigne was now faced with an increasing number of exultant Rajput cavalry, eager either complete their victory or wipe out the stain of past defeats and perceived slurs upon their high sense of their own honour. Many of these Rathor warbands engaged the Maratha horse who were pushed back and broken, being pursued by the Rajput cavalry until they came upon those Maratha allied horse sent by Tukaji Holkar a mile or more in the rear of the main Maratha army. These Marathas halted the Rajput pursuit and rallied some of Madhaji's fleeing horse but do not seem to have approached the main scene of the action immediately, preferring perhaps to await events.

---

32 Todd, *Annals and Antiquities*, Vol.2, pp.879–881, and the fascinating footnote on pp.881–882 of his conversations with De Boigne himself during the general's retirement in Chambery.
33 As quoted in Compton, *Particular Account*, pp.60–61.

In the meantime, the main wave of Rathor fury was to smash itself against De Boigne's square. The same letter to a 'Calcutta paper' continues:

> They then charged our main body in front, flanks and rear, but General De Boigne's foresight and incomparable presence of mind were the means of saving us, for upon perceiving the error which his officer had committed, and no doubt aware of the consequences, he formed us into a hollow square, so upon being surrounded shortly afterwards, we on all sides presented a front to the enemy.[34]

Nevertheless, despite the high courage of the Rathor cavalry, De Boigne's square was unbreakable. Platoon fire of muskets and those guns which still had crews caused carnage in the Rathor ranks. Outstanding valour and high honour were no match for musketry and discipline. As men and horses became exhausted the pressure on De Boigne's brigade lessened. The assaults became more piecemeal. Individual Rathor chieftains and their immediate followers walked up to the square intending to die rather than leave the field. By nine in the morning it was all over. Something approaching 5,000 Rajputs lay dead or wounded on the field. Yet even their enemies were in awe of their incredible bravery: 'It is impossible for me to describe the feats of Bravery performed by the "Jerd Kopperah Wallahs" or Forlorn Hope of the enemy. I have seen, after the line was broken fifteen or twenty men return to charge a thousand infantry and advance to within 10 or fifteen paces before all were shot.'[35]

Merta was stormed and ruthlessly pillaged later the same day, with the fort surrendering soon afterwards. De Boigne's casualties were not inconsiderable, falling mostly on the three battalions under the command of Captain Rohan. The brigade lost in total about 900 men. Captain Rohan though wounded survived. Captain Bahour or Baors also on the left did not. A Lieutenant Roberts was wounded by a ball from a multi-barrelled organ gun, 'Which is composed of about thirty six gun barrels so joined as to fire at once.'[36] This doubtless one of the 25 old guns in the Rajput artillery train.

Once again, De Boigne had proved the worth of his trained and disciplined infantry and artillery. Traditional Indian armies, no matter how courageous, could not stand up against their disciplined artillery and musketry. Nevertheless, De Boigne's quickness of mind in forming his battalions into a hollow square after Rohan's destruction certainly saved his brigade from possible destruction.

---

34 As quoted in Compton, *Particular Account*, pp.60–61.
35 The same letter to a 'Calcutta paper 'as quoted in Compton, *Particular Account*, p.61. *Jerd kopperah Wallahs* – Warriors wearing yellow garments (the Rajput colour of mourning) as a sign that they would win or die. When James Skinner first raised his famous cavalry regiment in 1803 they wore yellow coats.
36 Compton, *Particular Account*, p.61.

An Old Quarrel Resumed

Madhaji Scindia was now supreme in Hindustan, so the next two years were spent raising and training two more brigades to the pattern already described. A great cantonment and barracks was established at the city of Koil – close to the fortress of Alighur and the fortress itself was strengthened. These places became the centre of De Boigne's military and civil administration, all designed to improve the efficiency of the Army of Hindustan. Sufficient land revenue was set aside to pay for the establishment of the new brigades so that for all practical purposes De Boigne became civil governor of large tracts of Hindustan.

Yet all was not well in Hindustan, the generations old rivalry between the houses of Holkar and Scindia was about to erupt again. As was to be expected with a new round of an old quarrel this squabble centred on the division of the spoils at the end of the recent campaigns in Rajasthan. Holkar demanded an equal share of the Rajput tribute, despite his paltry contribution of a mere 5,000 horse, and sent in his predatory bands of Maratha Decani cavalry and *pindari* bandits to enforce his demands. Negotiations, despite repeated attempts by a 'peace party' on both sides and the intervention of the *Peshwa* (the nominal overlord of both Madhaji Scindia and Tukaji Holkar) were of no avail so the two rival houses slipped into war. Realising that they could not match De Boigne's brigade unaided, especially after a skirmish at Surauli in October 1792 when Holkar's cavalry fled and his commander's empty camp was captured. Holkar's family, led by the formidable lady Anhalya Bhai contracted the Chevalier Dudrenec to raise a brigade on the same model. However, as usual, a chronic lack of actual cash meant that the brigade numbered only four battalions, each of 400 bayonets, and with a mere five gun even though it was costing three lakhs of rupees per month.[37] As was usual with the mercenary infantry none were actually Marathas but, like De Boigne's *sepoys*, they were men of northern India; a mixture of men from Oudh and the Doab. Holkar's younger son, Malhar Rao, despised these new troops and was a fanatical and hugely boastful advocate of the traditional raiding style of Maratha warfare. To that end he demanded to be sent to the seat of the conflict in Rajputana with power to supersede the more experienced and cautious of Holkar's generals; Bapu Rao Holkar and Parashar Dadaji. Holkar's forces attempted to stop Scindia's army on the march on 29 May but the plan miscarried because of De Boigne's careful dispositions with both advanced guard and rear guard composed of his own battalions and guns. An attempted outflanking strike by Malhar Rao's division of cavalry upon the rear and baggage of Scindia's forces was beaten off by the infantry and guns supported by the Scindia's own household cavalry – the *kala-paga* – commanded by Lakwa Dada and a counterstrike by *pindaris* attached to Scindia's forces plundered Holkar's camp. At the head of the column De Boigne's advance guard deployed against the blocking force of irregular infantry and rocket men, and brushed them aside. At this, wiser

---

37 Sir Jadurnath Sarkar, 'The Battle of Lakheri', *The Modern Review*, February 1944, p.100.

heads in Holkar's army prevailed and they withdrew to fight another day. This engagement, the Battle of Panchilas, once again demonstrated the use of disciplined infantry and guns against the traditional styles of warfare in the Indian subcontinent. Malhar Rao's attempt at a sudden charge upon the rear of Scindia's forces had been a dismal failure.[38]

The Battle of Lakheri – 1 June 1793

However, the action at Panchilas was only the overture to the upcoming symphony. The main battle of the campaign would be fought a few days later and would be a much tougher proposition. The opposing forces for the upcoming contest were not dissimilar in numbers. Holkar's army consisted of roughly 25,000 assorted Maratha cavalry plus perhaps as many as 10,000 *pindari* freebooters who would be of little use in the coming battle. Of the infantry the best were Dudrenec's four battalions with their own guns, in total around 1,600 bayonets, the rest of the foot being a rabble of *ghoshais* and *baragais* and Nagas. The fighting monks of India were armed with the usual collection of matchlocks, swords and spears, but also provided with a plentiful supply of war rockets. There were perhaps as many as 10,000 of these irregulars. Of artillery there was a total of 38 guns all but five of these being the heavy immobile slow firing 'artillery of position' in the old Indian style. The remaining five, of course, belonging to Dudrenec's brigade. The army was commanded by Bapu Rao Holkar, who, with his Deccani cavalry took post on the right behind the irregular infantry and guns. In the centre of this second line stood Tukaji Holkar's own cavalry, commanded by Parashar Dadaji, and finally in this same second line stood the wild card Malhar Rao Holkar with this horse. Behind these stood a mob of *pindaris*. These large bodies of cavalry were some distance behind the first line. The irregulars in the first line were supported by Dudrenec's tiny force of four battalions with their few guns standing to their left. There do, however, seem to have been at least some irregular infantry and rocket men in the pass of Indegarh itself.

Unusually for a battle between Indian princes in the eighteenth century, and uniquely among De Boigne's battles, Lakheri was a fight where the terrain played a major part in the development of the contest. After their defeat at Panchilas the Holkarian forces retreated 30 kilometres (18 miles) south to the town of Lakheri which was effectively base camp for their army. Ghopal Rao Bhao and De Boigne followed up at a somewhat more leisurely pace and took station at the village of Balwan about 10 kilometres (six miles) northeast of Lakheri on 31 May. There they dropped their heavy baggage and camp followers while De Boigne reconnoitred the wooded pass through the nearby hills, behind which the enemy's camp lay. These hills separated the two armies and only the pass which led to the town of Indegarh would allow Scindia's army to come at Holkar's forces. The actual pass was 'three furlongs in width' (roughly 600 metres) but was cut by ravines and dry stream beds so that only one waggon could pass at once.[39] In addition the hills were covered in scrub and jungle making the manoeuvre of formed bodies of troops somewhat

---

38 Sarkar, *Fall of the Mughal Empire*, Vol.4, pp.73–74.
39 Sarkar, *Fall of the Mughal Empire*, Vol.4, p.75.

difficult. Nevertheless, De Boigne decided upon a reconnaissance in force and an attempt to clear the jungle (consisting mostly of babul, neem and dwarf tamarind trees) to enable easier passage for his guns. To that effect he sent a message to Gopal Rao Bhao: 'The path leading to the pass of Lakheri is just wide enough for one cart and the thick forest is unsuitable for cavalry movement. I am going alone with five battalions to cut down the jungle.'[40]

This would then enable the whole army to deploy and face Holkar's troops on the more open terrain at the other end of the pass. To that end De Boigne took five battalions and, one assumes, the *beldars* or pioneers, who would do the actual labouring, towards the pass on the morning of 1 June with the intention of improving the road thus enabling full deployment on the following day. Things did not go according to plan. While the *beldars* improved the track De Boigne's battalions entered the pass and almost at once came under a storm of fire from Holkars heavy 'artillery of position' at the other end of the pass. His battalions also came under fire from irregular musketeers and rocket men in the pass itself. De Boigne's first attempt to storm the pass using the 500 Rohilla irregulars attached to the brigade under their commander Abdal Khan, who were used to this type of mountain warfare, failed with some loss and De Boigne retired into the trees on the northern side of the pass where the enemy guns could do him little harm. He sent a message to Ghopal Rao but that worthy commander was already marching to the sound of the guns with the rest of the army, albeit with less speed than he liked because of the terrain.

However, as the rest of the infantry and all of the guns began to arrive in column of march and began their deployment under fire an unusual mischance of war occurred. A shot, described as 'a bullet', but equally possibly a rocket ignited an ammunition tumbril, and the resulting cataclysmic explosion and fire destroyed several more tumbrils and damaged the carriages of around a dozen guns in the crowded confines of the mouth of the pass.[41] The confusion caused was considerable, but once again discipline and training stemmed panic and officers and NCOs of the battalions immediately began to make order out of chaos. The austere and calm presence of their general gave the troops heart. As Bidwell puts it: 'Good soldiers are like iron filings in a magnetic field; they automatically seek for order and arrangement.'[42]

At least some of the infantry battalions were already in line at the head of the column, almost certainly those that had been involved in the initial reconnaissance, and these together with those least caught up in the conflagration were able to repulse a cavalry charge by Holkar's troops, though the uneven nature of the terrain was also of considerable help. To complete the enemy's discomfiture De Boigne personally led his bodyguard cavalry regiment in a counter charge at the large mass of Deccani horse facing him. As Sarkar puts it:

---

40 Sarkar, *Fall of the Mughal Empire*, Vol.4, p.75.
41 Charles, Comte de Boigne, *Mémoire sur la Carrière Militaire et Politique de M. le Général Comte de Boigne* (Chambery: Puthod, 1829), p.101, 'un boulet frappant sur le fer d'un caisson ouvert.'
42 Bidwell, *Swords for Hire*, p.73.

Just as the enemy horse stopped and hesitated, De Boigne launched his select cavalry on them. This body of only three hundred troopers mounted on superb horses and accoutred in the sumptuous style of the famous Bengal Cavalry of the British East India Company's army, charged with the compactness and force of a bullet. Their green coats and red turbans were at first lost to view in the wavy ocean of parti-coloured Jackets and tight twisted orange pugrees of the Deccani horse. The blow was struck at the psychological moment. At the impact of disciplined valour, Holkar's rabble on horseback began to scatter like chaff before the wind.[43]

This now meant that De Boigne could get his infantry and surviving guns, albeit somewhat scorched, out of the pass and onto the somewhat more open ground beyond. They were backed up by the cavalry of Ghopal Rao Bhao and the elite *kala-paga*, Scindia's own household troops, under Lakwa Dada. There may have been a lull in the fighting at this point, the sources are unclear. Holkar's forces were by now short of water and ammunition. June in Rajputana is very hot so water had become an issue for Holkar's soldiers, and the fire of their artillery had diminished. Scindia's forces do not seem to have suffered so badly as they had camels carrying water to the troops. The Holkar family chronicle says: 'Our troops began to cry for water. In Scindia's campo camels continued to bring skins full of water, but on our side there was no water. Therefore the Gosains and Bairagis ran away. Munitions ran short…. Even our Maratha horse took to flight.'[44]

Just after noon as De Boigne's guns, now finally in position, began to bombard their enemy. Holkar's army began to give way. First the irregular infantry and rocket men broke, they had fought in the pass for some time but regular infantry fire and artillery was too much for them especially as their own guns were out of ammunition and could make little reply. Then the Deccani horse, already under pressure from Ghopal Rao Bhao and Lakwa Dada, broke along with the already fleeing *pindaris* covering the terrain with panic-stricken cavalry. Of Holkar's army only the four steady battalions of the Chevalier De Dudrenec's brigade remained in place, saddled with the entirely unenviable duty of being the rear guard.

De Boigne offered them a chance to surrender but this Dudrenec declined to do. His brigade, in its first major action, fought on hopelessly. Outnumbered and outgunned these men nevertheless gave a good account of themselves. All of their European officers were killed or wounded, except Dudrenec himself who escaped death by hiding in a pile of the slain.[45] His brigade simply ceased to exist.

All 38 of Holkar's guns were captured together with camels of treasure and waggons of rockets, along with all the other impedimenta of an Indian army at war, when Ghopal's troopers looted Holkar's camp. His army scattered to the winds. In his capital at Indore Tukaji Holkar was devastated by the defeat

---

43 Sarkar, *Fall of the Mughal Empire*, Vol.4, p.78.
44 Sarkar, 'The Battle of Lakheri', p.103, quoting the Holkaranchi Kaifiyat.
45 Sarkar, 'The Battle of Lakheri' p.104.

and 'in impotent rage' sent a raiding party to Scindia's capital at Ujjain and, as it was undefended, sacked it mercilessly.[46]

Even more than others of De Boigne's battles Lakheri had been won by the discipline and training of his infantry. Despite the calamity of the munitions explosion they had not given way to panic and in the time bought by the timely charge of De Boigne's bodyguard cavalry had re-organised and continued to advance out of the pass and towards Holkar's army. While it is true that Scindia's own cavalry had completed the victory, the solid base provide by the First Brigade had enabled that victory to be grasped in the first place.

These six major battles – beginning with Tunga and ending with Lakheri – complete De Boigne's purely battlefield career. In all six of these engagements, he was in the field himself commanding his troops. For the last three of the six he was in effect operational commander for the whole Maratha army. After the battle of Lakheri De Boigne would not fight again, yet his status would continue to rise under his master Madhaji Scindia. Convoluted Mahratta politics would play its part and now De Boigne became *Subahdar* of Hindustan, the effective military and civilian governor of the rump of the Mughal Empire. This came about simply because Madhaji needed a man he could trust. One who was not burdened by the baggage of internecine Mahratta squabbles. De Boigne's measures to improve administration within his *jaidads* for the financial support of his army had already proved themselves successful. These measures were simply expanded. However, on 12 February 1794 Madhaji died unexpectedly. His successor was Daulat Rao Scindia, an ineffective boy of 15. De Boigne immediately gave his allegiance to the new regime, which lent it a temporary stability, but also prepared the way for his retirement. In 1794 only three small expeditions were mounted under Majors Fremont, Sutherland and Gardner, and then, at the very end of the year, Perron's First Brigade set out for the Kharda campaign.[47] It was during this time of comparative peace that James Skinner was given his first commission as ensign by De Boigne and posted to a *najib* battalion in the Second Brigade, at that time commanded by Sutherland.[48] Skinner's first battalion commander was the Hanoverian Pohlmann, at that time a captain.

De Boigne, suffering a bout of illness, plainly thought it was time to retire while he still had time and energy left to enjoy the fruits of his often monumental labours so, to that end, on Christmas day 1795 he left his headquarters at Koil attended by his bodyguard cavalry and a huge train of baggage including four elephants and 150 camels.[49] The army that he had recruited, trained and led to victory would now have to do without him.

He left an army that was the strongest, best trained, best equipped, and most experienced on the subcontinent, with the possible exception of the British. This army had three brigades, actually the size of small divisions, with a total of 30 trained battalions and over 100 pieces of up-to-date artillery.

---

46 Compton, *Particular Account*, p.75.
47 See Chapter 7.
48 Baillie-Fraser, *Military Memoir*, Vol.1, p.108.
49 Compton, *Particular Account*, p.92.

The First Brigade had a tradition of victory and a reputation which gave it the nickname of *Cherai Fauj* (Army of Birds) because of its precision and alacrity on the battlefield. At the time of De Boigne's retirement there was no comparable force amongst any of the other country powers capable of standing unaided against it.

As a general De Boigne was more than merely competent but hardly the military genius that Sarkar claims. De Boigne took an element that was already present in the lexicon of warfare in eighteenth century India, that of the trained mercenary infantry *campoo*, and honed a weapon already present into a truly formidable force. His battlefield tactics were somewhat formulaic but were sufficient unto the day. His only real tactical innovation, in terms of Indian warfare, was the use of the large multiple battalion hollow square, long familiar to European commanders but largely unknown in India (though the British had used it in Bengal once or twice) simply because of the lack of steady drilled infantry from which to make such formations a success. As a tactic against the almost medieval cavalry-heavy armies he faced it was a successful manoeuvre but could not have been contemplated without the careful application of European style drill and discipline. It was the imparting of this steadiness in the areas of drill and discipline that would give the Army of Hindustan its victories.

Most importantly, given most Indian rulers attitudes to actually paying their troops, it was by far the best and most regularly paid. This steady financial basis, more than any other single factor, gave the Army of Hindustan its edge. He left an armaments industry that was capable of producing muskets and cannon of as good a quality as those of the Europeans. He had placed his employer Madhaji Scindia at the zenith of his power and in his name had, under the Mughal Emperor, governed the rump of the Empire as *Subahdar* of Hindustan. Yet he had never lost sight of his objective. He was a mercenary so, when he had made his fortune, he hung up his sword and went home. First to London, and then in his old age back to his home town of Chambery in Savoy.

Plate 1 Maratha and Army of Hindustan Colours.

Maratha 'National Flag' variously described as yellow, yellow ochre, saffron, or even orange. This flag is also noted in triangular and square examples. Carried in various forms, even before the time of Shivaji in the late seventeenth century. The *Juri-pakta* carried at the battle of Khardha was small and square but there were also swallow-tailed examples. Individual Maratha chieftains each seem to have had their own flags and versions of the *Juri-pakta* – see Chapter 5.

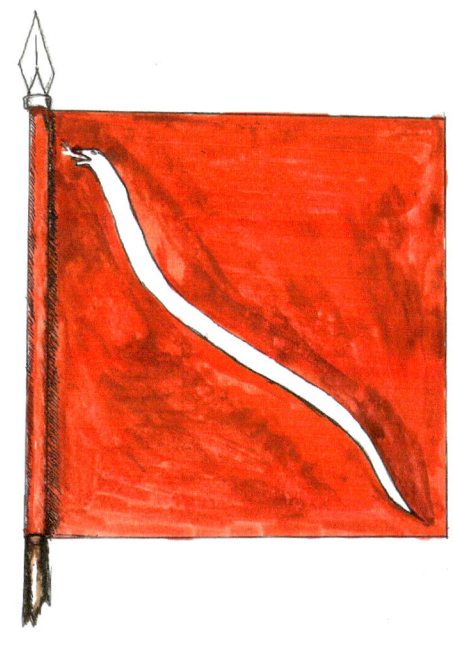

Scindia's flag as described by Captain John Pester, who saw multiple examples flying from the walls of Alighur. Since there were so many, they may have been unit flags.

De Boigne's cross of Savoy flag. Carried at the Battle of Merta and probably at all of his battles.

Conjectural combination of Scindia's and De Boigne's flags, postulated as a regimental colour of the Telinga battalions of the First Brigade.

Artwork © Andy Copestake.

Plate 2 Mughal Standards.

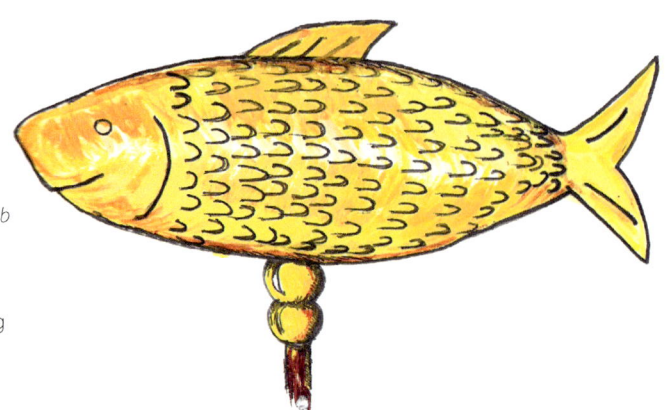

'Skinner's Brass Fish'. Actually the *Mahi Maratab* the symbol of the Viceroy of Hindustan, this version was awarded to Madhaji Scindia by the Emperor Shah Alam, but was lost at the Battle of Tunga. Skinner found it in his looting expedition after the Battle of Malpura some years later. Some versions were carried on elephants. See Chapter 8.

Mughal yak tail standard or *Touq*. Could also be pure white and have more than one tail, seemingly depending upon the power, rank and status of its owner. Only carried by cavalry. See Chapter 5 for more information on Mughal standards.

Mughal Hand standard. These could be of various sizes and examples are seen carried on elephants. Could also be a finial atop a silk standard. Again it all depended upon the status of the officer whose standard it was.

Artwork © Andy Copestake.

Plate 3 Telinga Sepoy, De Boigne's First Brigade, 1790–1803.

His appearance is very similar to the *sepoys* of the British East India Company. The only major difference being that De Boigne's *sepoys* carried swords as well as the usual musket and bayonet. Their muskets were made at the Army of Hindustan arsenals in Koil. (Artwork by Giorgio Albertini © Helion and Company)

Plate 4 Najib, De Boigne's First Brigade, 1790–1803.

The Najib battalions in each brigade were Muslim soldiers from Hindustan. Many were Rohilla tribesmen. Their clothing was more traditionally Indian in style. Weaponry consisted initially of a long-barrelled Indian matchlock musket, together with a sword and shield. These traditional weapons were later replaced by matchlocks with bayonets produced by the Army of Hindustan arsenals. Some battalions may have replaced matchlocks with flintlocks. This soldier's general appearance is also similar to many of the trained troops who did not wear European style uniforms, such as those of the Begum Somru.
(Artwork by Giorgio Albertini © Helion and Company)

Plate 5 Sowar, De Boigne's Bodyguard Cavalry Regiment. 1790-1803.

This *sowar* or trooper of De Boigne's personal guard, with his horse, arms and equipment supplied by De Boigne personally, is technically a *bargir* or retainer in De Boigne's service. The silver lace, in turban, sash and on his green coat may distinguish him from the other regular cavalry units of the Army of Hindustan, who may have worn a similar uniform but without the silver lace. Weapons are a carbine, a sword and two pistols, which are of course in saddle holsters. No details are known, but one may speculate that saddle cloths were, in this case, large green and red squares in similar style to Bengal Irregular Cavalry regiments in British service a few years later. Indeed the Second Bengal Irregular Cavalry, first raised in 1809, would wear an almost identical uniform. (Artwork by Giorgio Albertini © Helion and Company)

Plate 6 Mughal Cavalry Sowar. Second half of the Eighteenth Century.

This trooper in his mail armour and *char-aina*, 'four mirrors' style back and brest plate is typical of the middle ranking cavalry fighting for either the Mughal Emperor or many of the successor states. Were he wealthier, he might add mail leg armour to his panoply, and his armour and weapons could be highly decorated. He would most likely carry a lance to add to his sword and axe, and again depending upon his, or his leader's wealth, add other hand weapons such as maces or daggers to his collection. His shield is of buffalo or rhinoceros hide, but could be of steel, and again would be highly decorated in gold if he were wealthy enough. Firearms were the province of lighter cavalry with little or no armour. Though again were he wealthy enough he might have a pair of pistols. Bows on the Asiatic model had been popular in the previous century and were sometimes still carried but rather as a status symbol than as a battlefield weapon. Horse armour had been popular in the previous century but by now was rarely seen. (Artwork by Giorgio Albertini © Helion and Company)

Plate 7 Rajput Rathor Cavalier. Second half of the Eighteenth Century.

The Hindu Rajputs of such successor states as Jodhpur and Jaipur were possibly the most courageous cavalry in India. They made a fetish of courage and individual warrior skills. The charge to contact was almost their only tactic. Arms and armour were similar in style to the Mughals but differed in detail, a Rajput warrior was more likely to carry a straight Indian sword rather than the curved *tulwar* of the Mughals. This warrior's armour is largely of fabric with metal plates beneath, held by the brass rivets, and visible metal protection for the chest and thighs. Fabric armours were by no means uncommon in India and less wealthy troopers might go to war in little more than a padded coat and a helmet. He might equally wear armour similar to Plate 6 and vice-versa. Weapons are lance and sword. Other hand weapons such as mace and axe could be carried but firearms were the province of the lowly infantryman as they were dirty, and not fitting for nobly-born Rajput cavaliers to use. (Artwork by Giorgio Albertini © Helion and Company)

Plate 8 Maratha Cavalry of the Kala-Paga. Second half of the Eighteenth Century.

By no means all of the Maratha cavalry were the armourless mounted banditti, so often castigated by the British as ready to flee at almost the first shot. There were always a sizable minority of men who were quite capable of fighting in the line of battle. Such were the *kala-paga*, or household retainers, of the major chieftains. This warrior wears another version of the very popular *char-aina* 'four mirrors' body armour together with a helmet fashioned in Gwalior, a city held by Madhaji Scindia in the late eighteenth century. Leg armour was rare among the Marathas but was used by wealthier men. He carries a typical four-boss Indian shield similar to those carried by the figures in Plates 6 and 7. Weapons are a *tulwar* style sword and a lance together with a mace in his Kashmir shawl sash. Firearms in the form of matchlock muskets were certainly carried by some and pistols were not unknown but the Marathas did not have the mounted archery tradition of the Mughals so their cavalry did not carry the bow. (Artwork by Giorgio Albertini © Helion and Company)

7

General Perron Takes Command

The new commander of the three brigades which made up the Army of Hindustan in early 1796 was one Pierre Cullier, alias Perron. He was a very different man from his predecessor. To begin with, by no stretch of the eighteenth century imagination, was Perron a gentleman.

Pierre Cullier was born in 1755 at Sarthe in France, the son of a cloth merchant who went bankrupt when Pierre was still a teenager. After likewise failing as an itinerant silk handkerchief salesman he ended up working in the cannon foundry at Nantes, where he learned to cast cannon. He is said to have arrived in India in 1780 as part of the crew of the French frigate *Le Sardine*, one of the ships in *Amiral* Pierre André de Suffren's squadron.[1] However, this cannot be accurate as Suffren's ships did not arrive off the Indian coast until January 1782 when they captured the British 50-gun ship, *Hannibal*.[2] It is possible that he arrived with the earlier squadron under the Comte D'Orves which had arrived off the Indian east coast from the Isle de France in January 1781 and unlike Suffren's original command did indeed contain frigates.[3] The whole fleet would come under Suffren's expert eye when the unfortunate Comte died on the Isle de France later in the year. If Perron did desert from the French navy sometime in 1781 it would have been during the Comte D'Orves inconclusive contact with Haidar Ali of Mysore, then at war with the British, rather than earlier when no French naval vessels were in the vicinity. Equally there is some doubt over his position when he did desert. Compton says either common sailor or petty officer, Grey, without citing a source, calls him a 'sergeant of Marines.'[4] Whatever his precise rank or station once in India, like several other mercenaries, Pierre Cullier adopted Perron as an alias, or *nom de geurre*. He next turns up as a junior

---

1   Compton, *Particular Account*, p.221.
2   Alfred Thayer Mahan, *The Influence of Sea Power upon History* (Boston: Little Brown, 1916), p.427.
3   Mahan, *Sea Power*, p.420.
4   Charles Grey, *European Adventurers of Northern India* (New Delhi: Asian Educational Services, 1993), p.36.

General Pierre Cuillier Perron. Painted after his return to France. (Public Domain)

officer, or perhaps as an NCO or Gunner, serving in the *Rana* of Gohad's battalion commanded by George Sangster, that same Scot who would one day direct the arms industry that would supply the Army of Hindustan.

When Sangster's battalion was disbanded Perron took service with Lestineau's brigade and fought at Lalsot/Tunga, Chaksana and Agra.[5] This was when he first met fellow French mercenary Louis Borquien, for what became the start of a not quite so beautiful friendship.[6] When Lestineau decamped with his loot his three battalion brigade mutinied for lack of pay and was disbanded, though as we have seen De Boigne quite quickly picked up as many of its veteran *sepoys* for the First Brigade as he could get his hands on. Thus, Perron was engaged by De Boigne in late 1789 as a Captain Lieutenant and given command of the Burhanpore battalion of the First Brigade. Perron fought at Patan and Merta with his battalion and there, and in his subsequent service in Rajputana, carried himself so well that by 1792 he was given command of a four battalion task force to stiffen the Maratha troops engaged in the blockade of Kanaund. Upon arrival Perron found Ismael Beg with a rag-bag army of perhaps as many as 20,000, though the Persian news writers put the force at '10–12,000 horse and foot and 25 guns' who 'suffer hardships from lack of pay', camped under the walls of the city.[7] Given the parlous state of Ismael Beg's fortunes at this time, and his record of defeats, the lower figure is perhaps more likely. Perron and the Maratha cavalry with him thrashed this rag-bag army in under two hours and drove the remnants, including the unlucky Ismael into the city. He then began a formal siege as he did not have enough men for an assault. The end of the siege came about by chance. The lord of the city had been Najaf Kuli Khan, once the Emperor's *vizier* or prime minister and another enemy of the rising power of Scindia. However, he died in late 1791 abjuring his wife to hold the city unless De Boigne arrived, which the redoubtable *begum* and her loyal subjects did. Unfortunately, the poor noblewoman was killed by a chance cannon shot while playing chess with one of her ladies. Upon which sad event the garrison, declining to obey Ismael Beg, promptly mutinied and surrendered the city to Perron, along with Ismael. Perron promised the unfortunate Beg his life and eventually he was given a pension and lived out his few remaining years a prisoner, never to take the field again.

---

5   See Chapter 6
6   J.P. Thompson (trans.), 'An Autobiographical Sketch of Louis Borquien', *Journal of the Panjab Historical Society*, Vol.IX, p.37.
7   Compton, *Particular Account*, p.224; Joshi and Sarkar, *Persian Records*, Vol.2, p.58.

During the siege Perron lost a hand in an explosion, his troops therefore named him *Ekdast Sahib* (one handed sir) and, for his service at the siege and his victory he was promoted major and given the command of the newly raised Second Brigade. By 1793 he was firmly in command of this formation.[8] His first task with his new command was, as usual, pacification duties, bringing to heel the usual collection of petty *rajas* and chieftains who refused to either pay their tribute or acknowledge Madhaji Scindia's rule.

When Major Fremont died of an illness Perron transferred to the First Brigade while the second went to a Major Gardiner. According to Smith in his list of brigade commanders Gardiner commanded the Second Brigade in 1793, being superseded by Sutherland the following year.[9] However Compton in his appendix does not list a Major Gardiner but only William Lineaus Gardner who raised a brigade for Jaswant Rao Holkar and would eventually become a colonel of irregular cavalry in the British East India Company's Bengal Army. Clearly these are not the same person. So, precisely who Major Gardiner was, so far, remains a mystery. Nevertheless, Perron was in command of the Second Brigade in 1793 and by early 1794 he had been transferred to the First Brigade and sent out of Hindustan and into the Deccan, for great events were afoot in the south.

The Battle of Kharda – 11 March 1795

There had long been a mixture of rivalry and political alliance between the Maratha Confederacy and the State of Hyderabad under its ruler the *Nizam*. Hyderabad was one of the more successful breakaways from the Mughal Empire. Independent of the Mughals for almost a century Hyderabad had found itself squeezed between various encroaching powers; the British to the east, Mysore to the south, and the Marathas to the north and west. Militarily speaking French influence had been paramount as the Marquis De Bussy had based his army there during the middle part of the century. Indeed, French influence was still strong. The current *Nizam*, Ali Khan had a mercenary corps of his own, commanded by General Raymond and trained in the French style. There was even a women's battalion, the *Zuffar Paltan*, dressed in British style red coats, armed with musket and bayonet.[10] These martial women were primarily used to guard the *Nizam's* extensive *Zenana* where he kept his numerous wives but could apparently fight at need and were not merely ceremonial. There were two other smaller mercenary brigades. One commanded by a Colonel John. P. Boyd, of Massachusetts, the only recorded American mercenary, and another formation commanded by an Englishman named Finglass.[11] Finglass's corps does not appear to have taken part in the campaign though Boyd's command may have had some

---

8   Smith, *Regular Corps*, p.52.
9   Smith, *Regular Corps*, p.52.
10 William Dalrymple, *White Mughals* (London: Harper Collins, 2002), p.94.
11 Compton, *Particular Account*, p.226.

'THEIR INFANTRY AND GUNS WILL ASTONISH YOU'

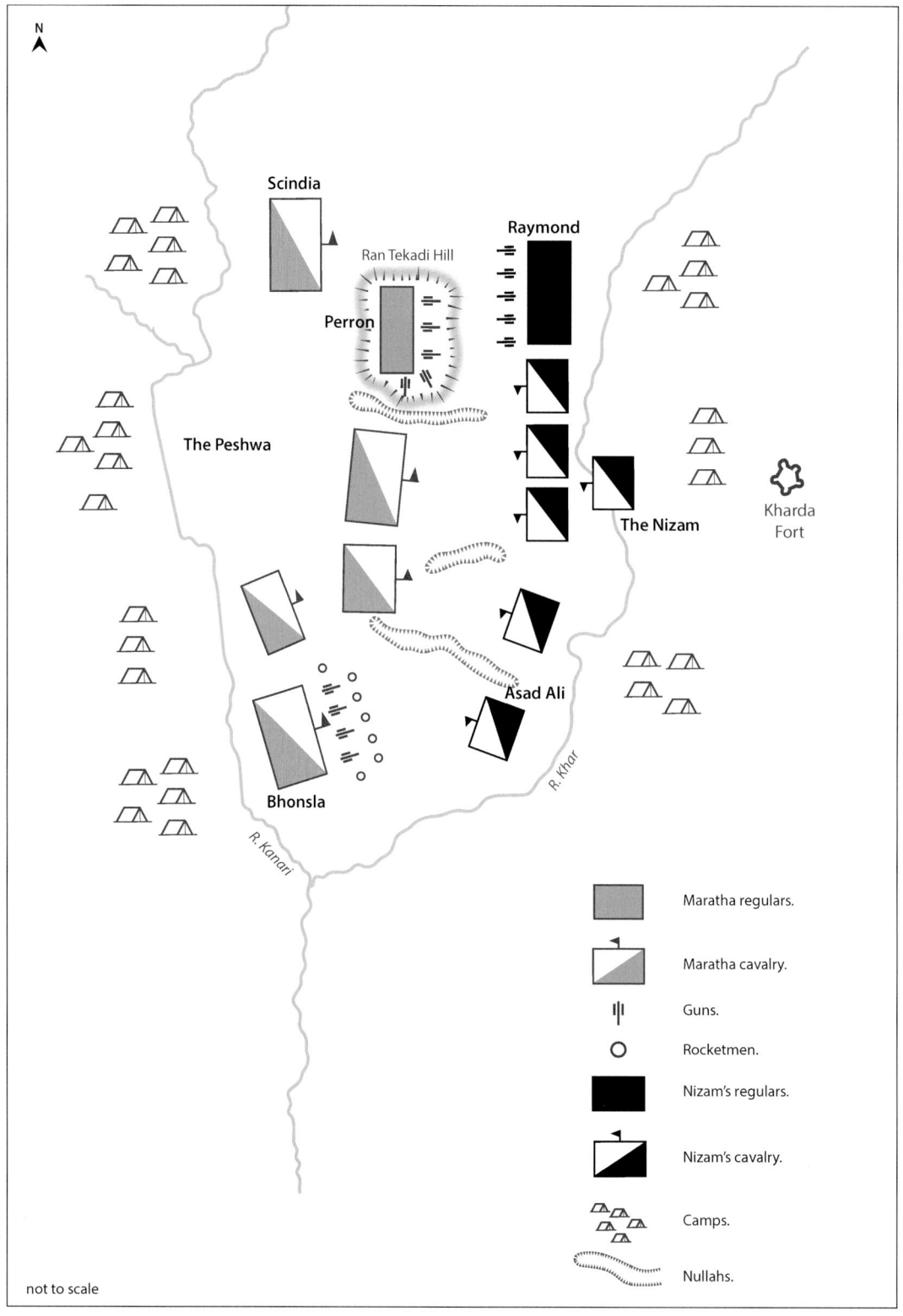

Sketch of the Battle of Kharda (not to scale) showing the deployment of the major commands. Perron's Brigade would hang on to the Ran Takardi hill despite several assaults.

part, but Boyd would be discharged from the *Nizam's* service and would later take his corps to serve the *Peshwa* in Poona.[12]

Other than Raymond's corps and the other mercenary brigades, and possibly the *Zuffar Paltan*, the rest of the *Nizam's* forces were the usual Indian collection of cavalry warriors, infantry mobs and ludicrously large artillery pieces. Two of these monster guns, 'Dhool-Dur' and 'Laxmi', required 250 and 200 bullocks respectively to move them, as battlefield artillery they were, of course completely useless.[13]

In terms of actual numbers, the *Nizam's* Mughal army (the Hyderabadis always thought of and referred to themselves as Mughals) may have topped the 100,000 mark, plus the usual huge amount of impedimenta and many thousands of camp followers. This huge train included the *Nizam's* collection of wives and all their servants, as well as the usual collection of *bazar-wallahs*, and other camp workers. Upwards of 50,000 bullocks were required to bring grain to the army and over 8,000 to move the artillery, there were also almost 400 elephants both to lend magnificence and acting as baggage animals. Like most Indian campaigns this was more of a tribal migration than an army on the march.

General Raymond. Commander of a large *compoo* in the service of the *Nizam* of Hyderabad. Narrowly defeated by Perron at the Battle of Khardha. (Author's Collection)

Of actual combat troops, Raymond's corps was around 11,000 strong including its own artillery contingent, the second in command of this brigade was also French; a Colonel Piron, not to be confused with Perron.[14] Compton gives the precise figure of 10,840 men with 28 guns and 46 tumbrils.[15] So Raymond's force was not dissimilar in size to a full brigade of the Army of Hindustan. Their standards featured the French revolutionary tricolour.[16]

As for the rest of the Hyderabadi army, there were around 45,000 cavalry with a significant proportion of these being heavily armoured.[17] There were some 3,000 rocket men and 33,000 infantry of sorts. There were also 59 heavy guns, including the two useless monsters mentioned above. Yet for all the numbers only Raymond's corps and the best of the cavalry were of any more than marginal combat value.

The Maratha army for this campaign was somewhat unusual, being as it was, composed of contingents from the whole Maratha Confederacy. This temporary appearance of unity was decidedly different and was brought

---

12 Dalrymple, *White Mughals*, p.142.
13 G. T. Kulkarni & M. R. Kantak, *Battle of Kharda: Challenges and Responses* (Pune: Deccan College, 1980) p.40.
14 Kulkarni & Kantak, *Battle of Kharda*, pp.43–44 has them as Peron senior in the Maratha forces and Peron junior as second to Raymond.
15 Compton, *Particular Account*, p.383.
16 Dalrymple, *White Mughals*, p.94.
17 Nicole, *Mughal India*, p.43, and Haidar, *Arms and Armour*, pp.112–113.

about by the idea that the *Nizam* owed several years unpaid *Chauth*. Of course, every Maratha chieftain worth his salt wanted his cut. The lure of the loot was even enough to still the usual Scindia-Holkar rivalry for a time, and bring in the *Bhonsla* of Nagpur eager for his share of the spoils. Both the houses of Scindia and Holkar contributed significant numbers of troops including trained brigades.

So, the army that gathered at Poona for the coming campaign was a large but somewhat polyglot force of over 100,000, perhaps more.[18] In terms of regular trained infantry there were four brigades totalling 24 battalions. The First Brigade consisted of 10 battalions, under the command of Major Perron.[19] Colonel Hessing's brigade was made up of four battalions. There was also a less than wonderful brigade under the Neapolitan mercenary Michael Filose. All three of these brigades were in Daulat Rao Scindia's contingent.[20] In addition Tukaji Holkar sent the Chevalier Dudrenec with four trained battalions. The Chevalier had been given another chance after his previous command had been destroyed by De Boigne at Lakheri two years previously. Compton puts the total of trained infantry at 24,000 but this must be far too high. Even factoring in the attached artillery and assuming that all battalions were at full strength, 24,000 is still too high. As has been seen De Boigne's *telinga* battalions, even at full strength, were only just over 700 officers and men, though the *najib* battalions were stronger. Even given an average strength of 700 and not really allowing for campaign wastage there cannot have been more than 17,000 regulars in total in the four trained brigades, including artillery crews, and the likelihood is that the actual total was a couple of thousand fewer.

As for the rest of the Maratha forces there was the usual horde of cavalry, with each major chieftain and all the minor commanders bringing their own contingents. In terms of quality, they ranged from the well-equipped and motivated *kala-paga*, the household troops of the major leaders such as Scindia and Holkar, down to the armed banditti of the *pindaris*. Scindia's total contingent was around 20–30,000 and the whole army may have had as many as 70,000 cavalry and 192 guns.[21] Though of course only the guns of the Trained Brigades were of proven battlefield effectiveness. Perron had at least 35 guns with his brigade and the other mercenary commanders perhaps 20 each though only Perron's guns are mentioned specifically.[22] There even seems to have been a select band of archers amongst Rhagoji Bhonsla's contingent. These were probably amongst the usual mob of infantry levies as Kulkarni and Kantak clearly separate them from the cavalry in their rather jumbled list of contingents and also mention that this group contained rocket men.[23]

---

18 Kulkarni & Kantak, *Battle of Kharda*, pp.41–43 gives a confusing list of *sardars* and commanders and a total 227,000, which is far too high. They also miss at least two of the regular brigades.
19 In a letter from Dualat Rao to the Governor General, quoted in Sinh, Sardesai, & Sarkar, *Poona Residency Correspondence*, Vol.8, letter 13.
20 Compton, *Particular Account*, p.226.
21 Kulkarni & Kantak, *Battle of Kharda*, pp.41–42.
22 Compton, *Particular Account*, p.227.
23 Kulkarni & Kantak, *Battle of Kharda*, p.56.

Despite the usual rather inflated numbers quoted by various authors what is clear is that the armies were similar in overall strength, hovering around the 100,000 mark. Each with more cavalry than infantry and both with large artillery trains, mostly containing guns whose actual military value was negligible.

From late February 1795 the two armies blundered slowly towards each other. The Marathas moving roughly south and the Hyderabdis/Mughals north, eating the country bare as they progressed. During these weeks each side tried both to suborn the troops of the other and carried our fruitless, and possibly insincere, negotiations. They finally came within scouting range of each other on 5 March and both armies immediately encamped. The Maratha camps (each contingent made its own) straggled along the west bank of the river Kanari; Scindia's division at the northern or left flank end of the line, then the *Peshwa* with his troops, followed by Holkar's contingent, and finally on the southern or right flank Rhagoji Bhonsla with his division.

The *Nizam's* forces were a bare five kilometres (three miles) away camped behind the River Khar with the small fortress of Kharda about two kilometres (just over a mile) or so to their rear. Between both armies lay an open plain intersected by dry watercourses, or *nullahs*, but dominated by a hill known as Ran Tekadi somewhat closer to the *Nizam's* position than that of the Marathas.

For several days each army watched the other. Cavalry skirmishing was constant but neither side gained a decisive advantage. Tiring of this the Marathas decided to attack on the morning of 11 March and, crossing the river Kanari, drew up in the same order as they were encamped with Scindia's contingent on the left and Bhonsla's on the right.

The Maratha leaders had pronounced Pureshram Bhao commander-in-chief and he rode forward with his bodyguards to view the *Nizam's* forces.[24] This party was attacked by a body of Pathan cavalry in the *Nizam's* service. First the Marathas sent in supports, including the *Peshwa's kala-paga*, then the Mughals sent in more units and a swirling cavalry fight developed. Indeed, there is a case to be made to suggest that the action was brought on somewhat by accident as the *Nizam* seems to have wished to shift his ground for tactical reasons.[25] If this was so the perhaps it explains why Raymond's brigade did not take part in the initial phase of the battle. One also might, in these circumstances, wonder how many of the *Nizam's* ponderous guns actually got into the action, this especially as only Raymond's guns seem to have been of the newer more mobile variety, similar to those under Perron's command. The *Nizam's* forces proposed shift of position would have meant crossing the Maratha front, at best a risky move. However, as each side fed in more and more troops, eventually the cavalry fight resulted in the Marathas being first pushed back and then being put to flight, until the pursuit was halted by Rhagoji Bhonsla coming in from the Maratha right and showering the Hyderabadi cavalry with rockets.[26] At one point it even looked as if the

---

24 Grant Duff, *History of the Marathas*, Vol.2, p.200.
25 Kulkarni & Kantak, *Battle of Kharda*, p.54.
26 Kulkarni & Kantak, *Battle of Kharda*, p.56.

Peshwa's personal standard the *jari pakta* would fall to the enemy but the *Peshwa's* contingent in the centre rallied and disaster was averted.

Meanwhile Perron with his brigade, and possibly Hessing's and Filose's as well, had climbed the Ran Tekadi hill and placed 35 of his guns there, giving them an excellent field of fire. He beat off initial attacks by the Hyderabdis and was therefore able to add his fire to that of Bhonsla's rocket men. The Hyderabadi cavalry centre, under fire from both flanks, wavered and eventually broke. Still, the sternest test of the day was yet to come. Raymond and Piron at the head of their battalions now advanced to clear Perron from his hill. Raymond's troops seem to have been fresher and despite courageous resistance, Perron's men slowly lost ground, but the collapse of his cavalry seems to have unnerved the *Nizam* and he ordered a retreat. As night fell the Hyderabadi army fell back on the small fortress of Kharda. Many of his troops were seized with a panic in the darkness, especially after a friendly fire incident, and plundered their own baggage before decamping at speed pursued by the Maratha *pindari* cavalry.[27]

Morning saw the *Nizam* with a bare tenth of his army remaining in and around Kharda fort in a very sorry state, with his personal baggage and his *zenana*, the ladies, understandably being in something of a panic. When Perron brought heavy guns within range of the fort the *Nizam* surrendered on 15 March 1795.

The battle had been a rather messy affair, lost by the *Nizam* rather than decidedly won by the Marathas. Holkar's contingent seemingly playing little part. Perron's defence of the Ran Tekadi hill had however proved to be the linchpin which had held the Marathas together, and together with Bhonsla's rocket men had given time for the Maratha centre to rally and prevent defeat.

Perron was now high in Daulat Rao Scindia's favour and constantly by his side, so that when De Boigne left for Europe Perron was ideally placed to take over. Fremont, who was actually the next senior officer after De Boigne, had died and Sutherland, the only other possible candidate, was away in the north pacifying the Bundelkhand region of Hindustan. This left Perron in close proximity to Daulat Rao as the best, and indeed only candidate, for that less than astute ruler to promote to general in September 1796.

At the time of his promotion Perron could command a field force upwards of 24,000 men with 120 guns divided into three brigades. In addition, there were garrisons in Delhi, Agra and Gwalior, as well as the arms factories and the cantonment at the army headquarters at Koil and its associated fortress of Alighur. When Perron took overall command the First Brigade went to Colonel Drugeon a Savoyard and therefore a countryman of De Boigne's.[28] Drugeon had been in Maratha service since before 1794 when he was recorded as brigade major to the Second Brigade.[29] This effectively made him the chief of staff of that formation and responsible for its administration. He moved with Perron to the First Brigade when that unit went south into the Deccan and became its commander when Perron was promoted. Robert Sutherland,

---

27 Grant Duff, *History of the Marathas*, Vol.2, p.201.
28 Smith, *Regular Corps*, p.52.
29 Compton, *Particular Account*, p.346.

ranked as Major in 1796, led the Second Brigade. The Third Brigade, the most junior formation, was commanded by Colonel Pedron (who Smith ranks as captain), a French officer of considerable age and experience who had entered De Boigne's First Brigade in 1790. Pedron had been in India since at least 1760 serving in several mercenary units. He became something of a creature of Perron's as the new general spent the year of 1797 establishing his power in Hindustan and taking over the administration of those *jaidads* previously assigned by Scindia for the upkeep of the army. All of this took time, and it was not until early 1798 that Perron was fully in control.

8

The Widows War and Other Stories

As he surveyed the scene from his newly built palatial residence at Koil at the beginning of 1798, Perron could not have been unaware of how much the situation had changed since De Boigne's retirement. He, Perron, would soon acquire all De Boigne's power and influence and more, but not only was Perron a very different character from his predecessor, his employer Daulat Rao Scindia was very different from Madhaji. Policy was dictated by whim and current court favourites. It was based around the idea of humbling the rival house of Holkar and attempting to ensure that the house of Scindia controlled the *Peshwa*. Yet Daulat Rao was neither politic nor consistent, plans fluctuated depending upon which sycophants and advisors had power at Scindia's court. Intrigue was ever present, and often murderous. Perron and the Army of Hindustan would be the instruments to carry out his assorted whims.

Nevertheless in 1798 Perron could, perhaps, be forgiven for thinking that all was well with his world. Although he was not yet supreme in Hindustan as he had necessarily to work with a Maratha *subahdar*, currently the talented and experienced General Lakwa Dada, he still had total command of his three brigades. The comparative peace in Hindustan and the administrative reforms of De Boigne had increased the land revenue which supported the army from 27 lakhs of rupees (Rs2,700,000) to 41 lakhs (Rs4,100,000). The relative efficiency with which collections were accomplished had also decreased the number of minor rebellions and enabled the Maratha forces to more easily coerce those independent princes still resisting Maratha dominance within the still nominally Imperial province of Hindustan.[1] Despite some minor expeditions there was no major war in Hindustan at the time Perron took command of the brigades.

Yet as always there was work for the Army of Hindustan. The three Brigades were scattered about through the lands controlled by Scindia as follows:

---

1 Sinh, Sardesai, & Sarkar, *Poona Residency Correspondence*, Vol.8, p.iv.

First Brigade – Colonel Drugeon – at Poona with Scindia
Second Brigade – Colonel Sutherland – in the cantonment at Koil
Third Brigade – Major Pedron – at Muttra, though Pedron himself was with Perron at Koil[2]

The strange nature of Maratha politics at this time, and the sometimes bizarre situations which arose, can best be illustrated by events involving the Army of Hindustan from the late 1790s to the very start of the new century.

The 'Afghan Menace'

Ever since their defeat at the Battle of Panipat in 1761 the Marathas had been understandably nervous of the possibility of invasion from Afghanistan. Every time the *Emir* Zaman Shah came over the Khyber Pass to Peshawar their nervousness increased, and when he came to Lahore in 1799 something close to panic erupted. This perceived Afghan threat temporarily put a stop to the never-ending internal squabbling of the Maratha Confederacy. Troops were moved into Hindustan and a huge concentration of units gathered around Delhi late in 1799 including the Second and Third Brigades.[3] Under pretext of this threat a Fourth Brigade was raised in 1799 and given first to Pedron, but by 1803 it was commanded by that unlucky soldier, the Chevalier Dudrenec.

As it transpired the Afghan threat was largely illusory, thanks in part to Zaman Shah's usual lack of money to prosecute his campaign and the customary internal squabbles within Afghanistan, but also due to the rising military power of the Sikhs in the Punjab who would, in time, form an effective barrier to Afghan expansion into the Indian subcontinent. Nevertheless, the Fourth Brigade came into being as part of the Army of Hindustan almost entirely because of this perceived threat.

The Widows War 1798–1799

Daulat Rao's insatiable desire for money to fund his personal excesses and to still the constant clamouring of his Maratha cavalry for their arrears of pay led him to commit, or cause to be committed, actions which drove Lakwa Dada and other more conservative Maratha *sardars* into open rebellion in 1798.

Daulat Rao was the nephew of the late Madhaji Scindia and had been used to taking advice from the wives of his late uncle. However, this easily led youth married a new young wife whose father, Sharza Rao Ghatkay, influenced young Scindia to dispossess his aunts of their property. This caused

---

2 The brigade commanders are taken as usual from Smith, *Regular Corps*, p.52. Compton, *Particular Account*, p.230 has Pedron in Sutherlands brigade and the Third Brigade commanded by Major Pohlmann.
3 Compton, *Particular Account*, p.235.

outrage. After all, having your respected widowed aunts flogged personally by your prime minister to persuade them to hand over their money is likely to cause some upset!

This was however only one of many of Daulat Rao's excesses in search of cash, '... and in February next year [1798] we find a reign of terror for extortion and personal vengeance let loose on Poona by Sharza Rao who was now supreme in Daulat Rao's court by reason of the marriage of his daughter Baiza Bai to that Prince.'[4]

The two outraged widow ladies, the *Bhais,* raised the banner of rebellion in the Deccan and appealed to the Maratha forces in Hindustan for aid. Disgusted by Dualat Rao's behaviour and that of his prime minister, the more traditional elements of the Maratha nobility were not slow to respond. Lakwa Dada and other captains had, by January 1799, 20,000 cavalry in the field. These then pursued the old-style guerrilla war and defeated those Marathas loyal to Daulat Rao sent against them. Large swathes of Hindustan fell under the control of the rebels and Lakwa added 'about fifteen Maratha battalions and twenty pieces of cannon' to his forces.[5] Daulat Rao appointed Ambaji Angria as the replacement for the rebellious Lakwa as *subahdar* of Hindustan, and ordered Perron to cooperate with Ambaji in supressing the revolt. Burdened as he was at this time with the sieges of Aligarh and Agra, whose *kiladars* had joined the rebels, Perron miscalculated badly, sending only two battalions from Sutherland's brigade under Captain Butterfield, with young Ensign James Skinner as the only other European commissioned officer, to reinforce Ambaji. These two battalions with their 10 guns joined the army assembling at Parie, about 50 kilometres (30 miles) west of Gwalior, under command of Ambaji Angria. Skinner describes the army he and Captain Butterfield joined: '... and found there a brigade under command of a native in that chief's service, named Colonel Kaleb Alee; four battalions under Khootub Khan, in the same service, and 15,000 Maratha horse under Ambaji's son called Bhow. Our force thus consisted of about 15,000 horse, 14 battalions of infantry and 30 pieces of cannon.'[6]

Although not specifically stated Colonel Kaleb Alee's brigade evidently had eight battalions, so we can estimate the total infantry number for the 14 battalions at around 6,000–7,000 men and certainly no more than 8,000. It should be noted that Butterfield's small command provided a full third of the available artillery.

Unfortunately, when Ambaji's forces found the rebels at a place Skinner calls Chaundkhoree things did not go according to plan. Lakwa, a fine general, well versed in the subtleties of Indian warfare and intrigue had 'tampered with' the troops of Kaleb Alee and Kootub Khan who first stood aside from the fighting and then changed sides.[7] Skinner wrote:

---

4   Sarkar, *Fall of the Moghul Empire*, Vol.4, p.126.
5   Baillie-Fraser, *Military Memoir*, Vol.1, p.118.
6   Baillie-Fraser, *Military Memoir*, Vol.1, pp.118–119.
7   Compton, *Particular Account*, p.234.

The troops faced each other at three P.M. and soon after a tremendous cannonade began. About five our whole line was ordered to advance, but we soon found that the whole brunt of the battle was to fall on our two battalions and that both Kaleb Alee and Khootub Khan had an understanding with the enemy.

After fighting for two hours we learned that both these traitors had joined; and, as soon as Bhow perceived it, he galloped up to Captain Butterfield, and directed him to retire and throw himself on the bank of a small river about a mile in our rear. We commenced retiring by wings in carrying which point we lost a great many men, but succeeded in effecting our object. Captain Butterfield then directed us to get the men under cover for the whole of the enemy's guns were now directed on us, and several charges were made by the Bhyes troops, all of which we managed to repulse, our men being steady and our cavalry behaving well.[8]

Lieutenant Colonel James Skinner in the European officer's dress of Skinners Horse. Skinner served in the Army of Hindustan for several years before entering British Service. (Author's Collection)

Defeat stared the Bhow in the face, so after a council of war he decided to break contact and retreat under cover of darkness to the fort of Shairghur, which entailed a difficult night march through a narrow pass. Not the easiest of military operations. Bhow's army abandoned their wounded and most of the baggage. Butterfield's much reduced two battalions being the rear guard (they had lost 500 of their original strength of 1,600) and the march began around 10:00 p.m. Skinner again takes up the story:

> On coming to the pass I was ordered to remain behind with two companies and a six pounder until the line had cleared the pass. This I accordingly did; and about two in the morning began to hear the enemy's drums. By this time the line had got well on through the pass and I commenced retreating. But I had scarcely gone a mile, when one of the wheels of our gun, which had been much shattered by the enemy's shot, broke down, and it took us an hour to determine what was to be done with the gun. We at length resolved to leave the tumbrils and with their bullocks to drag on the gun. With this view we threw away the other wheel also, and resumed our retreat.
>
> By this time the enemy's van had come up and there was nothing left but to abandon the gun, or stand like good soldiers and die defending it. The cry was 'not to leave the gun' so I immediately ordered it to be charged with grape and then for all to remain quiet until the enemy should come to the charge. The pass was narrow, being not above 200 yards broad, and very steep on both sides. The enemy thinking we had retired, their van, composed I think of about 500 men, came up within a hundred yards of us, when we gave them the round of grape and

---

8   Baillie-Fraser, *Military Memoir*, Vol.1, pp.119–120. Battalions were often split into two wings to manoeuvre.

a volley of small arms. We then rushed out upon them sword in hand, took three stand of colours and destroyed a great number. They retired in great confusion and we came back to our gun, then blowing up our tumbril we made good our retreat, and joined our detachment under the fort of Shairghur.[9]

Skinner's neat little rear guard action earned him an expensive *Khilat* (robe of Honour) and a promotion to lieutenant on a salary of Rs200 per month.

The campaign now petered out despite the rest of Sutherland's Second Brigade joining the army and Ambaji Angria hiring the Irish mercenary George Thomas with his six battalions and 20 guns to provide further reinforcements. Lakwa Dada had, with the help of the Rajputs of Udaipur, encamped and fortified himself and his army under the walls of Chittorgur, where Ambaji's forces could not come at him. Therefore, Ambaji and his army encamped some miles away and the two armies watched each other, skirmishing every day, and laying the surrounding country waste in search of provisions. Neither side seemed willing to bring the other side to battle. Yet each side was in communication with the other to try to achieve some kind of negotiated settlement, but also, it seems, to settle personal scores. Hatreds did not always follow the political map of the moment, as Skinner explains:

> One morning as I was exercising my horse, in full armour, I met Hurjee Scindia with about 500 chosen horsemen proceeding towards the river, and, riding up I asked him where he was going. He replied that he had been ordered to find out a ford and that as soon as he should have done this the army would be ordered to attack the enemy. He then asked me if I could go with him, to which I replied that I should be too happy to do so. I asked him in turn if he had any guides, to which he replied that Ambaji had sent two with him.
>
> Now Harji Scindia was a relative of Daulat Rao Scindia and both Ambaji and Lackwa Dada were his enemies and sought his destruction.[10]

These personal cross-party hatreds, whilst not uncommon, in this case led to the general of Daulat Rao's forces conspiring with the general of the rebels to allow the enemy to ambush and kill one of his own junior commanders. The bizarre nature of Maratha familial rivalries once again cutting across the major political events. Leaving aside the ridiculous nature of this, the incident itself, and Skinner's telling of it, allows us an eye-witness account of a cavalry fight between two bodies of Maratha irregular cavalry of the better quality. Skinner's narrative continues:

> I espied a single horseman on the bank who, immediately on seeing us, went down and disappeared. I mentioned this circumstance to Harji, next whom I was riding but he replied that he must be a Pindaree. Scarcely, however, had he said this, than we perceived several horsemen appearing from the various parts of the ravines, and in a few minutes they assembled to the number of 1,000 good horsemen with Balaram, a native chieftain of Lakwa's at their head. They instantly

---

9 Baillie-Fraser, *Military Memoir*, Vol.1, pp.120–122.
10 Baillie-Fraser, *Military Memoir*, Vol.1, pp.125–128.

charged us, but were repulsed with great loss. This had an excellent effect, and our men continued quite staunch. Harji, who was a noble soldier, called aloud that this was a snare laid for him, but that he put his trust in God who would assuredly defend him from all of his enemies. The men cried out that they were all ready to die for him. He then gave the word for a deliberate and orderly retreat; and we fell back skirmishing, for about a cos, when Balaram, heading his men, brought them again to the charge. We repulsed this attack also, but my mare was wounded by a sabre cut, and I received two or three sword blows on the body, from which I was only saved by my armour. Harji, who was also in armour, received a spear wound in his right arm. I happened to be close by when this happened and cut down the man who speared him. But in this attack we lost some of our best Sowars and one or two Indians of note and courage. We still had two cos between us and our camp and Balaram had become furious – charging us still on all sides. Our party now began to lose ground, the retreat became a flight, the soldiers to be disobedient to orders, and poor Harji to get confused. Balaram himself appeared in our rear, pressing us close, with about seventy or eighty sowars. On seeing this Harji Scindia called aloud, to the few who remained close to him, amongst whom I had the good fortune to be, telling them not to run like cowards but to die like Rajputs; that he well knew that Balaram, who was leading the party to his rear, and that he never would fly from him, About fifty men turned with him, and with this handful of heroes made a desperate push, and cut down Balaram himself while other levelled several of his sowars with the ground; the rest fled on all sides and we began once more to retreat with coolness. As soon as the rest of our pursuers knew that their chieftain had fallen they began to draw up and soon gave over following us … Had it not been for my armour I should have been cut to pieces this day, but my mare less fortunate received several cuts.[11]

It is interesting that firearms are never mentioned, nor indeed missile weapons of any kind. One might assume some firing of pistols and matchlocks in the skirmishing, but it is not specifically stated. The actual fighting is all sword and spear. Leadership is entirely personal, and the pursuing force gives up once their leader is cut down. Much of the actual hand to hand fighting is done by a relatively small number of men, perhaps no more than half of the total numbers on each side. As you might expect the longer the fighting goes on the more disordered and difficult to control each side becomes. The final fight where Balaram is cut down sees only about 10 percent of the initial forces involved. The rest, if not casualties, are scattered about the countryside, and possibly just keeping their heads down.

This minor action had an interesting sequel. Harji Scindia publicly rewarded Skinner with jewellery, a sword, shield and a 'very fine Dekhinee horse'[12] which animal Skinner's brigade commander, Robert Sutherland tried to persuade Skinner to part with under threat of telling Perron about Skinner's unauthorised activities with Harji. Skinner refused and indeed, thanks to a letter from Harji to Perron, received a letter of thanks from

---

11 Baillie-Fraser, *Military Memoir*, Vol.1, pp.125–128.
12 Baillie-Fraser, *Military Memoir*, Vol.1, p.129.

Perron which 'annoyed Colonel Sutherland.'[13] This must have led to the bad feeling between the two commanders as, despite a distant relationship by marriage, Perron and Sutherland appear to have loathed each other. Shortly after this Sutherland was moved to command the First Brigade, then in the Deccan, and Pohlmann, the Hanoverian, promoted first to major and later to colonel, took over the Second Brigade which remained in Hindustan.

Revenue Collection, Maratha style

A mixture of negotiations and the perceived Afghan threat caused Daulat Rao to reinstate Lakwa Dada as *subhadar* of Hindustan in November 1799. Lakwa's first task was to 'persuade' various Rajput chieftains including the *Raja* of Jaipur to hand over some of the tribute that they owed. Needless to say, the Rajput *rajas* refused the Maratha demands so force was the only answer. In essence this campaign was no different from the other tribute collections that the mercenaries and their troops were involved in. The only real difference was the size of the army needed to collect the 'taxes'. Thus it was that the Army of Hindustan was off to war once again.

The Battle of Malpura – 16 April 1800

The core of Lakwa Dada's army for the campaign of 1800 against the *rajas* of Jaipur and Jodhpur was Pohlmann's Second Brigade of the Army of Hindustan. Even before the battle this brigade saw some hard service and lost two of its European officers killed. Captain Donnelly and Lieutenant Exshaw, and a Lieutenant Turnbull were wounded at the siege of the fort of Jahazpur belonging to the Rajput 'baron' of Shahpurah in Mewar where the brigade also lost either 500 or 1,000 *sepoys* killed and wounded.[14] The Rajput garrison fought with their usual considerable tenacity and bloodily repulsed one storming attempt. As the brigade only had six of its battalions present, together with the siege train of six 18-pounder guns, four 12-pounder guns and two mortars, these casualties, of whatever precise number, did somewhat thin the ranks. The fort eventually surrendered in early March 1800.

Meanwhile the Rajput *rajas* were gathering their forces to resist what they perceived as the overweening power of the Maratha Confederacy. The *Raja* of Jaipur, Partab Singh, had officially declared war on the Marathas on 3 March 1800.

Skinner in his memoirs gives some impressive numbers for the Rajput field army:

> Towards the end of March we heard that the Jeypore Raja had arrived at his camp at Sanganeir, and his troops assembling daily. The spies reported that there were 50,000 Rajepoot horse, 10,000 of which were Rhattores commanded by Sewan Singh the Chela of the Jhoudpore Raja who would not himself join … The rest

---

13 Baillie-Fraser, *Military Memoir*, Vol.1, p.130.
14 Sarkar, *Fall of the Moghul Empire*, Vol.4, p.131. The higher casualty figure is Skinner's.

of the cavalry were Kutchawutees, Hurrowtees and Shekawutees ... There were besides about 50,000 regular infantry and 20,000 irregulars.[15]

However, the spies seem to have exaggerated somewhat, or perhaps Skinner's memory was at fault, as these numbers seem very high. Sarkar calls Skinner's figure 'an absurd exaggeration' and only gives the Rathors 5,000 horse.[16] He supports this assertion with figures from a letter written by another participant in the battle, an officer of the Second Brigade commanded by Major Pohlmann: 'The Jaipur Raja commanded his army in person, consisting of 18 battalions, 1000 Ruhelas (Rohillas) 2,000 Nagas and upwards of 15,000 cavalry and 56 guns.'[17]

The grand total given by this correspondent is 65,000, but this possibly includes non-combatant camp followers as 18 battalions are unlikely to have comprised more than 10,000 men and possibly somewhat less. However, it is also possible that the writer only counted the Jaipur troops and not the other contingents sent by Jodhpur and the lesser Rajput leaders. Given that possibility, and factoring in the usual mob of useless irregulars, perhaps the 65,000 total is conceivable but in the light of the course of the battle, still seems on the high side.

The same writer contends that the Maratha army was seriously outnumbered, as does Skinner. The Marathas had a total of 15 regular battalions. There was the Second Brigade, commanded by Major Polhman, which consisted of six battalions with at least 30 guns. Skinner's narrative refers to Polhman as 'our Colonel' and he was certainly ranked as a colonel by 1802.[18] Chevalier Dudrenec's brigade was also present fielding six battalions with again perhaps 30 guns, if the usual five guns to a battalion format was followed. There were in addition two battalions in the service of Lakwa Dada and a single battalion from the *Raja* of Kotah who was an ally – possibly under duress – of the Marathas. These last three battalions were probably commanded by Indian *sardars* though it is possible that William Henry Tone (brother of the Irish revolutionary Wolfe Tone) commanded Lakwa Dada's battalions as he was certainly in that general's service a little later. The Chevalier Dudrenec's six battalion brigade was a new formation actually in the service of Holkar but sent to 'aid' Scindia so that Holkar could claim a share of the loot of Rajputana.

At an average of 500 men per battalion this would give Lakwa's army 7,500 or so trained infantry of which the six battalions of the Army of Hindustan's Second Brigade were well trained veteran troops with 30 superbly served, mobile, by Indian standards, artillery pieces and therefore were by far the most formidable troops on the field. In addition there were a large number of Maratha horse possibly as many as 15,000 or even 20,000, enough to provide two bodies of 5,000 on each flank of the infantry line and a further body, or

---

15   Baillie-Fraser, *Military Memoir*, Vol.1, pp.142–143.
16   Sarkar, *Fall of the Moghul Empire*, Vol.4, p.132.
17   Sinh, Sardesai, & Sarkar, *Poona Residency Correspondence*, Vol.9, p.11.
18   Smith, *Regular Corps*, p.52.

bodies, in a second line a thousand paces behind the first.[19] Previous armies that had fought the Rajputs had consisted of similar numbers of cavalry so there seems to be no reason why, despite Sarkar's assertion to the contrary when he gives a total of a mere 16,000 men for the whole Maratha army, and 27,000 for the Rajputs, that this army should be so much smaller than its predecessors of only a decade or so earlier.[20] Whatever the precise numbers, the impression given by the two eye-witness accounts is that the Marathas were considerably outnumbered.

As was usual in large formal battles of this type, both armies encamped some distance from each other. Perfectly aware of each other's presence. Skirmishing between rival bodies of cavalry was an almost daily occurrence as each side plundered the surrounding district for fodder and food. In this case the armies were separated by the river Sohadra. The Maratha forces were camped to the south of this watercourse near the village of Hindoli. The Rajputs were on the northern side near the town of Malpura, some 88 kilometres (55 miles) south west of Jaipur, for which the battle is named.

The Rajput army was encamped some distance back from the riverbank and this gave Lakwa Dada his chance. Before dawn on 16 April the Maratha army left its camp and began to cross the river. The plan seems to have been to attempt to take the Rajputs by surprise while they were still encamped in a dawn attack. Skinner takes up the story:

> Luckwa then resolved to strike the first blow, and gave the different commanders of our army the signals of attack. The post these signals were to be given from was a hill in our rear. The first port-fire shown from thence was to be the signal for advancing, with our guns limbered; the second was to unlimber, and the third, to commence firing.[21]

At this point the Marathas had not yet crossed the river but could see the Rajput fires along their battle line as their guns and infantry slept under arms, in battle formation. The Rajput line 'extended upwards of a kos [roughly 2.5 km] greatly outflanking the Maratha army.'[22] Once the Maratha troops had crossed the river they shook out into the pre-arranged order of battle which was the tried and tested one of infantry and guns in the first line, flanked by cavalry with a second line of cavalry some distance behind. In this case Pohlmann's brigade was on the right with Dudrenec's brigade on the left. However, things did not go quite according to plan, as Skinner relates:

> At four o'clock in the morning we saw the first light when the army moved off in high order. I half an hour after the second was seen and we unlimbered, the lights of the enemy's fires along their line being in view. They had lighted their fires to keep themselves warm, in the belief that we dared not attack, and were completely surprised. Unfortunately before we saw the third light, our right had reached the

---

19 Baillie-Fraser, *Military Memoir*, Vol.1, p.145.
20 Sarkar, *Fall of the Moghul Empire*, Vol.4, p.132.
21 Baillie-Fraser, *Military Memoir*, Vol.1, p.146.
22 Sinh, Sardesai, & Sarkar, *Poona Residency Correspondence*, Vol.9, p.11.

enemy's left, and our cavalry finding them not on the alert, cut in and gave the alarm. In an instant the whole of their line was seen in a blaze, each golandaze, as he awoke firing off his gun.

By this time we had reached the river and every commander got his own corps over as best he could. Our brigade crossed and formed in a column on the opposite bank. Not a single gun was fired from our line until our Colonel gave us orders. The enemy's guns were, by this time, only about five hundred yards distant, and the day had dawned, when we received orders to commence firing. Our guns then opened; but after a few rounds the order to advance was given and on we went. The guns that were before us, about forty in number, we took immediately with the loss of about one thousand men killed and wounded, my horse was killed under me.[23]

The other contemporary account is more laconic but follows the same basic succession of events:

Major Polhman on this ordered the Second Brigade to advance with the great guns but to reserve their fire till they were close up to the enemy. These orders being punctually obeyed the artillery did great execution. This Brigade however, it seems, was in great danger; being ill-supported and pressed by eight times their number. A judicious movement of Major Polhman, by forming into square his six battalions, of which the brigade consisted, prevented the enemy's cavalry from surrounding them, which was attempted without success; and the brigade by an incessant and well-directed fire of the artillery finally succeeded in coming to close action with the enemy.[24]

Reconciling these two accounts would seem to split the battle into two distinct phases. The first phase consists of the Maratha forces crossing the river and the precipitate attack of the right wing Maratha cavalry upon the Rajput gun and infantry line. In essence this line was a trip wire for just such an eventuality and the Rajput gunners fired off their guns in some surprise. At this point the Rajput cavalry in all likelihood were neither mounted, armed nor formed. The Rajputs saw off the Maratha horse but their infantry were not able to withstand the assault of the Second Brigade. It was at this point that Polhman's men first captured the Rajput guns. The sacrifice of the Rajput infantry had, meanwhile, bought time for their superb but rather lackadaisical cavalry to form up, and upon seeing this Polhman formed his battalions into a large hollow square with their guns in front of the infantry. This was a formation that the Army of Hindustan had previously used in battles with the Rajputs at Tunga and Merta, to name but two.

The second phase of the fighting involved a series of cavalry charges upon the Second Brigade square which were entirely unsuccessful, but also on the Chevalier Dudrenec's brigade which seems to have fared rather badly, losing at least two of its guns.

---

23 Baillie-Fraser, *Military Memoir*, Vol.1, pp.146–147.
24 Sinh, Sardesai, & Sarkar, *Poona Residency Correspondence*, Vol.9, p.11.

Skinner, describing the event later to Baillie-Fraser put it thus:

> The Rhattores, more than ten thousand in number, were seen approaching from a distance, the tramp of their immense and compact body rising like thunder above the roar of the battle. They came on first at a slow hand-gallop which increased in speed as they approached; the well served guns of the brigade showered grape upon their dense mass cutting down hundreds at each discharge; but this had no effect in arresting their progress;– they came, like a whirlwind, trampling over fifteen hundred of their own body, destroyed by the cannon of the brigade; neither he murderous volleys from the muskets nor the serried hedge of bayonets could check or shake them; they poured, like a torrent on and over the brigade and rode it fairly down leaving scarce a vestige of it remaining.[25]

While the incident obviously remained in Skinner's mind he exaggerates somewhat. Dudrenec's brigade was roughly handled and suffered 70 killed and 250 wounded as well as the loss of two of his guns, which Pohlmann recaptured and returned.[26] Yet this is hardly the destruction that Skinner relates. The Rathor cavalry carried on into the Maratha second line horse and routed a good number of those, pursuing them from the field.

Raja Partab Singh now gathered a body of his own cavalry, Skinner claims 5,000–6,000, but it was probably no more than half that number and probably less. The *Raja*, leading them on his elephant, approached Pohlmann's command with the intention of charging it. However, the elephant was brought down by artillery fire and the charge failed. At this the *Raja* mounted a horse and fled the field. The Rathor cavalry, returning from their pursuit of the Maratha cavalry, kettledrums beating in victory, were soon disabused of their supposed triumph by a few rounds from Pohlmann's guns. Being Rathors they immediately charged and, according to Skinner, some managed to break into the square but again this may be an exaggeration as the other source in the *Poona Residency Correspondence* never mentions this incident. However, the discomfited Rathors then retreated to their camp and, unable to find the departed *raja* likewise fled. At this point the only organised units remaining on the battlefield were Pohlmann's Second Brigade and those battalions of Dudrenec's *campoo* who had survived the Rathor assault.

Sending forward the 300 cavalry of his brigade, to which Skinner attached himself, Pohlmann discovered that the Rajput army had dispersed and had entirely abandoned their camp. It was here that Skinner picked up the Rs2,000 worth of loot noted in an earlier chapter. In addition, he also accidentally recovered the *mahee muratib* (the brass fish) an emblem of the Mughal Empire conferred upon Madhaji Scindia but lost at the Battle of Tunga, for this he was rewarded with a ceremonial palanquin and parasol, as well as a valuable *khilut* (robe of honour) this last, with the other trinkets he had picked up, he valued at Rs15,000. Not a bad day's work for a young officer of 22.

---

25 Baillie-Fraser, *Military Memoir*, Vol.1, pp.147–148.
26 Sinh, Sardesai, & Sarkar, *Poona Residency Correspondence*, Vol.9, p.12.

The battle had been hard fought and while we can dismiss Skinner's vast exaggeration of the casualties the butcher bill was still considerable. Lakwa Dada, in a letter to Colonel John Ulrick Collins, the British Resident at Scindia's court, put his own losses at around 700 and those of the Rajputs at 2,000. The Second Brigade seem to have lost 'not above 75 killed and wounded.'[27]

Tactically the battle had followed the format of many of the other combats in the history of the Army of Hindustan. The brunt of the fighting fell upon the artillery and the trained infantry. Their ability to maintain their discipline and formations in the face of medieval style Rajput cavalry charges once again won the day.

After their defeat the Rajput *rajas* once again came to terms with the Marathas. The *Raja* of Jodhpur even requesting Perron's aid to coerce some of his own refractory chieftains into paying the arrears of their tribute. However, the endless whirligig of Maratha politics was once again to take an unexpected turn. Intrigue, and not a little murderous bloodletting, would be the order of the day at Scindia's court.

Interlude: A small campaign in Hindustan – July–September 1800

Now, as Skinner put it 'war broke out on all sides' and, as ever in troublesome times, opportunistic bandits saw their chance.[28] In this case one Simboonauth (Skinner's spelling, Smith spells his name Sumboonaut) *subahdar* of the district of Seharunpore gathered 5,000 Sikh mercenary cavalry, 10,000 more or less regular infantry, and 20 or 30 guns to invade the *jaidad* of the Army of Hindustan.[29] This invasion of the lands that paid for and supported the troops could not be tolerated and Colonel Pedron, with the Third Brigade at Koil, sent Ashref Beg whom Skinner describes as an 'old soldier held in much respect by the soldiers' to counter this incursion.[30] Beg commanded three battalions with 10 guns and 1,000 cavalry, plus some Rohillas. What is interesting about this is that initially at least no European officers were sent with this expedition. It is also typical of the many small expeditions mounted by the Army of Hindustan but here, thanks to Skinner and Baillie-Fraser, we have more detail than in the laconic paragraphs of Lewis Ferdinand Smith.

Upon receiving information of the invasion from Pedron, Perron immediately detached Captain Smith with another two battalions to join Ashraf Beg. The outnumbered Beg had, with his infantry numbering around 2,000 bayonets, already met Samboonauth's army and beaten off the initial attack capturing six of the enemy's guns. Retreating overnight to the town of

---

27 Sinh, Sardesai, & Sarkar, *Poona Residency Correspondence*, Vol.9, pp.12–14.
28 Baillie-Fraser, *Military Memoir*, Vol.1, p.162.
29 Compton, *Particular Account*, p.248, calls Samburnath 'a faithful adherent of Lakwa' but cites no source for this assertion. It is quite possible but given the time and distance involved Samburnath was very quick off the mark if he was supporting Lakwa Dada. It is just as likely that this was an audacious plundering expedition made with the assumption that most of the available troops of the Army of Hindustan were elsewhere.
30 Baillie-Fraser, *Military Memoir*, Vol.1, p.163.

Khandowlee, his base for the operation, Beg prepared to withstand a blockade as Samboonauth's army encamped within five kilometres (three miles) of the town. Beg was made of stern stuff and decided to launch a surprise attack at three in the morning. Taking 1,000 of his surviving infantry and all his cavalry he launched them against the blockading camp:

> He succeeded completely in surprising them, and took several pieces of cannon which, however he could not bring away. The day had broken, however before he commenced his retreat, and the enemy recovering from their fright attacked him on all sides, Ashraf Beg then ordered he horse to set off for the town, which they reached with the loss of 100 men; while he threw his infantry into a square and made good his retreat, with all his cannon, thought the Sikhs pressed him hard and fought nobly. His loss in this gallant affair was about 300 men, but several brave and good native officers were killed, which disheartened him so much that he remained inactive for five days.[31]

Captain Smith now belatedly appeared with his two fresh battalions and news reached Samboonauth that Perron was not far behind with further reinforcements. He therefore retreated to his own district, not without the loss of more guns, taken by the re-energised Ashraf Beg, and the desertion of one of his battalions commanded by Mahomed Azim Khan to the Beg's service. Smith now took command of the whole force and marched to Seharunpore but Sanboonauth had already taken flight with his Sikh cavalry. Smith therefore took the surrender of the remaining infantry and guns.[32] It is more than likely that some of these men transferred their allegiance to the Army of Hindustan to replace casualties and recruit the battalions up to strength, though we are not told this specifically, it certainly happened in other cases, such as when De Boigne snapped up the disbanded *sepoys* of Lestineau's brigade to recruit the First Brigade a decade previously. Over the next few years the Army of Hindustan would need every man it could get.

The Widows War Part II: Lakwa Dada's Last Stand

Immediately after his victory over the Rajputs, Lakwa Dada was once again dismissed from his offices in an act of deliberate revenge by Daulat Rao and his re-appointed minister Sharza Rao, who had promised Daulat Rao Scindia 25 lakhs of rupees (RS250,000) as payment for his path back to power. Orders were sent to arrest Lakwa and other *sardars* of his party. Several who were seized were murdered by being blown from guns or tied to rockets, or even having their heads smashed with tent mallets. All these men had been chieftains and commanders serving Madhaji Scindia. Skinner calls this 'the

---

31 Baillie-Fraser, *Military Memoir*, Vol.1, p.165.
32 For Smith's almost dismissive report of the same small campaign see Chapter 6 of this book. Compton, *Particular Account*, pp.243–244, never mentions Ashraf Beg and gives all the credit for the victory to Perron, who is never mentioned by either Smith or Skinner.

most fatal blow Scindia ever gave his army.'³³ Needless to say Lakwa and his commanders fled in fear of their lives. At the same time Daulat Rao's officers once more attempted to seize Madhaji Scindia's widows who appealed in desperation to the new head of the house of Holkar, Jaswant Rao, for aid. The Widows War was on again. This time however it would broaden into a complicated civil war that would eventually engulf most of the Maratha Confederacy.

The Seondha Campaign – March–May 1801

Lakwa Dada and the other rebel leaders managed, despite the usual lack of funds, to raise a force of 10,000 cavalry 5,000 foot and 32 guns.[34] Including 400 cavalry from the *subahdar* of Jhansi and more significantly the *Raja* of Datia joined the rebels with 'three thousand Infantry, two thousand cavalry, all well appointed, and six field pieces.'[35] In addition Lackwa had a brigade of regular infantry commanded by Colonel William Henry Tone. How strong this formation was is unknown, but it must have been larger than the '200 *sepoys*' mentioned by Compton as at least one other European officer, a Captain Evans was present.[36] It is possible that there were as many as 2,000 of these regulars as Lakwa Dada had possessed two battalions of his own in the Malpura campaign the previous year. Also present was a second brigade under *Raja* Burar Singh. The rebels were however seriously overmatched by the forces that could be brought against them. Nevertheless, despite some fruitless negotiations, Lakwa fought on.

Once more confirmed in the office of *Subahdar* of Hindustan, Ambaji Angria was given charge of subduing his one-time ally. He had considerable forces to call upon as he collected his army at Gwalior. Skinner puts his forces at 20,000 Maratha cavalry and three brigades of regular infantry. Skinner himself was now with the Third Brigade under the rather aged Colonel Pedron, after a short stint commanding the two battalions of Perron's bodyguard. These two battalions were drafted into the Third Brigade. Possibly to stiffen it for the upcoming campaign.[37] In addition to the Third Brigade's eight battalions Ambaji also had two other brigades, both directly in his own employ. One of these was commanded by two English officers, James Shepheard and Joseph Bellasis.[38] The third was led by Colonel Kaleb Ali, and this was almost certainly the same brigade that Lakwa had 'tampered with' when he faced it in the first round of the Widows War in 1798.

Ambaji was however, loath to start the campaign and remained at Gwalior for several weeks despite repeated orders from Scindia to move against the rebels. It transpired that Jaswant Rao Holkar had not only declined to aid the widows as he had promised but had actually attacked and despoiled the

---

33 Baillie-Fraser, *Military Memoir*, Vol.1, p.162.
34 Sarkar, *Fall of the Moghul Empire*, Vol.4, p.147.
35 Sinh, Sardesai, & Sarkar, *Poona Residency Correspondence*, Vol.9, letter 243, p.424.
36 Compton, *Particular Account*, p.244.
37 Baillie-Fraser, *Military Memoir*, Vol.1, p.183.
38 Compton, *Particular Account*, p.245 and Baillie-Fraser, *Military Memoir*, Vol.1, pp.183–184.

ladies and their entourage by night as they lay in their camp near Ujjain, using one of his trained battalions from Dudrenec's *campoo* under a Captain Plumet to do this unchivalrous and treacherous deed. The ladies escaped with little more than the clothes they stood up in. Since he then plundered the city of Ujjain in November 1800 it became obvious that the real trial of strength between the houses of Scindia and Holkar was fast approaching and that the current campaign was merely the overture to what was to come.[39] Ambaji was perhaps wise to bide his time until he could see which way the wind was likely to blow.

Even so under the constant prodding of Scindia, and under threat of losing his *jaghirs*, Ambaji finally took the field. Despite winning two small victories over the supporters of Daulat Rao, Lakwa Dada and the other partisans of the widow ladies were slowly herded towards the fort at Seondha, about 64 kilometres (40 miles) due east of Gwalior, which belonged to his most steadfast ally the *Raja* of Datia. With his customary skill Lakwa took up a strong position with the fort and the river protecting his rear and impassable ravines to protect his flanks and parts of his front:

> The position he had chosen was an exceedingly strong one. In his rear was the fort of Sounda; in his front a network of ravines extending seven miles: and his flanks were defended by broken country and several strong forts. Through these natural defences there were only three clear passes or passages for the advance of an enemy, all strongly protected with infantry and artillery.[40]

The Scindian forces under Ambaji and Pedron arrived before this formidable position in March 1801 and for the next month or so did very little. The usual cavalry skirmishing took place but Ambaji seemed disinclined to assault any of the three passes into Lakwa's position.

Perron therefore decided to deal with this impasse personally. He had other problems, such as the Irish freebooter George Thomas and his war with the Sikhs causing mayhem in the north west, also part of this same Widows War. Perron's erstwhile comrade, Louis Borquien, with elements of the Fourth Brigade, was making very slow work of the siege of Ajmir in Rajputana, which at this time also belonged to Lakwa Dada. This currently stalled campaign was tying up troops needed for other tasks and needed to be resolved as soon as was practical.

So it was that on 1 May 1801 Perron arrived at Seondha with five battalions of the Fourth Brigade and 5,000 of the newly raised Hindustani Horse.[41] His arrival injected new purpose into the campaign and on 3 May a three-pronged assault was launched on Lakwa Dada's positions.

The right column was commanded Colonel Pedron and comprised of the battalions of the Third Brigade. There were at least four of these, and more likely six, since they had already been stiffened by the two battalions

---

39 Sarkar, *Fall of the Moghul Empire*, Vol.4, p.144.
40 Compton, *Particular Account*, pp.244–245.
41 Baillie-Fraser, *Military Memoir*, Vol.1, p.185. Compton, *Particular Account*, p.245 says 'a battalion of Infantry and 2,000 Hindustani Horse' but cites no source.

of Perron's bodyguard. Skinner was with this column. The centre column under Colonel Shepheard was supported by the troops of Colonel Kaleb Ali. Potentially this was numerically the strongest column, though no source states this directly. Kaleb Ali had, in a previous campaign against Lakwa, a *campoo* of eight battalions and the European led formation must have had more than two battalions since they lost five European officers killed and wounded, so a sensible estimate for Shepheard's brigade would be a minimum of four battalions, and possibly six. The left column comprised of five battalions of the Fourth Brigade under Captain Syme. Supported by the Hindustani Horse.

There was to be no tactical subtly here. This was to be a simple brutal storming of a difficult position, well defended, as Skinner relates:

> Colonel Toone's brigade happened to be opposed to our column and he defended his pass with great bravery; we carried it however, though with great difficulty, making prisoners of Colonel Toone himself, Captain Evans and several other officers.
>
> Colonel Sheppard attacked Raja Burar Singh and succeeded, also with difficulty; but Captain Syme, who had to deal with the Duttea troops was beaten back with great slaughter, Perron, on hearing this, galloped up, and placing himself at the head of the column, led them on with great bravery and coolness and beat back the Duttea troops in their turn.[42]

The action seems to have been very fierce and, even allowing for Skinner's possible exaggeration, casualties were heavy amongst the battalions of both the Third and Fourth Brigade elements present:

> Our Brigade (the Third) took sixteen guns belonging to Colonel Toone's [sic] force; our loss on the occasion being two officers killed, one wounded and about 1,000 men killed and wounded. Captain Sheppard had three European officers killed and one wounded and about 1,500 men killed and wounded. The third column lost Captain Syme and Lieutenant Arnold killed and Lieutenant Paish wounded. The fifth battalion lost half their men and had it not been for Perron's prompt and gallant assistance the whole would have been cut up. Perron himself was slightly wounded by a spear.[43]

The British resident at Scindia's court, Colonel Collins, though not himself present, wrote to the British Governor General in Calcutta in somewhat more concise terms:

---

42 Baillie-Fraser, *Military Memoir*, Vol.1, p.186.
43 Baillie-Fraser, *Military Memoir*, Vol.1, pp.186–187.

> From J. Collins Resident
> To– The Governor General Fategarh 7th May 1801
>
> I have this instant received intelligence that on 1st instant Mr. Perron attacked, and after a sharp conflict, carried a redoubt of the insurgents, erected by them for the purpose of retarding the approach of Scindia's forces towards Seondha.
>
> In this engagement both Lakwa Dada and the Datia Raja were slightly wounded. The insurgents have lost five pieces of artillery a stand of colours and several horses and camels which were taken by Mr. Perron. The chiefs of the insurgents and the Bais likewise seem greatly dispirited by this defeat."[44]

Although from Skinner's narrative we might assume that all three assaults went in on the same day. Collins' letters might imply otherwise.

> Since yesterday when I had the honour to address your Lordship, I have received an express from the camp of Mr. Perron mentioning that in consequence of the loss of a second redoubt, which was carried by Mr. Perron, the bais, Lakwa Dada Jagoo Bapoo and Durjan–sal had fled from Seondha and effected their escape … The flight of the insurgent Chiefs was conducted with too much precipitation to admit of their carrying off either camp equipage or artillery.[45]

Since both Lakwa Dada and the Raja of Datia would die of the wounds received in the fighting at Seondha the Widows War was finally over. Pedron plundered the town of Seondha capturing another 20 guns.[46] The battalions of the Third Brigade then returned to their cantonments at Alighur for a well-earned rest.

The Army of Hindustan with Perron the Frenchman as its commander-in-chief was now the paramount military force in northern India. Only the British had the resources to match the army that the Savoyard De Boigne had created and that Perron had expanded, and that in regard to its junior European officers and its military doctrine was paradoxically British in character. Like many mercenary forces this multi-national aspect was its main weakness. However, in 1801 such a weakness was not in the least apparent.

---

44 Sinh, Sardesai, & Sarkar, *Poona Residency Correspondence*, Vol.9, letter 250, p.434.
45 Sinh, Sardesai, & Sarkar, *Poona Residency Correspondence*, Vol.9, letter 251, p.435.
46 Sinh, Sardesai, & Sarkar, *Poona Residency Correspondence*, Vol.9, letter 252, p.436.

9

Mercenaries and Freebooters: George Thomas's War

By mid-1801 the Army of Hindustan was the most formidable military force in Northern India. Its commander, Pierre Cuillier Perron, the onetime handkerchief salesman and cannon foundry labourer, was by now, also the *subahdar* (governor) of Hindustan with seven great fortresses as his to command. He was Daulat Rao's paramount officer in the rump of that Mughal Empire where the poor blind Emperor was now merely a cypher:

> General Perron had now succeeded in bringing all of Hindustan under subjection; and every raja and soobah from the Nerbudda to the Sutlej regarded him as lord and master. He had now under his command four regular brigades of 8,000 effective men each and 10,000 regular Hindustani horse, besides the command of all the troops of every Raja and chief in that wide territory.[1]

However, paramount is not the same as unchallenged. Perron and the Army of Hindustan still had work to do.

In the second half of 1801, once the Widows War was finally concluded, Perron had two areas of conflict with which to contend. In the south, away in the Deccan, his master, Daulat Rao Scindia, was at war with Jaswant Rao Holkar and was bleating piteously and urgently for help. There were regular troops already down there. Colonel Sutherland still had the First Brigade with Daulat Rao and there were other regular infantry brigades not directly part of the Army of Hindustan, but still in the service of Scindia, also in the Deccan. Colonel George Hessing, son of John Hessing, had a four battalion formation near Ujjain, which was only half of his eight battalions, the other four being in Agra.[2] There was also a brigade led by Fidel Filose son of the Neapolitan mercenary and sometime muleteer Michel Filose, who had served under De Boigne. At its strongest this brigade had 14 battalions but by 1801 only 11 remained, scattered about the Deccan. At least six of these marched into Hindustan and joined Perron's forces in August 1801,

---

1 Baillie-Fraser, *Military Memoir*, Vol.1, p.188.
2 Smith, *Regular Corps*, p.57.

possibly adding to the strength of the Fourth Brigade.[3] These troops should have been enough to satisfy Daulat Rao but his total lack of tactical or strategic insight made sure that they were not sufficient as we shall see in a later chapter.

The point of course is simply that Perron refused to send troops to his employer's aid. There were political reasons for this but the main, indeed only, purely military reason which concerns us here is a certain Irish mercenary by the name of George Thomas.

The Astounding Career of Jehazi Sahib

Of all the European military adventurers to take part in the wars of the various Indian princes of the last quarter of the eighteenth century, be they gentlemen or common soldiers, one-time mule skinners or cashiered officers, no individual career, even De Boigne's or Perron's, is quite so unlikely or remarkable as that of George Thomas, the so called 'Raja from Tipperary.'[4]

Thomas dictated much of his life story to Captain William Francklin who published *The Military Memoirs of George Thomas* in Calcutta in 1803, after Thomas's death. Despite Francklin's pedestrian style it is a work that still fascinates, although it says almost nothing about Thomas's early life before he became a mercenary.

George Thomas was born in Roscrea County, Tipperary in 1756 of a Roman Catholic family.[5] His early life is shrouded in mystery. As Francklin puts it:

> From the best information we can procure it appears that Mr. George Thomas first came to India in a British ship of war in 1781–2. His situation in the fleet was humble, having served as quartermaster, or, as is affirmed by some, in the capacity of a common sailor.
>
> Shortly after landing in the vicinity of Madras, the activity of his mind, overcoming the lowliness of his situation, he determined to quit the ship, and embrace a life more suitable to his ardent disposition.[6]

In this regard he was really no different from many of the ex-sailor mercenaries who joined the various brigades at this time. Perron himself started his career in India in an almost identical way.

For some years Thomas seems to have served the various minor rulers in the south of the subcontinent known collectively as 'Poligars,' but seemingly tiring of their limited scope he travelled first to Hyderabad where he served

---

3   Smith, *Regular Corps*, pp.54–55.
4   Maurice Hennessy, The Raja from Tipperary (New York: St Martin's Press, 1971).
5   Hennessy, *The Raja from Tipperary*, pp.6–7.
6   Capt. William Francklin, *Military Memoirs of Mr. George Thomas* (Calcutta: Hukaru Press, 1803), p.2.

the *Nizam* for a time but then north, arriving in Delhi in 1787.⁷ He obtained a command in the mercenary brigade of the *Begum* Somru. That enterprising lady always needed European officers to command her often unpaid and therefore unruly troops. At the time this brigade of four battalions was in the service of the Emperor Shah Alam. Madhaji Scindia's first attempt at a takeover had failed with the defeat at Tunga and the Emperor – or his advisors – had decided upon a campaign against Najaf Kuli Khan who, like many Mughal nobles, saw any relaxation of control by central authority as an excuse to assert their independence. In this particular case the Emperor himself took the field with an armed rabble, disguising itself as an army, a mere 7,000 or so strong, with the *Begum's* brigade in addition being the only worthwhile formation in the whole force. This collection of military ineptitude then sat down near Najaf Khans fortress of Gokakgargh, a little to the north west of Agra. Najaf Khan himself was encamped under the walls of the fortress with a force of similar size and on the night of 12 March 1788 launched a surprise cavalry attack against the unwary Mughal forces. As with many of the more irregular troops in Indian armies of this period this unwelcome surprise caused huge panic. The sortie penetrated the siege camp as far at the Emperor's tent and Shah Alam's life was in some danger. The *Begum* Somru's brigade, encamped close by, was not affected by the panic and the *Begum* herself took steps to remedy the situation: 'A hundred men and a six pounder gun under the command of Thomas, were hastily ordered to advance, while the Begum, seated in her palanquin accompanied them to the scene.'⁸

A blast of short-range canister shot and a bayonet charge saw off the importunate raiders and the Emperor was able to take shelter in the approaching square of the main body of the *Begum's* troops.⁹

This incident was the foundation of Thomas's career. The rapid advance, often accompanied by a blast of canister from a handy 6-pounder gun, would become something of a trademark of his over the next few years. He remained in the *Begum's* service for almost four years as governor of the district of Tappal to the north west of Delhi where his primary task, after that of revenue collection, was to protect the frontier from the raids of the Sikhs who were endeavouring, with some success, to advance their territories at the expense of the ailing Mughals. Although details are lacking, these years of border warfare must have honed his military skills. Raid and counter raid meant rapid movement. Especially against Sikh forces who were made up almost entirely of *ghoracharra* irregular cavalry. Thomas's own cavalry were mostly Pathan, deadly enemies to the Sikhs and as adept at the kind of irregular warfare that Thomas was involved in as were the Sikhs themselves.

---

7   Compton, *Particular Account*, p.110.
8   Compton, *Particular Account*, p.111.
9   Sarkar, *Fall of the Moghul Empire*, Vol.3, p.255 makes light of this incident and does not mention Thomas, but Francklin, *George Thomas*, p.3, makes it clear that it was Thomas who led the *Begum's sepoys* but also that it was the *Begum* herself who organised the despatch of the troops.

'THEIR INFANTRY AND GUNS WILL ASTONISH YOU'

The *Begum* Somru and her household. Note the two *sepoys* in the background in Indian style dress but with muskets and bayonets. The whole of her brigade were dressed in this fashion. The *Begum* herself in the front row centre was a small woman, apparently only four feet and five inches tall. (Public Domain)

By 1792 Thomas was apparently on the rise. He had gained some influence with the *Begum*, but this had made her other European officers, who were mostly French, jealous of the relative newcomer's influence. They therefore plotted to oust him from his place as governor of Tappal and were successful, though the *Begum* spared his life.[10] It was probably this plot, at least as much as the international situation of the times, that gave Thomas a poisonous dislike of the French.

Thomas was not out of work for long. After a few months in British territory he was contracted to the Maratha chieftain Appa Khande Rao, often known as Rao Sahib. Thomas himself enjoyed the sobriquet of Jehazi Sahib (Sailor Sir). Many Indians had trouble with western names and most of the mercenaries had local nicknames. Sutherland, for example, was Sutlej Sahib. Perron was Ekdast Sahib (Sir One-hand) after he lost a hand from a prematurely exploding grenade at the siege of Kananund.

Appa Khande Rao was the same general who had been De Boigne's first employer but who had since fallen out with Madhaji Scindia and was now trying to establish his independence in the territory to the south west of Delhi. To do this he needed trained men and as Thomas was in need of mercenary employment a deal of sorts was struck. As usual Appa was loth to part with actual cash but, armed with the usual collection of hollow

---

10 Compton, *Particular Account*, p.113.

promises, Thomas raised 700 infantry and with his own following of Pathan horse, which may have numbered 250 men and a couple of guns set out to govern the lands Appa had assigned to him to pay his troops, with of course the surplus going directly into Appa's own coffers.[11] Needless to say these territories were as usual in rebellion. The Mewati people who lived in these districts saw no reason why they should bend the knee, or more importantly loosen the purse strings, to a Maratha, acting in the Emperor's name or not, in faraway Delhi. Thomas eventually succeeded where previously the forces of the *Begum* Somru had failed and thereby gained considerable status for his ability in collecting revenue from these turbulent and recalcitrant people. Thomas's speed in action and severity to the rebels meant that Appa used his slowly growing army as a kind of quick reaction force to stifle the constant petty, and sometimes not so petty, rebellions that plagued his territory. The relationship between Appa and Thomas was always stormy simply because Appa so often refused to part with any actual cash to pay Thomas what he was owed.

Nevertheless, Appa needed him and slowly Thomas increased the revenues of his territories and was therefore granted more territories to administer around the north western side of Delhi. Panipat and Sonnepat were added to his territories as *jaidad* to pay his troops and Thomas was awarded the district of Jhajjar as *jaghir* for his own upkeep. Thomas was therefore able to increase his strength to 2,000 infantry, 200 cavalry and 16 guns. At the instigation of Lakwa Dada Thomas was given the task of protecting the frontier from the Sikhs. In effect he was back in his old job of border warden. He kept this post and the territories assigned to it until the death of Appa Khande Rao in 1797. These were years of almost constant campaigning, Francklin's biography is a constant litany of battles and the storming of rebellious villages and forts, either against Sikh raiders or rebellious subjects.

Perhaps his employers feared his success but once Appa was dead Thomas's position became increasingly insecure and sometime in 1797 he was stripped of his offices and his *jaidads* by Appa's successors. At this point his army numbered some 3,000 men with their dependants and he had no means of paying them other than to become a bandit 'levying contributions' wherever he could, as his only remaining possession, Jhajjar, could not support his army from its own resources.

Thomas's ambition however, wanted more and such was the turbulent state of the country that he was able to occupy the district of Hariana with its capital of Hansi. This lay somewhat to the north west of Jhajjar and owed allegiance to no master. Thomas took over the territory in a swift campaign and, by dint of enormous effort and the bayonets of his army, imposed a kind of peace upon the population. He repaired the walls of the city of Hansi and over 1798 became de facto ruler of an area of some three thousand square miles. With an imposed peace Thomas was able to repopulate an almost deserted city. As he told Captain Francklin:

---

11 Francklin, *George Thomas*, p.5.

> I established a mint and coined my own rupees, which were current in my army and country; as from the commencement of my career at Jhajjar I had resolved to establish an independency, I employed workmen and artificers of all kinds, and I now judged that nothing but force of arms could maintain me in my authority, I therefore increased their numbers, cast my own artillery, commenced making muskets matchlocks and powder and in short made the best preparations for carrying on an offensive and defensive war.[12]

Thomas spent much of his time in raid and foray, levying contributions upon the Sikh territories on the eastern bank of the River Sutlej, varying this with employment for himself and his army as a jobbing mercenary for various Maratha chieftains most notably Ambaji Angria who used Thomas's skills during the Widows War when he was trying, and failing, to contain Lakwa Dada. Thomas did, however, manage to drive that wily general out of Mewar.

It was during this campaign that Thomas first encountered troops of the Army of Hindustan, these being Sutherland's Second Brigade who, during one encounter with the rebellious Lakwa Dada rather left Thomas in the lurch, marching away overnight while the rebel forces were within striking distance. As ever political intrigue was in the air and Perron had seemingly made some private arrangements with Lakwa to embarrass Ambaji Angria who was Thomas's employer. Perron even attacked Thomas's *jaghir* of Jhajjar which merely served to stoke the fires of the Irishman's hatred of the French.[13] One suspects the real reason for the attack was some attempt to bring Thomas to heel. He had been offered several contracts to permanently enter the service of Daulat Rao, which would mean that he would serve under Perron's command. This Thomas had no intention of doing under any circumstances. He would not serve as a subordinate to Perron.

Equally, Perron did not need an independent minded loose cannon such as George Thomas on his borders levying contributions whenever he was short of funds to pay his men, especially one whose dislike of the French mercenaries was so well known. While it is overstating the case to declare that Perron had a plan to establish a French state in Hindustan his actions certainly would give the new Governor General Richard Wellesley, Lord Mornington, serious cause for concern and a real fear of that possibility. By 1800 Perron's power within Hindustan was paramount. He was promoting French officers to senior positions within the army despite the fact that many, if not most, of the European officers in the individual battalions were of British extraction. At this time, of the four brigades existing in 1801, two were commanded by French officers. The Third Brigade by Louis Borquien who had replaced Pedron and Fourth Brigade under the Chevalier Dudrenec. Robert Sutherland, the Scot, still had the First Brigade and Colonel Pohlmann, the Hanoverian, the Second Brigade. All of the major fortresses had French commanders. Pedron for example would be given Aligarh once the war with Thomas was over.[14]

---

12 Francklin, *George Thomas*, p.93.
13 Compton, *Particular Account*, p.163.
14 Compton, *Particular Account*, p.379.

With the benefit of hindsight, we can see that war between two such characters as Perron and Thomas was almost inevitable. The collision between Perron's growing paranoia and Thomas's intense dislike of the French and his fear of the loss of his independence would fan the smouldering coals of mutual distrust into the bright flame of war.

The Irish Raja's Military Machine

While the Army of Hindustan had, by 1801, a decade long history of almost unbroken success, with its own arsenals and garrisons the forces at Mr Thomas's command for the upcoming war were considerably more extemporary. Thomas simply could not command the resources available to Perron. Despite this, his 'party' was far from inconsiderable. Lewis Smith described Thomas:

> This man was one of the most uncommon characters I have ever seen; and I knew him well; he was bold, indefatigable, active, cautious, and possessed of at strong natural sense: he formed a considerable party from his own personal exertions unassisted by the power or treasure of any prince-without money and without country– opposed by all and supported by none, he raised a strong party which was nearly destroying the gigantic power of Perron; but, in the struggle between Thomas and Perron. The former wanted decision, prudence and activity; qualities which never failed him in less important contentions.[15]

Smith's summary of Thomas's qualities and abilities is fair and to the point. His military talents were none the less astonishing for being almost entirely self-taught, for Thomas was probably illiterate, as were most of the Royal Navy's ratings in the eighteenth century.

A few examples of Thomas boldness in action must suffice to illustrate his methods of warfare. There were times in Thomas's career where he was no more than an armed robber.

As Smith writes: 'Thomas commenced his ambitious career in 1794 after he left the Begum Somru's service by collecting a few men near Delhi with whom he stormed a large village. The little money he acquired from this village, laid the foundation of his future hopes and prospects.'[16]

Yet he was never afraid of actual combat indeed he seemed to rather relish it. In his first foray into the Mewati country with his new command of 700 or so infantry and around 200 cavalry this newly raised force was ambushed by that warlike people:

> The party had not proceeded far, when they were attacked and obliged to retreat. Orders were given for the cavalry to advance and cover the detachment. And Mr. Thomas himself leading the infantry hastily marched, and with his collected force attacked the enemy at the village … By this time they had assembled and became

---

15 Smith, *Regular Corps*, p.20.
16 Smith, *Regular Corps*, p.20.

formidable. The centre division of Mr. Thomas's troops set fire to the village and there seemed no doubt of a complete victory, when the divisions on the right and the left, giving way, fled with precipitation …

The centre division under the special command of Mr Thomas, now following the example of their brethren, left him, of his troops only a dozen infantry and a few cavalry.

Thus discomfited and vexed by the unsteadiness of his troops, Mr. Thomas, as a last resort, encouraged his small party to exert themselves in extricating a nine pounder, which unfortunately, previous to the battle, had stuck in the bed of a nullah. In this he had just succeeded, when the enemy as certain of victory, recommenced a furious attack, and endeavoured to seize the gun.

The commandant of cavalry, a man of distinguished bravery, still adhered to Mr. Thomas and desperately with a few others threw himself between the gun and the enemy. They were cut to pieces but the gallant effort afforded time to remount and oppose a well directed fire of grape from the nine pounder. This saved Mr. Thomas and the brave few of his surviving party.[17]

During his conquest of Hariana he was somewhat incommoded at his siege of Khanori in the southern part of his proposed conquests. The garrison of the place made a sudden sortie against one of the redoubts that Thomas had constructed:

In the confusion attendant upon a business of this nature, the greater part of his people being panic struck, ran away. Mr Thomas was reduced to a situation truly critical. Five men only remaining with him of the infantry, to whom had been allotted the particular charge of his firearms, consisting of pistols and blunderbusses of a large size; with these, and the assistance of a few horsemen, who had likewise adhered to him, he maintained the post for a considerable time against every effort of the enemy, and at length by repeated and well directed discharges compelled them to retreat.[18]

In both of the above examples Thomas's opposition were the usual Indian irregular troops. In these two cases all seem to have been infantry, armed variously with matchlocks swords and spears. However, when defending their own homes they put up a far better showing than the average irregular.

As Thomas settled himself into his new domain, he was able to increase his forces so that when he went to negotiate with Perron in August 1801 he had in hand 10 battalions of drilled infantry with 60 guns as well as 500 cavalry and 1,000 or so Rohillas. Six more battalions were in the process of being recruited.[19] This was a considerable improvement on his early forces.

In July 1800, over a year before Thomas's war with Perron, Colonel Collins, the British resident at Scindia's court, wrote to the Governor General in Calcutta and amongst the news of the Widows War he felt it incumbent to mention Thomas:

---

17 Francklin, *George Thomas*, pp.15–16.
18 Francklin, *George Thomas*, pp.85–86.
19 Smith, *Regular Corps*, pp.21–22.

Though I can have little doubt that Mr. Perron is jealous of the growing power of Mr. George Thomas and would willingly crush it whenever a convenient opportunity occurs, yet I am inclined to think he will, if possible, avoid coming to immediate hostilities with that officer as well on account of the force he commands which is far from contemptible, as is the consideration of Mr. Thomas's connection with Begum Somru. Who now accompanies Mr. Perron and whose assistance is of importance in this juncture,

Yusef Ali Khan, who was detained a whole day in the camp of Mr. George Thomas as Sossnah by the late heavy rains, states his present force to consist of seven battalions of infantry, five hundred cavalry, twenty field pieces of artillery and four howitzers. The whole well equipped, regularly paid, and in strict subordination.[20]

As far as is known Thomas's troops wore no uniforms other than the civilian dress of the time with European style cross-belts in natural leather or possibly in black, but this last is speculation. His battalions carried colours as he mentions 'a stand of colours' during another of his personal fights but gives no clue as to their form.[21] Skinner gives a useful description of a part of Thomas's forces as he saw them during the abortive negotiations: 'We saw his troops who looked well, but were not over disciplined. His artillery was very fine, and the bullocks particularly good and strong. The only European officers he had were Captains Hearsey, Hopkins and Birch; and there were some Europeans acting as sergeants in his artillery'.[22]

At the meeting between the two mercenaries in August 1801 Perron offered Thomas Rs60,000 for his party and the rank of colonel if he would enter Scindia's service. Neither trusted the other and the two parted with mutual recriminations, each determined upon war.

Both protagonists had tried to build an alliance against the other. Perron, having more money and being the more powerful, was the more successful. The Sikh rulers of Patalia and Jhind in particular were anxious to come under Perron's protection. This was hardly surprising as Thomas had been a flail for their backs for almost a decade and their most earnest desire was to be rid of him. They and other Sikh chieftains offered Perron a subsidy of five lakhs of rupees (Rs500,000) and 10,000 cavalry for the coming campaign.[23]

Thomas made alliances with *Begum* Somru and even with Jean-Baptiste La Fontaine who commanded part of Filose's brigade.[24] He was also negotiating with Jaswant Rao Holkar who was already at war with Scindia in the Deccan. Holkar promised troops and money but when the grip came that wily chieftain, needless to say, did nothing, while Thomas's other allies left him in the lurch and in the end he was left to fight alone.

---

20 Sinh, Sardesai, & Sarkar, *Poona Residency Correspondence*, Vol.9, letter 19.
21 Francklin, *George Thomas*, p.24.
22 Baillie-Fraser, *Military Memoir*, Vol.1, p.216.
23 Compton, *Particular Account*, p.185.
24 Compton, *Particular Account*, p.185.

According to Smith who was present: 'Hostilities commenced after the retreat of George Thomas and the flight of Perron from his army.'[25]

The mainstay of the forces deployed against Thomas would be the Army of Hindustan's Third Brigade commanded by Major Louis Borquien. Both of the brothers Smith and both of the Skinner siblings would be involved in this campaign. It is, therefore, comparatively well off as regards source material since in addition to those incidents Thomas himself dictated to Francklin, we have Skinner's lively and entertaining memoir, and Smith's rather more terse account.

The campaign opened with the Third Brigade marching to Thomas's undefended *jaghir* of Jhaijar and occupying it. Thomas himself had concentrated his forces at his city of Hansi where his arsenals and supply depots were situated. Smith takes up the story:

> I was ordered with three battalions to lay siege to Georgeghar a small fort forty cos [approx. 96 kilometres/60miles] to the eastward of Hansi– Thomas and his forces were encamped under the fort of Hansi. Borquien was ordered with seven battalions and five thousand horse to lie between me and Hansi to cover the siege of Georgegarh, which must have fallen in a week; but with singular ignorance, Borquien encamped at Gin– ten cos (24 kilometres/15 miles) further from me than Thomas's army– the consequence was obvious – three days after I laid siege to Georgegarh I was attacked by Thomas with eight battalions. Compelled to raise the siege and retreat to Jaijjar.[26]

Smith's force, which also had a siege train with it and 100 cavalry did not get away unscathed. He lost a gun, and one of his three battalions was destroyed in a brutal little rear guard action on 27 September 1801 at a cost of 700 casualties which did however allow the rest of his force with their remaining guns to retreat.[27] Thomas's army, tired from the forced march to relieve Georgegarh, could only send a few cavalry in pursuit. These picked up 'several stands of colours and small arms which had been thrown away in the retreat' but otherwise Smith was able to extricate is men, guns and baggage and avoid complete disaster.[28]

The following day Smith was reinforced by a body of 2,000 cavalry commanded by his brother Captain E.F. Smith who had forced marched to get to Jhaijar. The following day Thomas's *hicarrahs* (scouts) brought news that Borquien with the bulk of the Third Brigade was approaching from the rear. Declining to be caught between two fires by a force with a far more numerous cavalry than his own, he therefore decided to retreat. Thomas now returned to Georgegarh and fortified his camp to await the showdown which was not long in coming.

---

25 Smith, *Regular Corps*, p.23.
26 Smith, *Regular Corps*, p.23.
27 Francklin, *George Thomas*, p.227.
28 Francklin, *George Thomas*, p.226.

The Battle of Georgegarh – 30 September 1801

Thomas's army had time for no more than a brief respite when the Third Brigade appeared before his camp. For the coming contest the Irish *Raja* had 10 battalions of infantry 500 cavalry, 600 Rohilla irregulars and 50 pieces of artillery.[29] The whole force not exceeding 5,000 men. This would put his average battalion strength at something under 400 once the artillery crews for his 50 guns are deducted from the total. The opposition had roughly the same number of infantry, in perhaps nine battalions but perhaps as many as 5,000 cavalry mostly of the usual irregular type, either Maratha or Sikh *ghorracharra*, neither type being 'battle' cavalry.

Smith relates the commencement of the action:

> Major Borquien with the Third Brigade reached Georgeghar after a surprising march of forty cos [approx. 95 kilometres/60 miles] in thirty-six hours; the brigade arrived about midday. The troops were harassed, fatigued and famished. With destructive imbecility, Borquien ordered the troops consisting of seven battalions, to storm Thomas's entrenched camp at four o'clock in the afternoon.[30]

Smith has little time for Borquien's lack of military skill yet Skinner, admittedly writing somewhat later, paints a somewhat more measured picture:

> There we halted for one day to rest and next morning moved to Baree, within two cos of Georgeghar. Borquien then went to reconnoitre the place and I accompanied him. We found that Thomas had drawn up in one line, having Georgeghar on his right flank, and a large village which he had fortified; on his left he had a small fort or ghuree in which he had stationed 1,000 Rohillas and four pieces of cannon. His rear was likewise defended by a large village.[31]

As was usual in many Indian battles the field was a large open plain. Yet this one was a little different in that the plain was made up of loose sand. Indeed, Thomas's entrenchments seem to have been little more than piled sand banks behind which he placed his artillery. Although Skinner says Thomas had all his army in one line Thomas himself says: 'Of this force 5 battalions were opposed to Mr Lewis (Borquien) two were assigned for the battalions opposite the centre of his line and three to sustain the shock of the enemy's horse.[32]

Rather than the linear battle which both Smith and Skinner describe, each seemingly taking part in the main infantry assault, the action appears somewhat more complex. Thomas being at least partially surrounded in his camp by the far superior (in numerical terms at least) cavalry of Borquien's army. Borquien himself did not lead the main assault and according to Smith 'prudently remained with the cavalry two thousand yards in the rear

---

29 Francklin, *George Thomas*, p.228.
30 Smith, *Regular Corps*, p.24.
31 Baillie-Fraser, *Military Memoir*, Vol.1, p.219.
32 Francklin, *George Thomas*, p.228.

of George Thomas's line.' Skinner says quite deliberately that 'two battalions and two eighteen pounders together with some horse were sent to try his rear.'³³ These two battalions would, as was normal practice in the Army of Hindustan, have had their own guns with them so the total of this force would have been two battalions with their five guns each plus the two larger pieces from the brigade siege train plus the 2,000 horse all in theory commanded by Borquien himself. While Skinner does not give us a total for his 'some horse' it seems highly unlikely that there would have been two entirely separate columns of cavalry sent to attack Thomas's rear. This would mean that the total force deployed against Thomas would have been nine infantry battalions of roughly 500 men each including their artillery company, of which seven took part in the main assault. In addition, there was a total of 5,000 cavalry including those that were with Borquien, with the rest on the flanks of the main assault.

Francklin describes Thomas's situation on the morning of the 30 September as follows:

> On the ensuing morning the enemy prepared to attack him, his situation was at this time critical; the battalions who had before retreated from Georgeghar now came back, and took post within cannon shot to the eastward of his encampment; the force under Mr. Lewis was stationed to the south west; while the enemy's numerous cavalry attacked him in front.
>
> About 4 o'clock in the afternoon the action commenced by a heavy cannonade on both sides; the motions of the enemy had induced Mr. Thomas to divide his army according to the ground he occupied, the advantage of which, allowing for the quality of the troops, was much in his favour, but his battalions not being accustomed to be exposed to a cannonade, he drew up his army on a loose sand which thereby deadened the shot and prevented their rising after first graze.³⁴

This loose sand not only made Borquien's artillery less effective by deadening the round shot by not allowing the balls to graze (bounce) as they would have done on harder ground, but it also made dragging the guns forward much more difficult. The main assault on Thomas's position was carried out by seven battalions of the Third Brigade. This was of course one of the formations originally raised by De Boigne:

> The seven battalions of De Boigne with calm intrepidity, advanced with their guns through heavy sand exposed to a dreadful and well directed fire of fifty-four pieces of cannon, and attacked Thomas's ten battalions in their entrenchments; but they were repulsed with the severe loss of above one thousand and one hundred men killed and wounded which was nearly one third of their number.³⁵

---

33 Baillie-Fraser, *Military Memoir*, Vol.1, p.219.
34 Francklin, *George Thomas*, p.228.
35 Smith, *Regular Corps*, p.24.

In this bloody assault Captain L.F. Smith lost his brother Captain E.F. Smith who was killed leading the battalions of the left wing. Skinner provides more details of this phase of the battle:

> At three p.m. we moved to the attack, in open columns of companies … Having come within gunshot we formed line, under a heavy cannonade of thirty-five pieces. [Skinner seems only to count the guns facing him rather than the full total of Thomas's artillery] The cavalry were on our flanks, but took good care to keep out of cannon reach. Our right had come into a line with Thomas's left, when the word was given to wheel into line and thus we moved to the attack. Both parties fought well, and disputed the day with great courage. About four p.m. we came within musket range, but found that Thomas had thrown up sand banks in his front, which brought our line to a halt. Both musketry and cannon now showered on us like hail, and the men began to fall by hundreds. Two of Thomas's battalions now moved out in columns of companies, under command of Captain Hopkins, a gallant officer. They formed just in front of our left wing, and gave their fire exactly as if they had been at a review: when all had formed, they gave a volley and came to the charge, which completely succeeded in driving back our left wing. However our golundauze kept to their guns; and the gallant Hopkins, having his leg shot off, by one of our six pounders, whilst advancing at the charge, the battalions gave way as soon as he fell, and ran back taking their leader along with them. Our left wing then rallied and resumed their position, but the fire was so murderous that our whole line was ordered to sit down; as for Thomas's men, they were sheltered by the sand hillocks in his front.[36]

The heavy sand on which the battle was fought caused other problems. Writing of the same assault Smith comments upon the speed of the advance:

> Their slow progress through the heavy sand which lay in front of Thomas's line. Owing to the guns, which they would not leave in their rear, occasioned not only their defeat but their dreadful carnage. Thomas's loss was not so great, as the guns of De Boigne's battalions were mostly dismounted by their recoil on the sand, when fired, which snapped their axel trees.[37]

What, you may ask, was the supposed commander of the Third Brigade doing while his infantry units were being shot to bits by Thomas's guns? Well, in short, not very much. Neither Skinner nor Smith make any further mention of Borquien until the fighting is over. We may assume that he remained with that body of troops in Thomas's rear which does not seem to have done any more than threaten without actually advancing against the Irish Raja's position, though the cavalry may have taken part as Thomas's own cavalry had some hard fighting. Thomas's narrative as written by Francklin does not mention him directly but his account of the battle while more or less agreeing with those of Smith and Skinner differs in some details:

---

36 Baillie-Fraser, *Military Memoir*, Vol.1, pp.220–221.
37 Smith, *Regular Corps*, p.24.

> Mr. Lewis's division came on briskly having their guns at the drag ropes. [this would be the main assault] Mr. Thomas by a rapid discharge of round and grape shot from his artillery, at first threw them into confusion, and had he been able at this moment to prevent his troops from giving way, would have entirely defeated the enemy, but the centre of his line, being at that time hard pressed by the enemy's cavalry, gave way and no effort could prevent the remainder from following their example.
>
> This rendered an immediate and spirited advance necessary to support; for this purpose Mr Thomas ordered Mr. Hopkins with the right wing and Mr. Birch with the left to advance and charge with bayonets their respective wings, which service they performed with no less gallantry than success.
>
> The enemy halted, and began to retreat, but a heavy fire being still continued, from their numerous and well served artillery, Mr. Thomas's people fell in great numbers, which the enemy's cavalry perceiving charged a second time.
>
> They were not only repulsed with loss, but pursued by Mr. Thomas's horse a considerable distance from the field of battle, at this time intelligence was brought to Mr. Thomas who was on the left wing that Mr. Hopkins had received a severe contusion, by a cannon shot, which broke his leg, this circumstance so disheartened his men, that they fell back in disorder and increased the confusion in the centre of his line.
>
> A strong detachment of the enemy, who were stationed in Mr. Thomas's rear prevented his receiving any support from the troops opposed to them, and he could only spare one battalion to support the centre. This body, however conducted themselves with so much gallantry, that could Mr. Thomas have afforded the additional aid of 100 resolute men, they might have advanced, and would, in all probability, have decided the fate of the day.[38]

Thomas's narrative indicates that the cavalry opposing him did take some part as they charged at least twice. It would not be correct to think of this as similar to a European cavalry charge of the same era, nor yet, a charge by cavalry, such as the Rajputs could command. Such a charge in this context may mean more of an attempt to intimidate rather than a full-blooded charge to contact. Skinner mentions no such charge and Thomas's infantry and outnumbered cavalry were able to counter the threat, though it is unclear if these attacks were from the front, or from Borquien's troops in Thomas's rear.

As night fell the fighting petered out and both sides being exhausted they remained on the field. The battle was a bloody draw which both sides thought they had lost. Smith writes: 'Had Thomas taken advantage of Borquien's ignorance and folly and sallied out on the beaten back troops of Perron he would have overturned his power.'[39] Similarly Skinner wrote:

> The state of our guns and the spirit of our soldiery was such that had Thomas shown any inclination to move towards us we should have got out of his reach; for our commander Major Louis Borquien was not only a coward but a fool. He was one of those who had got on by flattery; and had it not been for Captain

---

38 Francklin, *George Thomas*, pp.228–230.
39 Smith, *Regular Corps*, p.25.

Burnear [Bernier] a Frenchman, we should certainly have lost the day, for the Major was not seen during the battle– and our being saved from total destruction was entirely owing to the exertions of Captain Burnear who was a brave and able soldier.[40]

Thomas lost some 700 men in this action including the gallant Captain Hopkins, who died of his wounds a few days later, while Borquien lost some 2,000. These figures being from Francklin, as Skinner, as usual, magnifies the numbers considerably in his own account, though he also names the European officer casualties: '… out of seven European Officers we had two killed, namely Lieutenants Smith and M'Culloch and two wounded Captains Oliver and Rabella. Twenty-five of our tumbrils were blown up by the enemy's shot and 15 of our guns dismounted'.[41]

Thomas also lost some 20 of his guns dismounted because of the recoil on the heavy sand and Borquien's forces now blockaded Thomas in his camp.[42] For his own part Thomas seems to have been somewhat unmanned by the death of Hopkins and the mauling his army had suffered and for several days lost his usual decisive manner and took solace in drink. On the other side the aged but experienced Colonel Pedron arrived and superseded Borquien. With more troops arriving the blockade tightened. Almost daily skirmishes and contacts took place and slowly Thomas's forces began to fall apart even though he maintained to Captain Francklin that his troops had the better of many of these skirmishes. Perron had ordered forward more troops as soon as he heard of Borquien's poor performance, five battalions of the Fourth Brigade marched from their cantonment at Koil with Colonel Pedron in command.[43] Five more of Colonel George Hessing's independent brigade started from Agra, and various local *rajas* and Sikh chieftains also contributed more cavalry.[44]

Of course, Thomas's real problem, as always, was lack of money. Perron bribed some of Thomas's Indian officers, whose families lived within Perron's reach, and Thomas began to suffer serious desertions amongst his force as the difficulty of procuring food and fodder became more acute. An attempt to organise a breakout to Hansi with his available forces failed as the *sepoys* would not obey orders. The Jehazi Sahib's aura of victory had deserted him and after a 15 day blockade his Indian troops could see no alternative but to surrender. Some joined their erstwhile enemies and others simply went home. Pedron captured all of Thomas's baggage, artillery and stores including 50 guns. Thomas's army was finished.

---

40 Baillie-Fraser, *Military Memoir*, Vol.1, p.223.
41 Baillie-Fraser, *Military Memoir*, Vol.1, p.221.
42 Francklin, *George Thomas*, p.231.
43 Compton, *Particular Account*, p.196, says these five battalions were from the Second Brigade. At this time that formation was commanded by Colonel Pohlmann so this does seem a little unlikely.
44 Compton, *Particular Account*, p.196.

Thomas himself, with his two surviving European officers – Captains Birch and Hearsey – broke out on the night of 10 November with his bodyguard of 300 horse and racing past Hessing's piquets, rode hard for Hansi.[45]

The Last Fight of the Irish Raja: The Siege of Hansi November–December 1801

When Thomas arrived at his capital, he found the defences in a parlous state. His own account says that in the fort of Hansi only two guns were fit for service. In the time allowed by the slow advance of Perron's forces Thomas cast and mounted eight more guns and sent out patrols to fill in the wells and pollute the water to make the enemy advance more difficult. His garrison consisted of around 1,200 men, of which only 300 Rajputs could be entirely relied upon. Thomas is scathing about his Rohilla troops in his account to Francklin calling them 'treacherous' and 'clamorous for their pay' and asserting that they offered to surrender and join Perron's army in return for their money.[46]

Meanwhile the Third Brigade was being rebuilt by Pedron with drafts from those five battalions of the Fourth Brigade which had come with him from Alighur. Major Louis Borquien was again placed in command of this army. Pedron, thinking that little was left to be done in the campaign returned to Alighur. The army, now marching at a somewhat leisurely pace towards Hansi consisted of 10 battalions of trained infantry 500 Hindustani horse and 5,000 Sikh cavalry, plus a substantial siege train.

Thomas did not idly await his fate. Aside from the casting of new guns he built three outworks, one in front of each of the three gates to the city of Hansi, 'about one hundred yards from the town.'[47] His reliable Rajputs he placed in the fort while his Rohillas garrisoned the city and these outworks.

Once Borquien had reconnoitred he decided to storm the three outworks simultaneously, each with a column consisting of two battalions. One of these was commanded by Skinner, another by Lieutenant Mackenzie and the third by that Captain Bernier who, according to Skinner, had saved the army from defeat at the Battle of Georgeghar. Two of the outworks were carried easily, their garrisons retreating to the city. Captain Bernier's column had a little more trouble. He had put his force between the outwork and the city walls, cutting off the garrison's retreat, which forced them to fight. Bernier was then killed in the ensuing melee.

Batteries were then erected on these three captured outworks and the serious business of breaching the city walls began. The besiegers managed this without any serious interference from the garrison and on the morning of 3 December 1801 mounted their assault. Again using three storming columns each of 1,500 men commanded by Skinner himself, his brother Lieutenant Robert Skinner, and Lieutenant Mackenzie.

---

45 Baillie-Fraser, *Military Memoir*, Vol.1, p.225.
46 Francklin, *George Thomas*, pp.242–244.
47 Baillie-Fraser, *Military Memoir*, Vol.1, p.226.

MERCENARIES AND FREEBOOTERS

Skinner's narrative of the actions of his column show the sometimes odd nature of combat between two mercenary forces:

> At dawn of day, on the 3rd of December, the signal of attack was given. Mackenzie was opposed to Captain Hearsey: my brother to a native, Ellias Beg; and I had to contend with Captain Birch. Both Mackenzie and my brother made good their way in, after some resistance; but Birch, who defended his post well, beat me back twice with great loss. Burning powder choppers [*chopra* – chopped hay bales], powder pots, and everything he could get hold of were showered upon us; but our greatest loss was from the powder pots [these pots would be primitive grenades] which greatly disheartened the men: however, after a desperate struggle I drove them from the breach. Just as I had got up, I saw Birch about twenty yards from me taking aim at me with a double barrelled gun, the contents of which, both barrels, he fired at me; but 'the sweet little cherub' saved me from them. I immediately levelled my javelin, and, putting my shield to my breast, darted it at him, and took off his hat, on which he set off and joined his men, who were now leaving the wall and retreated about two hundred yards behind houses.
>
> All my storming party had now got in, and we moved towards the chowk or centre of the bazar where we saw our columns. The fight now became desperate. Thomas had come down from the fort with 1,000 of his chosen men, attacking the column commanded by Lieutenant Skinner, drove it back to the walls of the town. I immediately hastened to my brother's assistance, and beat Thomas back to the gate of the fort.
>
> All our columns now having joined in the chowk, Thomas made another attempt, bringing up a six-pounder, and, after great resistance, drove us out of the chowk. We were then joined by our reserve of a battalion, with a couple of six-pounders, and, in spite of a very obstinate resistance, by Thomas, drove him back to the fort. About noon we had a complete possession of the town; but it cost us dear, as the slaughter on our side was very great, for several times we had to come to the sword [that is hand to hand with the sword]. My brother got a cut at Thomas but his armour had saved him.[48]

The fighting was evidently intense as Thomas himself acknowledged to Francklin:

> The assault was accordingly made; on the entrance of the enemy to the town, a desperate conflict was maintained on either side, Mr Thomas's remaining troops fighting with the most determined valour. Three different times the enemy were repulsed with loss, but numbers at length prevailing, Mr. Thomas could no longer persuade his men to continue the conflict. He was therefore reluctantly compelled to take shelter within the fort.[49]

Thomas had finally been beaten into his last refuge. On the morning of 4 December a battery of eight 18-pounder guns was erected within 200 yards of the fort in the open space of the *chowk*, or market square. Thomas's

---
48 Baillie-Fraser, *Military Memoir*, Vol.1, pp.228–229.
49 Francklin, *George Thomas*, p.243.

remaining troops, around 700 men, were now short of provisions and water, but were not yet quite prepared to give up. The guns had little effect upon the walls of the fort so Borquien's men tried mining and, according to Skinner, made it to within 10 yards of the wall. Borquien however tried the more certain method of bribery using messages tied to arrows to suborn Thomas's men, who replied the same way. Borquien had decided to imprison Thomas if he could get hold of his person but the country-born and English officers of the besieging forces deemed this underhand and as Borquien was the only French officer in the brigade the majority prevailed and Borquien, always more of a talker than a doer, was persuaded to offer terms. All of this took time, so it was not until 20 December that Captain Smith opened negotiations:

> Borquien had subdued the garrison with gold, which in India is always more irrefutable than in Europe. In this critical situation I came forward once more to assist Thomas, to mitigate the severity of his misfortunes and dissipate the dangers with which he was environed– I advised him to an honourable surrender, before the garrison delivered him over to his enemy, with eternal disgrace to themselves and ignominy to him.[50]

The formal surrender of Hansi fort took place on 1 January 1802 and Mr George Thomas was no longer ruler of his own state. He was allowed to depart to British territory with all his personal wealth and baggage. The escort commanded by Captain Smith, took him to the British frontier where he arrived in middle of January 1802. He spent some time at Benares, where he dictated his memoirs to Captain Francklin, and died en route to Calcutta at Berampore on 22 August 1802, aged 46.

Perron had emerged victorious from the unequal contest. His focus now turned to the affairs of his paymaster Daulat Rao Scindia in the Deccan, where a civil war had raged for much of the past year between the house of Scindia and the house of Holkar and which shook the Maratha Confederacy to its foundations.

---

50 Smith, *Regular Corps*, p.26.

10

Holkar and Scindia: The Civil War in the Maratha Confederacy

While Perron was busy swatting the angry Irish wasp that was George Thomas, far away in the Deccan and in the lands of the Maratha Confederacy the Widows War had morphed into a much more serious internecine conflict between the two most powerful houses of the always squabbling confederates. This current outbreak was significantly more serious than the usual raiding and territory grabbing by the various *sardars* and chieftains who felt temporarily strong enough to get away with it. This would be all out war. The usual tortuous political wrangling of the Confederacy need not detain us except in very broad-brush terms.

Almost the only consistent policy of Daulat Rao Scindia was to humble the rival house of Holkar. The rulers of these rival houses, Scindia and Jaswant Rao Holkar, were the two most powerful members of the Maratha Confederacy. That grouping's titular head, the *Peshwa*, at this time Baji Rao II, had few troops of his own and those little more than an armed mob. So when the *Peshwa* murdered one of Jaswant Rao's relatives by having him flogged and then tied to the foot of an enraged elephant, it is little wonder that Jaswant Rao swore revenge. This forced Baji Rao to come to some accommodation with Daulat Rao Scindia, despite the deep distrust that existed between them. Daulat Rao had also managed to alienate the other major members of the confederacy, such as Bhonsla of Berar, so he found himself virtually friendless for the coming war.

Jaswant Rao was a soldier of significant skill in the old *gamini kava*, guerrilla warfare, mould of Maratha fighting, but he also had some understanding of the need for trained infantry and guns on European lines. There had been a four battalion brigade under the Chevalier Dudrenec in the service of the house of Holkar, destroyed by De Boigne at Lakheri. Dudrenec had been allowed by Holkar to raise a second formation as a replacement. However, when that officer tried to leave Jaswant Rao's service with this brigade, the troops preferred to remain where they were. Dudrenec therefore took service with Scindia, and Perron eventually placed him in charge of the Fourth Brigade.[1] Those troops remaining with Holkar became part of his trained infantry and artillery brigades, on the by now usual model, led by mostly British officers. There were, in fact three of these brigades, each of four battalions, with their own complement of light artillery, as usual, in the region of four or five guns per battalion. These brigades were commanded by Captain William Gardner, Captain Dodd and a French officer Captain Plumet who seems to have taken over Dudrenec's command. In addition, Holkar could command a large force of Pathan mercenary cavalry led by Amir Khan, no mean soldier himself, who had in his youth been turned down by De Boigne for a place in the First Brigade as being too young. Amir Khan had then raised a band of followers and maintained them, like George Thomas, largely from exacting contributions, in other words plundering. Such was his success that by 1801 his personal following was several thousand strong and while in the service of Holkar was often seen as much as an ally rather than as a mercenary.

By 1801, therefore Holkar was well equipped to take on the might of the Army of Hindustan. Needless to say, because of the army's other commitments, mostly against George Thomas but also the usual problems of garrisoning and revenue collection, by no means all of the four brigades were available for service in this war. Aside from the veteran First Brigade, commanded by Colonel Robert Sutherland, Daulat Rao Scindia had other formations of regular troops to hand for the coming campaigns. George Hessing commanded four battalions of his brigade at Scindia's capital of Ujjain. Scindia also had the rather doubtful assistance of the *compoo* of Fidel Filose, or at least four battalions of it, the rest being in Hindustan at the fortress of Agra where they would become the foundation of the Fourth Brigade. In addition there was also the supposed *compoo* of one Captain (or perhaps Major) Brownrigg, an Irishman who had his own corps in the service of Daulat Rao according to Compton.[2] However, Smith, who knew Brownrigg personally, says that these were 'four battalions of De Boignes brigades.'[3] So, it is possible that Compton has made an error. If therefore these four battalions were indeed De Boigne's they could only have come from the veteran First Brigade under Sutherland as this was the only specifically Army of Hindustan formation in the Deccan at this time, the other three brigades being engaged in various tasks further north in Hindustan. Sutherland's brigade, and this detachment from it under Brownrigg, were both to play a pivotal role in the campaign of 1801.

The Indore Campaign – June–October 1801

Daulat Rao Scindia was no general. He wasted the first half of 1801 in idle self-indulgent personal pursuits, such as tiger hunting and kite flying, as he progressed rather aimlessly and with long periods of inaction towards the

---

1 Compton, *Particular Account*, p.350.
2 Compton, *Particular Account*, p.348.
3 Smith, *Regular Corps*, pp.14–15. Smith calls Brownrigg 'my amiable friend' but does not mention him having his own *compoo*.

A single Maratha trooper, better equipped than some he is probably of the *sillhadar* or volunteer classes. He could just as likely be one of Holkar's troopers as one of Scindia's. (Anne S.K. Brown Military Collection)

river Narbada (Narmada). He sent piecemeal detachments ahead of him to reinforce George Hessing at Ujjain, with gaps of 30 or 40 miles between each detachment. Militarily speaking this was arrant folly as it invited Jaswant Rao and Amir Khan to destroy each of these detachments in detail at a time of their own choosing. Daulat Rao was, at the same time, sending piteous appeals for help to Perron in faraway Delhi, which, for his own reasons, the Frenchman saw fit to ignore. At the same time Daulat Rao was also receiving equally piteous appeals for help from his local garrisons and tax collectors as their villages were looted and despoiled by Jaswant Rao's and Amir Khan's predatory cavalry. Inertia and indeed idiocy seemed to be the order of the day.

Sarkar's description of the geography over which the coming campaign would be fought cannot be bettered:

> Daulat Rao Scindia's main camp and family rested near Handia on the south bank of the Narmada. On the north bank of the river facing Handia lay the town of Nimawar, which served as the other bridgehead to his army. A broken plain stretched for eighteen miles to the town of Satwas, and the route was intersected only by small nullahs draining southwards into the great river. Fourteen miles northwest of Satwas stood Bijwara, at the eastern end of a pass after crossing which, and debouching on the plain at the village of Dhantalav at its western mouth, the road reached the town on Unchaud another thirteen miles from Bijwara. Sixteen miles west of Unchaud lay the city of Newri and sixteen miles further off in the same direction lay Dewas. Ujjain was twenty-two miles northwest of Dewas and Indore (Jaswant Rao's capital) thirty-two miles south of Ujjain.[4]

---

4   Sarkar, *Fall of the Moghul Empire*, Vol.4, p.150.

There was, of course Hessing's four or possibly five battalions at Ujjain but two other smaller detachments were on the march to reach Ujjain and join Hessing's small force. The first, under an otherwise unknown mercenary – Lieutenant MacIntyre – consisted of two battalions, one from Filose's brigade, the other the remaining battalion of Hessing's briagde, and therefore neither technically part of the Army of Hindustan at this time, and 500 cavalry. They seem to have been understrength as they had only seven guns. This force had reached the city of Newri in late June 1801. Some distance away, at the fortified village of Satwas lay Captains Brownrigg and Gautier with four battalions and an additional train of heavy artillery pieces numbering 52 guns. This force had originally been despatched by Scindia in two separate detachments but by the end of June 1801 they had managed to unite.

On 25 June 1801 Jaswant Rao, after bypassing Hessing at Ujjain, fell upon MacIntyre's isolated and hugely outnumbered force outside Newri like a thunderbolt and, after a stubborn fight, forced to surrender when MacIntyre's infantry ran out of ammunition. Holkar captured 200 horses, 400 muskets and seven guns. MacIntyre and his two other European officers were both taken prisoner. Holkar's army may have suffered as many as 1,000 casualties though the total was probably less.[5] Nevertheless, Jaswant Rao had won a victory.

In Satwas, Brownrigg and Gautier had a problem. They too were isolated from any meaningful aid, but they were also encumbered by the heavy guns and the assorted impedimenta of a large artillery train. Fortunately, the veteran Brownrigg knew what he was about and his four battalion command, for he seems to have been senior over Gautier, was from the First Brigade; the oldest of the Army of Hinduatan's formations. When Holkar's fast riding *pindari* light cavalry approached the village of Satwas, Brownrigg shooed them away with a few rounds of gunfire. He then set his baggage and guns on the road to begin a 22 kilometre (14 mile) retreat to the river Narbuda where, within reach of the bridgehead at Nimawar, he entrenched. He was joined by two more battalions under the Maratha commanders Devji Gauli and Sadashiv Rao, bringing his total force to six battalions and a possible maximum of 72 guns.[6]

Brownrigg had chosen his position well. His men had their backs to the river, so there was nowhere to run. His flanks were protected by nullahs and ravines which would inhibit Holkar's vast numbers of cavalry. Despite his large numbers of available guns Brownrigg's force cannot have numbered more than a maximum of 3,000 bayonets and with the addition of gunners, *kelsais* and 100 Rohillas, cannot have been more than 4,000 combatants.[7]

---

5   Sarkar, *Fall of the Moghul Empire*, Vol.4, p.150.
6   Compton, *Particular Account*, p.343 and Smith, *Regular Corps*, pp.14–15, both ignore the two extra battalions under their native commanders who are only mentioned in Sarkar, *Fall of the Moghul Empire*, Vol.4, p.151. But Smith gives the number of guns in Scindia's grand park of artillery as 52 pieces. We must assume that the four battalions of the First Brigade each had their own usual complement of four guns and one howitzer with them. This would bring the grand total of available guns with Brownrigg's force for the coming action to a rather impressive 72 pieces.
7   Compton, *Particular Account*, p.254.

Smith states that Jaswant Rao's force numbered 10 battalions, 4,000 Rohillas, and 10,000 cavalry.[8] Compton puts the total at 14 battalions and an improbable 50,000 cavalry but even he calls this an exaggerated figure, citing 'a Bombay Journal' which also gives Holkar 'twenty-seven heavy guns and forty-two light field pieces.'[9] Whatever the precise numbers Brownrigg was certainly outnumbered at least four to one and quite possibly by as much as twice that figure.

On 4 July 1801 Jaswant Rao began his attack on Brownrigg's position. We do not know precisely how Brownrigg positioned his slender force, but he was a veteran campaigner having been in the service since at least 1799. We can conjecture that in the normal manner of Indian battles the guns were placed in front of the infantry, 'skilfully dispersed along his line' as Sarkar puts it.[10] The battle began with the usual mutual cannonade which, according to Compton, lasted up to four hours, though again he does not cite his source.

Jaswant Rao's first attack was led by the French officer Plumet, who brought four battalions and eight guns to the assault supported by a large force of cavalry commanded by Kushaba Bakhshi. The cavalry charged first to pin Brownrigg's command but were met by showers of grape and canister from the guns. Plumet's *sepoys* then assaulted Brownrigg's position and actually broke through, though Plumet was wounded. Brownrigg was equal to the contest however and, as Plumet's *sepoys* and their supports attacked the heavy baggage park behind Brownrigg's main line, they were cut to pieces by chain shot from the heavy guns placed there in reserve. Plumet's men broke and seemingly abandoned their guns. Jaswant Rao at this point rallied his men in person and a second attack went in which recovered all but two of the abandoned guns. Nevertheless, Brownrigg's position could not be stormed and Holkar therefore retreated to Satwas

Smith's account of the action is short and to the point:

> Brownrigg had skilfully chosen a strong position with the river in his rear and his front and flanks protected by woods where Holkar's horse could not act– he received the victorious troops of Holkar with firmness and intrepidity, beat back their repeated attacks and took two of their guns. The cool valour of Brownrigg animated the troops and their position rendered them desperate– there was no alternative but death or victory, the rapid river would have engulfed those who could have escaped the unrelenting sword of Holkar had they once recoiled. Lieutenant Rowbotham an officer with Brownrigg was killed in this glorious and unequal contest.[11]

Holkar lost at least 400–500 men and two or three *sardars*. Brownrigg's total loss was 107 men. Holkar's invasion had been halted.

Jaswant Rao was too good a soldier to let a simple setback, such as this defeat, stop him for long. He retired to his capital at Indore to rest and refit

---

8 Smith, *Regular Corps*, p.14.
9 Compton, *Particular Account*, p.255.
10 Sarkar, *Fall of the Moghul Empire*, Vol.4, p.151.
11 Smith, *Regular Corps*, pp.14–15.

his army for a few days. He next moved to Scindia's capital of Ujjain where he was joined by Amir Khan and his Pathan cavalry. As we have seen Ujjain was defended by Colonel George Hessing, with four or five battalions and 30 guns. He had been joined by roughly 5,000 Maratha horse who had been falling back under pressure from Holkar and Amir Khan.

Hessing had been in the Ujjain area since late May, trying to uphold Scindia's authority in the surrounding countryside, with the aid of Maratha commander Atmiram Wadke. However, as Amir Khan advanced westward, Wadke and Hessing fell back on Ujjain and encamped under the walls of the city. So, on the 17 July 1801 Holkar and Amir Khan joined forces at Ujjain and after a cannonade blockaded Hessing's position by entrenching their two trained infantry brigades overnight. There was little Hessing could do, outnumbered as he was, except hold his position.

The army which Holkar and Amir Khan brought to Ujjain was basically the same force that had fought Brownrigg but with the vital addition of several thousands of Amir Khan's cavalry. Although often referred to as Pathans by no means all of the Khan's mercenary cavalry were actual Pathans, indeed as a freebooter, Amir Khan had always enlisted any man who would swear loyalty to him whatever his tribe or religion. Basically, if you had a horse, a sword, and a predatory nature then you were welcome in the ranks of his horde.

On the following morning, 18 July, Holkar's assault began. At first his trained infantry, led by one Captain Fleury (Plumet being wounded), were repulsed by Hessing's *sepoys*. Unfortunately, Amir Khan's cavalry had seen off Wadke's Maratha horse in a series of charges so Hessing's command was now isolated, but still holding its own. Until the weather intervened decisively. It rained 'like Noah's flood',[12] rendering gunpowder weapons useless and allowing Holkar's and Amir Khan's cavalry to take Hessing's guns and ride down his demoralised infantry. Hessing himself escaped, but of the other 11 European officers present eight were killed, of whom six or seven were 'country-born' of British extraction. At least three were the sons of East India Company army officers. Major Derridon, a 'country-born' French officer, was captured. Perron had married Derridon's sister and John Hessing ransomed him from Jaswant Rao for Rs40,000, which unusually Daulat Rao actually repaid.[13]

The British resident in Poona, Colonel John Collins, was surprised by Holkar's victory:

> The inhabitants of Ujjain are, as your Lordship will readily conceive, in the utmost consternation, the defeat of Mr. John Hessing's troops being an event altogether unexpected and unprovided against. Indeed had this officer chosen a judicious position for defensive operations, it is not easy to comprehend how his detachment could have suffered so total an overthrow, since it consisted of five

---

12 Sarkar, *Fall of the Moghul Empire*, Vol.4, p.153.
13 The account of the Battle of Ujjain is an amalgam from Sarkar, *Fall of the Moghul Empire*, Vol.4, pp.152–153; Compton, *Particular Account*, pp.255–256; and Grant Duff, *History of the Marathas*, Vol.2, p.250. Only Sarkar mentions the rain. Compton is the source for the casualties.

battalions of Sepoys and, at least, four thousand cavalry, exclusive of a strong park of artillery.[14]

After his victory Holkar did not let his *pindaris* loose on the now defenceless city. Rather he extracted a huge fine before returning to his capital.

In the meantime despite the rains making campaigning difficult Brownrigg advanced to the Unchaud pass with a force which Collins reported to Calcutta as nine battalions of Sepoys, 3,000 cavalry and 60 guns.[15] Serious campaigning began again in October as Scindia's main army advanced on Indore, Daulat Rao seemed intent on exacting revenge upon Holkar's people for the temporary losses he had recently suffered in terms of material but, more importantly, in the mind of Daulat Rao, also to his prestige.

Colonel Collins also sent a report to the Governor General detailing the strength of Daulat Rao Scindia's forces, which can be viewed in Table 7.[16]

Table 7

	Guns of various calibres	Guns attached to Infantry Corps	Hindustani and Deccani Cavalry	Pindaris	Battalions	Mewati Piadahs
With Scindia	25	24	5,000	–	(A) 4	500
Under the command of Sardar Sheo and Mr Brownrigg.	20	36	10,000	5,000	(B) 9	500
Under the command of Shahzaji's elder brother and Ghopal Bhao, now on their march to join Scindia	–	22	6,200	–	(C) 4	–
Total	45	82	21,200	5,000	17	1,000

(A) One of these battalions is attached to Mr. Sutherland's brigade and the other three to M. Filose's
(B) Six of these corps are subject to the command of Mr. Sutherland and the other three to Filose.
(C) These battalions belong to Mr. Sutherland's brigade.

The overall number of guns, as was usual in the Indian armies of this period, is impressive. Far more guns than would be seen in a contemporary European army of comparable size. Even if we ignore the larger guns not attached to infantry battalions that still leaves a fearsome 82 guns divided amongst 17 battalions. Individual battalions would be at most 700 strong with perhaps an average of 500 bayonets in each. So, a total of perhaps 9,000–10,000 trained infantry and gunners is not too wide of the mark. Most European armies at the time would manage barely half of that number of guns or less, for the same number of battalions at roughly the same numerical strength. Even assuming that the European army in question used regimental artillery, or battalion

---

14 Sinh, Sardesai, & Sarkar, *Poona Residency Correspondence*, Vol.9, letter 258, 29 July 1801, Collins to the Governor General.
15 Sinh, Sardesai, & Sarkar, *Poona Residency Correspondence*, Vol.9, letter 28, 26 August 1801, Collins to the Governor General.
16 Sinh, Sardesai, & Sarkar, *Poona Residency Correspondence*, Vol.9, letter 30a, 19 September 1801, Collins to the Governor General.

guns, the usual ratio was two guns per battalion rather that the four to six that we see in the Army of Hindustan. Collins gives Sutherland's brigade a total of 11 battalions; somewhat over strength for the official organisation of one of De Boigne's brigades. This is echoed by Smith but neither give any explanation, however there is no reason to doubt the veracity of either of these reports.

To return to the campaign, Daulat Rao and this rather impressive army marched towards Indore making initial contact with Holkar's forces on 5 October, as Collins informed the Governor General:

> Since the 5th instant there have been several skirmishes between the contending armies in Malwa but the general result thereof has been of little or no importance to either party. It is however, supposed that a decisive action will shortly take place, Jaswant Rao having been joined by all his infantry and as he expects no further reinforcements it is evidently his interest to bring on a battle before the arrival of the battalions now advancing towards Indore under the command of M. Pohlman.[17]

Indeed, Jaswant Rao Holkar needed to fight as early as he could but most of his infantry and guns were at Indore or marching to that place. The skirmishes that Colonel Collins alludes to in his letter were in fact Holkar's attempts to impede the progress of Scindia army using the *gamini kava* tactics in the traditional Maratha light cavalry style.

Sutherland and Brownrigg, in executive command of Scindia's army, countered this by marching as far as possible in a large hollow square with the baggage in the centre, and infantry and the more mobile guns on the front and flanks. Even with these precautions the approach march to Indore was not easy, as George Carnegie related his mother: 'On the 26th of September when the roads became passable after the rains, the First Brigade, with some Cavalry crossed the Nerbudda at Hundea and marched directly to Indore, Holkar's capital. This was the most fatiguing march I ever experienced being harassed day and night by large bodies of the Enemy's cavalry.'[18] Yet the march continued, as a Maratha news writer put it: 'Holkar is not fighting face to face but practising ghanimi, He cannot make a stand before our guns and our troops are chasing him back.'[19]

Holkar made a serious effort to stop the square on 11 October, breaking some of Filose's battalions in the first charge. They were the vanguard that day and things looked bad for a time as Filose' men retreated behind the cavalry of Sharza Rao who made a stand. Sharza abused Filose in 'the filthy language of which he was a master' charging him with cowardice and treason. Filose committed suicide sometime afterward by cutting his own throat, possibly to avoid punishment for treacherous correspondence with

---

17 Sinh, Sardesai, & Sarkar, *Poona Residency Correspondence*, Vol.9, letter 31, 23 October 1801, Collins to the Governor General.
18 Cormack, *Maratha Wars*, p.38, George Carnegie to his mother 12 December 1801.
19 As quoted in Sarkar, *Fall of the Moghul Empire*, Vol.4, p.155.

Maratha light cavalry. This late Victorian image shows the usual view of Maratha light horse. (Author's Collection)

Holkar.[20] Sutherland's battalions restored the position and Holkar's assault was beaten off with loss.

Despite this temporary check, Scindia's army continued its march, arriving before Indore on 14 October where the climactic battle of the campaign was to be fought. Holkar's masses of cavalry had been joined by his regular infantry and guns, though the recent defection of Dudrenec, and later Plumet, seems to have left Jaswant Rao's regulars without any European officers. Compton mentions a 'Major R. L. Ambrose once in Holkar's service' as saying that the desertion of these European officers shortly before the battle was the cause of his defeat.[21] That of course is too simplistic, though it cannot have helped the morale of Holkar's regular troops.

European officers or not, Jaswant Rao's army for the upcoming action was still considerable: He had 10 battalions of regulars in two brigades; 5,000 Rohilla irregular infantry, matchlock armed; and 12,000 Maratha cavalry. In

---

20 Compton, *Particular Account*, p.352.
21 Compton, *Particular Account*, pp.266, 337.

addition to this host Amir Khan brought another 15,000 cavalry into the field. The army was well provided with guns having '110 pieces of cannon.'[22]

Holkar entrenched his infantry and guns behind a nullah (ravine), but a considerable distance back from it, with his Maratha horse behind and on the flanks in support. Amir Khan with is cavalry was about five miles away threatening Sutherland's rear. Daulat Rao did not himself take the field but remained in his camp with the baggage and women guarded by three battalions, one from Sutherland's command and two from Filose's.[23]

Sutherland therefore had a maximum of 14 battalions of infantry, 10 of his own and four of Filose's, plus perhaps as many as 20,000 Maratha horse, though Smith says only 10,000. The infantry battalions must have suffered during the approach march, so it is unlikely that the trained infantry and gunners totalled much more than 7,000 men. It can assumed that the 1,000 or so Mewati irregulars were left in camp as this was their normal role. As usual the *pindari* irregular cavalry on either side would be of little or no military value in the combat to come. To approach Holkar's position Sutherland and Sharza Rao had to traverse some difficult ravine strewn country, which they managed without interference. Amir Khan was too far away to take advantage of the choke point.

In the absence of precise details it must be assumed that Sutherland formed his infantry line in the accustomed manner, guns in front pulled by the *kelsais* as the gun bullocks would be useless crossing the nullah. As in other formal battles, the infantry probably formed up in two lines. Sutherland evidently managed to get his guns across this nullah without too much difficulty as neither Smith nor Carnegie mention it in their admittedly very brief accounts of the action. Holkar's foot and guns, snug behind entrenchments, did not interfere and indeed seem to have been rather supine for most of the action, only reacting to events rather than taking part in them.

Once Sutherland and Brownrigg had crossed the nullah they were met by a hail of fire from 95 guns. However, this did not prevent the veterans of the First Brigade storming the entrenchments at bayonet point and putting Holkar's regulars to flight after some stern resistance which cost the First Brigade some 400 casualties.[24] This retreat immediately spread to Holkar's *pindaris* who, as you would expect, promptly left the field at high speed. Meanwhile Holkar's own cavalry seem to have been fighting Sharza Rao's horse on the flanks of the infantry advance, but also getting involved with Sutherland's orderly advance and not doing too well in either case. Amir Khan belatedly appeared in Sutherland's rear, but Sutherland was alive to the threat, forewarned as he had been by some of Sharza Rao's cavalry who had been trying to delay the Khan, and, turning his second line about, Compton says 'boldly faced around with a portion of his force' and gave the newcomers a fire of grape and canister as they emerged from the nullah.[25] Amir Khan was

---

22 Cormac, *Maratha Wars*, p.39. Carnegie gives Holkar's total strength as 40,000 horse and foot and 110 pieces of cannon.
23 Smith, *Regular Corps*, p.15.
24 Smith, *Regular Corps*, p.16.
25 Compton, *Particular Account*, p.267.

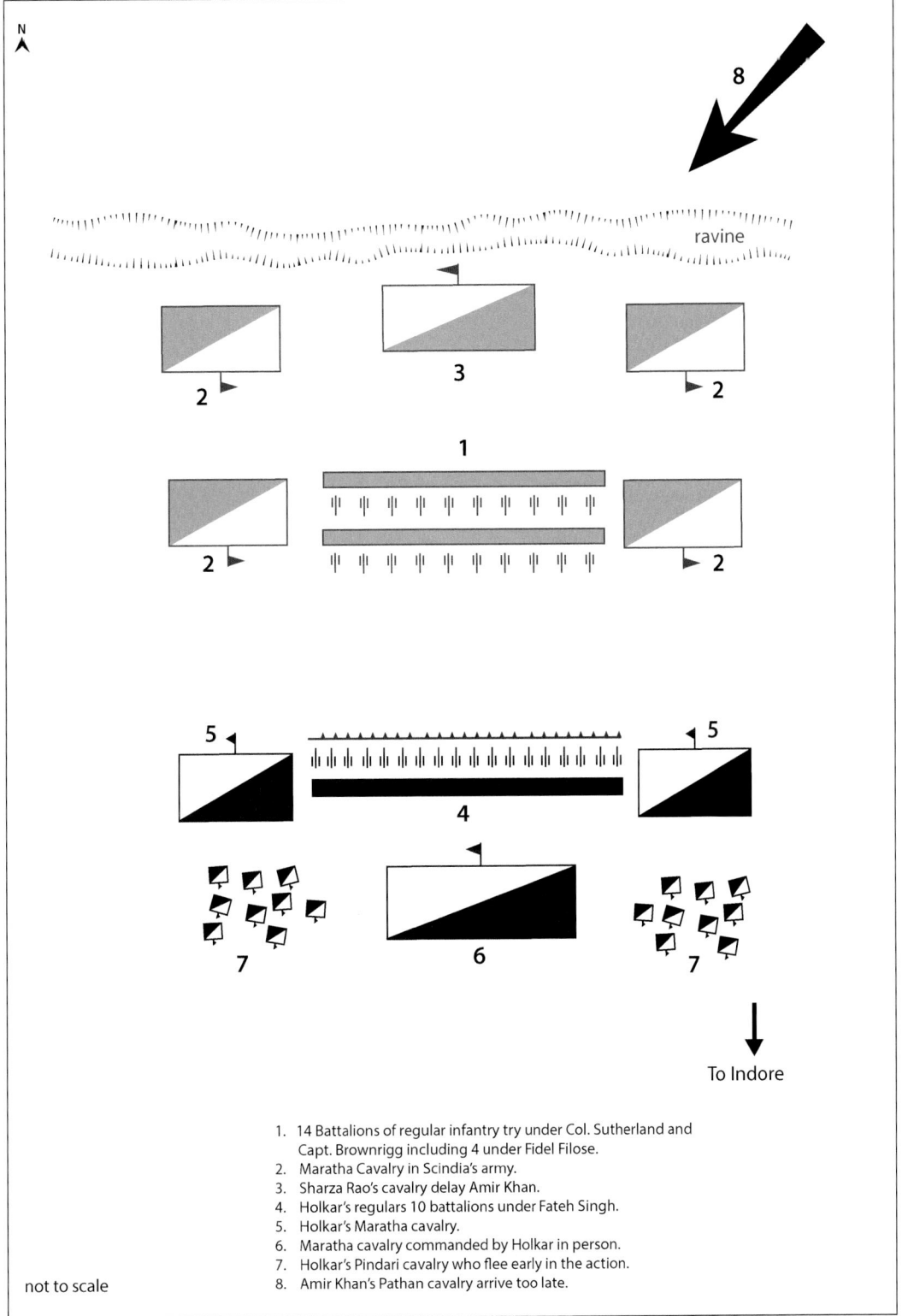

Sketch of the Battle of Indore. Colonel Robert Sutherland's victory over Jaswant Rao Holkar (not to scale). The deployment of the regular infantry has not changed in essence since the Battle of Merta over a decade earlier.

unhorsed and his troopers thinking him dead, broke and fled.[26] Jaswant Rao seems to have put in a last neck-or-nothing charge with his personal cavalry which recaptured three of his lost guns but this was simply not enough to restore the situation.[27]

With his infantry now in tatters, his ally possibly dead, and his own cavalry in none too good a condition to charge formed regular infantry, Holkar realised the game was up and left the field. He abandoned his baggage and guns, most of which had already fallen into Sharza Rao's or Sutherland's hands. The victors took 98 guns and 160 tumbrils.[28] Indore fell the next day and was ravaged by Scindia's predatory cavalry.

So, the Army of Hindustan had another victory, once again gained by the discipline of its infantry and guns. Without that discipline and training it is difficult to imagine Sutherland being able to turn part of his force about to fend off, and indeed defeat, Amir Khan's attack, or to take yet another entrenched position held by copycat regulars who simply were not as well trained or led as Sutherland's veteran First Brigade.

Holkar and much of his cavalry escaped, but without infantry and guns he could not hold territory and was forced back upon the old Maratha staple of predatory guerrilla warfare to support the remains of his army. Holkar was down but he was by no means out.

The Poona Campaign and the Battle of Hadapsar

After the victory at Indore, Daulat Rao Scindia did nothing of note for almost six months. He had it in his power to finish off Holkar but declined to do so. The pursuit after the battle of Indore was at best languid. It was not until February 1802 that Captain Dawes was sent, '… with four weak battalions of De Boignes Brigades and six ragamuffin battalions of Umbahjee [Ambaji Angria] commanded by a native, with 10,000 horse were sent to pursue Jaswant Rao Holkar and destroy or disperse his discomfited forces.'[29]

Needless to say, this was both too little and far, far too late. Holkar's hard riding cavalry devastated large swathes of territory in Malwa and the Deccan, to raise funds to rebuild his regular forces. He managed this in a remarkably short time so that by the second half of 1802 Holkar once again had regular infantry and guns present in his armies. He was able to do this simply because of the large reservoir of manpower available to him at that particular time. Mercenary soldiering was a proud profession in India, and the continuing wars always left considerable numbers of men in the market for employment from disbanded or unpaid units, and of course from the remains of those units previously broken and defeated. In the same way that De Boigne had recruited the men of Lestineau's command after that gentleman fled with his ill-gotten gains, so Jaswant Rao could recruit from

---

26 Compton, *Particular Account*, p.267.
27 Sarkar, *Fall of the Moghul Empire*, Vol.4, p.156.
28 Smith, *Regular Corps*, p.16.
29 Smith, *Regular Corps*, p.16.

similar bands of disbanded soldiery scattered about, the military detritus of years of warfare, eager for any employment in the only trade they knew. Of course, the speed of recruitment could not guarantee the quality of the result but Holkar managed to engage several European officers, either British or 'country born' of British descent. There were a total of four nominal brigades of which three were commanded by British officers. These consisted of six battalions commanded by Colonel Vickers, four by Major Harding, and four by Major Armstrong.[30]

With this newfound strength Holkar invaded the Deccan. His main force, as usual, was preceded by swarms of light cavalry *pindaris* who plundered and ate up the country. Holkar also altered his strategy by concentrating on defeating the *Peshwa* Baji Rao II. Nevertheless, there was considerable skirmishing between Scindia's local forces and Holkar's raiders, but none of this involved the regular infantry and guns of either side. Threatened by Holkar, the *Peshwa* could do little but appeal to Scindia for help. Baji Rao's own troops, such as existed, were deserting him for want of pay and no competent commander existed to lead those who were left. Baji Rao's 'sole confidents and agents were the pimps and sycophants who formed the inner circle of his court.'[31] Little wonder then that one of Holkar's generals, Fateh Singh Mane, was able to disperse the few thousand irregulars Baji Rao's commanders had been able to scrape together at Bharamati on 8 October 1802 where, despite the presence of the *Peshwa's* own *juri pakta* banner, the fight was over almost before it began and Fateh Singh captured all of the *Peshwa's* artillery pieces with scarcely any loss to Holkar's forces.[32]

Captain Dawes with his four weak battalions and the 'ragamuffin' battalions of Ambaji had arrived at Poona along with some 10,000 of Scindia's cavalry under Sadashiv Bhaksar by 22 October. The sorry remnants of the *Peshwa's* forces were already in position. They had been joined by other cavalry forces supporting Scindia so that the total was considerable. One of Holkar's British officers wrote an account of the action which was published in the Asiatic Annual Register for 1803 and he supplies the following numbers for the contending forces:

4 battalions of Sutherland's Brigade commanded by Captain Dawes	3,000
7 battalions of Ambajee's commanded by a Musselman	4,500
4 battalions of the Peshwa's, badly paid and appointed commanded by natives	2,500
Cavalry mustered by Scindia's officers the day before	68,000
Peshwa's cavalry	6,000
Total	84,000

---

30 Smith, *Regular Corps*, p.16.
31 Sarkar, *Fall of the Moghul Empire*, Vol.4, p.168.
32 Grant Duff, *History of the Marathas*, Vol.2, p.255.

His [Holkar's] army being at this time assembled, was immense, and was composed as follows:

4 battalions under the command of Colonel Sutherland [probably a misprint, should be Harding]	5,000
5 battalions of Major Vickers	4,000
4 battalions of Major Armstrong late of Scindia's service	2,600
3 battalions under natives	2,300
Shermeth Khan's infantry	1,500
Meer Khan's infantry	600
Irregulars, mostly Rohillas	6,000
Cavalry, at a very moderate statement	125,000
Total	144,000[33]

The numbers, especially of cavalry seem huge and are certainly far too large. Grant Duff gives Holkar a mere 25,000 cavalry.[34] However, this number probably excludes the hordes of *pindaris* as Smith gives this number as 'good cavalry, for Holkar's cavalry are the best in Hindustan.' Smith also gives the strength of Captain Dawes detachment as 'one thousand four hundred men' rather than the 3,000 noted above.[35] Equally Smith gives the number of Rohillas as 5,000. It is possible that the 'three battalions under natives' were in fact those under Shermeth Khan and Mir Khan, and so have been counted twice in error. Also, it might be sensible to halve the numbers of Scindia's cavalry, based upon those numbers that were present at other battles of the time. Such adjustments could tend to reduce the numbers quoted in the Asiatic Register by roughly 50 percent. Grant Duff asserts that the combined forces of the *Peshwa* and Scindia, commanded by Scindia's general Sadashiv Bhaksar, consisted of: 'His cavalry and irregular infantry, including those of the Peshwa,' and 'were in point of numbers, at least equal to those of Holkar.'[36]

Whatever the precise strength of the two armies actually was, they drew up for battle on the plain outside Poona on 25 October 1802. The combined forces of the *Peshwa* and Scindia with the city itself behind them. Precise dispositions are impossible to determine but the usual formations of an infantry centre with guns to the fore, backed by cavalry on the flanks and to the rear, is indicated for both sides simply because of the way the actual fighting developed.

As normal the action began with a long mutual cannonade which was sustained for two hours or more. The Asiatic Register gives Holkar 'at least 200 capital guns, some of very large calibre, with plenty of ammunition and stores.'[37]

---

33 *The Asiatic Register for 1803* (London: Debrett, 1804), Bengal occurrences, December 1803, p.59.
34 Grant Duff, *History of the Marathas*, Vol.2, p.256.
35 Smith, *Regular Corps*, p.17.
36 Grant Duff, *History of the Marathas*, Vol.2, p.256.
37 *The Asiatic Register for 1803*, p.59.

Contemporary print of the 'Advance Guard of the Mahratta Army'. This is the usual British view of Maratha cavalry. As the advance guard these men on their smallish ponies are most likely *pindaris* eager to be first in at any loot. (Anne S.K. Brown Military Collection)

Holkar's Pathan horse dispersed some of the *Peshwa's* cavalry but Fateh Singh Mane, attacking the *Peshwa's kala-paga* paid cavalry was repulsed with loss, Bhaksar followed up with a charge of his own and Holkar's cavalry began to waver. At this point Jaswant Rao once again proved himself a soldier of note. He had been in the rear of his line, possibly watching the progress of his infantry centre as it advanced against Captain Dawes' veteran battalions and Ambaji's ragamuffins. Seeing his cavalry wavering, and indeed some fleeing, he dismounted from his elephant and mounted his horse. Collecting his body guards, he rallied the fugitives, and reformed them into a compact body. He then personally led a charge into the pursuing cavalry crying 'Now or Never for Jaswant Rao' which not only halted the pursuit but threw back Scindia's cavalry.[38]

Meanwhile, in the centre, the mercenary battalions of both sides had been fighting it out. The four battalions of the *Peshwa's* forces had not stayed long. They had broken and fled into Poona soon after the commencement of the action. Ambaji's battalions had lasted a little longer, but had eventually given way under pressure from Major Vicker's brigade. Thus, as Holkar, flushed with his success against Bhaksars cavalry, came up the only troops still offering effective resistance were the four veteran battalions of the First Brigade under Captain Dawes. The likelihood is that they had formed a hollow square, beset as they were by large numbers of cavalry. As the Asiatic Register puts it: 'Jaswant Rao, seizing this important moment, charged furiously, sword in hand upon the battalions, who encompassed on every side and deserted by the Maratha horse, after a very brave resistance, were thrown into confusion and put to death without mercy.'[39]

Of the four European officers present in Dawes' detachment three were killed; Dawes himself, Captain-Lieutenant Catts and Ensign Douglas. Over 600 of their men also fell.[40] All 20 of Dawes guns were taken by Major

---

38 Bidwell, *Swords for Hire*, p.216.
39 *The Asiatic Register for 1803*, p.60.
40 Smith, *Regular Corps*, p.17.

Armstrong, whose own brigade suffered severely in their capture losing 400 men from the four battalions. Dawes' detachment died hard as befitted the veterans of the First Brigade. His guns were the first ever lost by the Army of Hindustan in action.

Holkar's victory was to have serious consequences both for the Maratha Confederacy in general and the Army of Hindustan in particular. The imbecile *Peshwa*, scared out of what few wits he had, fled into British territory. Jaswant Rao installed a puppet as *Peshwa* and Baji Rao therefore negotiated the Treaty of Bassien with the Governor General, which basically gave control of the Confederacy to the British in return for his restoration to his throne in Poona. The road to war with the British, which Madhaji and De Boigne had striven to avoid, now became almost inevitable.

11

'Their Infantry and Guns will Astonish You' The Last Campaigns of the Army of Hindustan: The Campaign in the Deccan

Perron had, for the most part, managed to keep himself out of any serious campaigning in 1801 and 1802. He had used the excuse of the war against George Thomas for much of 1801 but he had also refused to assist his paymaster in the campaigns against Holkar. It was left to his rival Sutherland to win the Battle of Indore which put a temporary halt to Holkar's ambitions.

Pierre Cuillier Perron was, by 1802, as *Subahdar* of Hindustan, de facto ruler of Hindustan. Under the firman of the old blind Emperor Shah Alam II and by the permission of Daulat Rao Scindia he ruled the last province of the Mughal Empire with almost absolute power. The fortresses and cities of Delhi, Agra, Aligarh, and other fortresses, were garrisoned by troops being paid by, and therefore owing loyalty to, the Army of Hindustan and therefore to General Perron. His last personal appearance on a battlefield had been at the Battle of Seondha at the beginning of May 1801. Since then, his chief activity had been, as usual, revenue collection. He had extorted significant sums from the Rajput principalities in return for leaving them alone but had, seemingly, not remitted these sums to his employer, in part at least, due to the huge sums that were being eaten up by the continued expansion of the Army of Hindustan.

In 1802 this army stood at four brigades of regular infantry each of at least eight battalions and 50 guns, including each individual brigade's battering train of heavier pieces and mortars for the inevitable sieges. There were in addition, garrison troops and regular cavalry. Technically outside of the Army's organisation stood Filose's brigade and the *Begum* Somru's troops, yet these also had come under the overall commend of Perron. He stood at the head of a regular drilled field army of some 46 battalions and possibly as many as 300 guns. All of this military might owed ultimate allegiance to Daulat Rao Scindia, whatever Perron might think to the contrary.

While Madhaji Scindia had lived there was little chance of war with the British. He had carefully rebuilt the power of the house of Scindia after the catastrophic defeat of the Maratha Confederacy at the Battle of Panipat in 1761. As we have seen it had been a slow and often painstaking process. The first Maratha War against the British had shown Madhaji the value of drilled infantry and artillery on the British model, assuming he had not already known this from the usefulness of Ibrahim Khan Gardi's drilled troops in the period before their destruction at Panipat. Madhaji had therefore employed De Boigne to train and lead his regular army on the model of the East India Company's Madras army, in which De Boigne had served, and the two men had built up a trust and rapport such that Madhaji had never even been tempted to tangle with the East India Company, nor had De Boigne ever been tempted to interfere in the snake pit that was Maratha politics. However, Daulat Rao was no Madhaji Scindia and Perron was no De Boigne.

Equally, the arrival of Richard Wellesley as Governor General signalled a significant change in British policy. Previous governor generals had always paid at least some attention to the Board of Directors of the East India Company in London, after all the EIC was, first and foremost, despite appearances, still a trading company anxious to earn a healthy profit. Richard Wellesley, however, took a more imperial line, frequently ignoring the directors strictures to limit his expenditure.[1] Wellesley's objectives was simple, to destroy French power in India. The Wars of the French Revolution had, needless to say, brought about the usual outburst of British paranoia where the machinations of the French, real or imagined, were concerned. The British had already neutralised the French trained brigades of the *Nizam* of Hyderabad without having to fight, and had destroyed the somewhat less solid forces of Tipu Sultan at the final storming of his capital Seringpatam in 1799. So now Wellesley's only remaining target was the so called 'French State' in Hindustan, and the military force that controlled that state. His target was therefore the Army of Hindustan.

Wellesley was undoubtedly given unwitting aid by the often bizarre actions of those very people he was soon to be at war with. Jaswant Rao Holkar's victory at the Battle of Hadapsar had far reaching repercussions. It threw the *Peshwa*, Baji Rao II, into British hands and gave the Governor General a perfect pretext for war. After all, the British were only returning the *Peshwa* to his rightful throne in Poona, and adhering to the articles of the Treaty of Bassien which had been ratified at the end of December 1802. Baji Rao had agreed to a British subsidiary force and to all intents and purposes had sold the Maratha Confederacy to the British. There was, of course, no chance that the other Maratha leaders would agree to sign away their independence without a fight. The treaty made war, already inevitable, imminent.

Far to the north of Poona, in Hindustan, Perron was not without problems of his own. His relationship with his paymaster, Daulat Rao Scindia, had

---

1   Dalrymple, *The Anarchy*, p.368.

never been as smooth as that De Boigne had enjoyed with Madhaji Scindia. As he sat in his palatial residence in the city of Koil he must have pondered upon his likely future. After all it was a long way from his days at the cannon foundry in Nantes and he was now a wealthy and powerful man. But what was the use of a fortune if you didn't live to spend it?

Perron had summarised his situation as it stood in February 1802 in a letter to De Boigne in faraway Europe:

Camp Bandares
February 28th 1802

My Dear General
Since your departure from this country there have been nothing but troubles. Four years ago the widows of the old Prince fled from their nephew, the reigning prince, and collected a considerable force in opposition to him.

Three years ago Luckwadada, who also turned traitor to the Prince, took the part of the widows. I was obliged to march against these two factions who opposed us. Having brought them to action I was fortunate enough to defeat them. Luckwadada was wounded in the battle and since his defeat the widows have petitioned the Prince to grant them terms.

He has just pardoned them and they have returned to their allegiance. Luckwadada died of his wounds; had he got the better of me he would never have spared me.

Jaswant Rao of the house of Holkar has also been at war with the Prince for the last two years. He is plundering and desolating the country everywhere, and I am on the march against him with my cavalry.

A man named George Thomas who took advantage of my stay in the Deccan to raise a party of 12,000 men with 60 guns, seized a considerable tract of territory on the Sikh frontier where he built a strong fort and devastated all the countryside even up to the walls of Delhi. I was obliged to destroy his force with my third brigade, and I have allowed the scoundrel to go, but prohibited him from again entering the Prince's territory.

You are a soldier, my dear General, and you know that we always lose brave soldiers in time of war. M. Rostock whom you recommended to me was killed at the battle of Indore. M. Bernier, one of the best and bravest officers in the brigades met the same fate; also the younger Smith, Donelly your protégé and several others whom you do not know.

At the present moment the Prince has only Jaswant Rao to subdue to ensure complete peace in his immense possessions. The brigades of which you yourself, my dear General, were the creator and in which your name is daily invoked. Are as efficient as ever. It is in reality you who have conquered this immense territory.

Following your example in the discipline, which I insist on, and which is not only most necessary for an army but the basis of its success, I have been everywhere victorious with the brigades. My command is made happy by the attachment and confidence the troops express for me. And I have always won, remaining master of the situation even under the most critical of circumstances.

You recommended M. Drugeon to me. A year ago I reinstated him in the brigades, but in consideration of the ability you know he possesses, I appointed him to an even more honourable position than any I could have given him in the army itself. I have made him Governor of the fort of Delhi and Guardian of the Emperor's person. In giving him this post I have overlooked his former shortcomings and I feel perfectly compensated by the interest you take in his welfare.

Yes I will receive with pleasure any one whom you may recommend for an appointment in the brigades. My friendship for you demands this, and it is also due to you as the creator of the brave soldiers who compose this force. It is the least I can do for you, and both my duty and gratitude require that I should not fail in fulfilling your wishes.

CUILLIER PERRON[2]

Little could Perron have foreseen that a bare 18 months after he wrote this letter he would be riding hard for British territory with all the portable wealth he could muster.

Perron was, at least in part, the author of his own fate. Although he had resisted leaving his base at Koil and travelling south to meet his paymaster for several years, he had finally been persuaded to comply in March 1802, meeting his employer at Scindia's capital of Ujjain. With him he took his own bodyguard cavalry regiment 500 strong, several thousand of the newly raised Hindustani Horse, as well as the Second Brigade under Pohlmann. Sutherland and the First Brigade, less the four battalions under Captain Dawes in their ultimately futile pursuit of Holkar, were already at Ujjain with Daulat Rao. The two brigades joined at Ujjain around 20 March 1802.

Captain George Carnegie was present with the First Brigade, at this time commanded by Carnegie's family friend and mentor Colonel Robert Sutherland: 'I have seen our Commander in Chief General Perron. He came in great state to Ujjain escorted by 4,000 cavalry and 12 light guns. He has made many changes in the army, and I am sorry to say, few of them for the better.'[3] The '12 light guns' would of course be the galloper guns attached to the *rissalahs* of the Hindustani Horse.

Daulat Rao and his abominable minister and father-in-law, Sharza Rao Ghatkay had shown themselves fickle and not to be entirely trusted. Old Maratha *Sardars* who had served Madhaji faithfully such as Ghopal Rao Bhao were now treated with disdain by Daulat Rao and his sycophants. There had always been some bad feelings between the Maratha commanders and the European mercenary officers but under Madhaji and De Boigne this had barely surfaced as each had their own spheres of responsibility, however under the less politic and more lackadaisical regime of Daulat Rao these enmities resurfaced.

Eventually after being kept waiting for some time, while Daulat Rao enjoyed himself flying kites, Perron was able to attend the audience or Durbar. The meetings were less than comfortable, as Smith relates:

---

2 From St Genis, *Life of De Boigne* translation quoted in Compton, *Particular Account*, pp.271–272.
3 Cormack, *Maratha Wars*, p.42.

THE CAMPAIGN IN THE DECCAN

> Perron was obliged to risk his authority and his person by proceeding to the presence of his Prince:– he had many motives for this dangerous step, by which he endangered not only his power but even his personal safety. Colonel Collins, the British Resident was at Ujjain, and Perron wished to know from a closer inspection what were his views, for he was ever jealous of the Company; moreover he began to dread Colonel Sutherland who commanded the 1st Brigade, which was then with Scindia and to fear Sharza Rao Ghatkay, Daulat Rao's father in Law, who was avowedly hostile to Perron's power. He went to Ujjain in March 1802 with the firm determination to quit his station and resign his authority, if he could not quell the storm that was forming in the Prince's durbar, but his apprehension was, perhaps, greater than his real danger, for he soon hushed the turbulence of his enemies; or perhaps the five lakhs, he gave to Scindia as a present dissipated the dangers which threatened his ambition. He returned to Koil with his former power and in perfect safety, however it was clear to every discerning eye that his influence with Daulat Rao Scindia was much diminished.[4]

Doubtless the 'present' of five lakh of rupees (Rs500,000), the rough equivalent of around £550,000 today, mollified Dualat Rao's greedy anger a little but Perron had managed to build up a considerable number of personal enemies, including Ambaji Angria his recently displaced rival for the lucrative position of *Subahdar* of Hindustan. Smith, however, was not an eyewitness to the meetings, though he doubtless spoke to eyewitnesses after the event, being still with the Third Brigade.

Skinner, having transferred back to the Second Brigade was present and his account while somewhat different in detail, and omitting the five lakhs of rupees, concurs in its essentials:

> Perron aware of the intrigues of his enemies became depressed and perturbed; when at length, matters seemed likely to be brought to a crisis. A day was appointed for holding a Durbar, to which Perron and all his European officers were invited. At this Durbar Scindia together with his father in law Sharza Rao Ghatkay had formed a plot to lay hold of him; and had employed 500 Pathans belonging to Bahadur Khan… And several others of his own favourites – his companions in vice and debauchery – to carry this purpose into effect.
>
> Perron, however, was made aware of this plot. And ordered all the native officers of both brigades, as low as the rank of jemadar, as well as all the European officers to come fully armed to attend his visit to Scindia. Our full uniform included a brace of pistols attached to our sword belts, and these he directed us to bring loaded. We amounted in all to 300 native and 30 European officers; and in this state of preparation we marched to the durbar, a large tent pitched for the occasion…
>
> Scindia rose to receive us and we all presented out nuzzurs. We were then directed to sit down on the left side of the presence, the right being occupied the Pathans who regarded us very fiercely.[5]

---

4 Smith, *Regular Corps*, pp.26–27.
5 Baillie-Fraser, *Military Memoir*, Vol.1, pp.243–244.

The meeting was obviously very tense with each group eyeing the other speculatively and waiting for the bloodshed to begin. However, violence was avoided for the moment, largely at the instigation of Ghopal Rao Bhao. The Pathans were then dismissed by Scindia. Perron threatened to resign his command but was at length persuaded to continue and, up to a point, relations were patched up, despite Perron's continued misgivings. His wish to leave Scindia's service seems to have been well known to the British. As the Governor General wrote:

> M. Perron's forces are said to be at present concentrated a Koil and to consist of about 8,000 infantry and an equal number of cavalry, Scindia it is generally believed has no confidence in M. Perron's attachment to his government. In the event of War with the British Government it is probable that Scindia will endeavour to conciliate M. Perron; and the prospect of this crisis of affairs, which would render M. Perron's conduct and object of attention to both states may have contributed to induce M. Perron to postpone his avowed intention of relinquishing Scindia's service in the hope of more advantageous offers from Scindia or the British Government.[6]

On the purely military level things were not as they should have been even within the two brigades. Feelings were running somewhat high:

> A misunderstanding subsisted for some time between General Perron and Colonel Sutherland which threatened disagreeable consequences (they are related by marriage). Happily however this affair has been brought to light and amicably settled. The French Officers are suspicious (without cause) of the British forming Cabals against their interest and the General being a weak man, lends an open Ear to the false insinuations of designing interested men.[7]

In fact, the suspicions ran both ways. Perron certainly favoured non-British officers for the senior commands. Sutherland was transferred to command the Second Brigade and Pohlmann given the First. This was probably because Sutherland, having been with the First Brigade in attendance on Dualat Rao for several years, had the Prince's ear and his victory over Holkar at Indore had raised the Scottish officer's stock with Scindia such that, were Perron actually to resign, Sutherland would take over command of the whole of the Army of Hindustan.

Lieutenant, soon to be Captain, George Carnegie certainly believed that Sutherland would take over the command. So much so, that when Sutherland was transferred to the Second Brigade, Carnegie went with him. However, it did not turn out that way and although Sutherland appears to have retained command of the Second Brigade until March 1803, he did leave the service

---

6   Sinh, Sardesai, & Sarkar, *Poona Residency Correspondence*, Vol.9, p.299, letter 186, from the Governor General to Lake.
7   Cormack, *Maratha Wars*, p.42.

soon after this and proceeded to Agra.[8] Colonel George Hessing took over command of the Second Brigade but does not seem to have held it for long, being succeeded before the beginning of hostilities with the British by the French officer Major Geslin. Hessing became Governor of Agra.

However, the Battle of Hadapsar, or Poona as the British termed it, and the subsequent flight of the Peshwa into British territory threw the plans of both Perron and Scindia into confusion. Once the terms of the Treaty of Bassien were ratified at the end of 1802 the Marathas had little choice but to fight if they were to retain any authority and independence within the territories both of the Confederacy and of Hindustan. The European mercenaries, most especially those of non-British origin, would have been effectively forbidden from future employment by a clause in the treaty which allowed the British to bar any officer they felt came from a nation whose interest clashed with that of the Company and the British Government. Reinstated by the British, Baji Rao would have been no more than a puppet *Peshwa*. Yet even at this desperate juncture there was dissension and prevarication. While the British prepared two armies to invade the Maratha territories from the south, under Major General Arthur Wellesley, the future Duke of Wellington, and from the North East, under General Gerard Lake, a one-time Guards officer and a soldier of considerable experience. The various Maratha leaders argued amongst themselves and conducted desultory negotiations with the British resident Colonel Collins.

In Calcutta, Governor General Richard Wellesley, older brother of Arthur, was convinced, or pretended to be convinced, that there was a French plot to seize India in which Perron and his French officers were deeply implicated. It was of course largely imaginary simply because of the tremendous time it took for letters and messengers to reach Europe from India and visa-versa. Perron had sent an 'Ambassador' to France in 1801, a M. Desoutee, but that gentleman had not returned, and nothing was known of any results of the journey.[9]

For propaganda reasons this plot was amplified, and even lent a little colour, by the arrival of the French General Decaen and his small force to reclaim the French outpost of Pondicherry. This had been handed back as a result of the Treaty of Amiens, which had brought a very temporary halt to the war between Britain and France. Both sides knew that the war would re-start, but the French hoped to get into their outpost before any re-commencement. Decaen's small fleet left Brest on 6 March 1803 bound for Pondicherry carrying around 1,400 men, including extra officers to command newly raised *sepoys*. The British believed that these extra officers were to command Perron's Army of Hindustan, but this is scarcely credible as very few of these officers had any Indian experience, and of course Pondicherry is in the far south east of the subcontinent; a very long way from the area that the Army of Hindustan controlled and recruited from. In the event only a small portion of Decaen's force actually landed and, knowing that a renewal of conflict was more than

---

8   Cormack, *Maratha Wars*, pp.46–48, letter from George Carnegie to his mother dated 12 March 1803, camp near Jeypore 'Colonel Sutherland is in good health.'
9   Compton, *Particular Account*, p.285.

likely, the British spun out negotiations until Decaen abandoned the 180 men of the 109e *infanterie de ligne* who were in the Pondicherry barracks and sailed off to Ile de France and Reunion, leaving *Adjudant-Commandant* Binot and his men to hold out against the British until 10 September.[10]

Even had Decaen been able to land all of his men it is hard to see what he could have achieved. As for bringing French aid to Perron that, given the distances involved and the British territory to be crossed, was utterly unlikely. One cannot escape the conclusion that the so called French plot was no more than a mixture of Napoleon's wishful thinking and British propaganda. It suited the British to refer to Hindustan as 'the French State' and Scindia's regular infantry as French trained for obvious propaganda purposes despite the fact that De Boigne's model, as we have seen, had been the British East India Company's Madras army that he had served with. Referring to the brigades of the Army of Hindustan as French continued long after their demise, as can be seen in this example from 1895: 'The Marathas were estimated at 250,000 of which 40,000 were organised and drilled by French officers under M. Perron.'[11] This statement is, as we have seen, misleading to say the least, yet historians would continue to refer to the Army of Hindustan as French.

With the minor irritant of Pondicherry well in hand the British were able to concentrate on the coming Maratha War. Calcutta struck an obvious and, as it turned out, extremely effective blow at the regular brigades of the Marathas even before the first shot was fired. In August 1803 Calcutta issued a proclamation stating that any officer of European origin who left Maratha service would be awarded a pension equal to his pay in his former service. As Smith says: 'The Proclamation having induced most of the European and all of the British subjects in the Maratha armies, on point of war, to quit their chiefs has made such unfavourable impression on the minds of the Native Princes.'[12]

Smith gives a list of 37 officers who left Maratha service over the next few weeks as news reached them. Some were not actually being discharged until mid-September. The list includes himself, both of the Skinner brothers, and George Carnegie. There were others who are not on the list; Major Brownrigg for one and, tragically, Colonel Vickers and Majors Dodd and Ryan, the commanders of Jaswant Rao Holkar's regulars, murdered by Holkar when they refused to fight against their countrymen. The fourth of his regular commanders, Major William Linaeus Gardner, managed to escape and may be the 'Major Gardiner' on Smith's list but he is more likely to be the Major Gardiner who Smith notes as commanding the Second Brigade in 1794, especially as William Gardner does not seem to have served under Scindia's banner.

Bloody though Holkar's action was, he could not understand why these officers would not continue in his service, after all, Maratha fought Maratha on a regular basis so why could English not fight English. From Holkar's perspective the three officers were being 'false to their Salt' (the taking of

---

10 Chartrand, *Napoleon's Overseas Army*, pp.34–35.
11 Lt. F.G. Cardew, *A Sketch of the Services of the Bengal Native Army to the year 1895* (New Delhi: Today and Tomorrow's Printers and Publishers, 1971), p.81.
12 Smith, *Regular Corps*, p.49.

an oath of allegiance often included the ritual taking of salt) and therefore mutineers. Needless to say, the Europeans did not see it this way.

The proclamation had the obvious effect of significantly weakening the command element of the Army of Hindustan. Experienced battalion commanders were removed at a stroke. These men had been trusted by the soldiers they commanded. The foundations of the *sepoys*' and *sowars*' ordered military world was severely shaken. Which of their European officers could they now trust? While not all the European officers resigned there is no doubt that the resignation of so many at once shook the Army of Hindustan to its foundations.

So, in the months leading up to the outbreak of war with the British the now five brigades of the Army of Hindustan stood as follows:

> First Brigade commanded by Colonel Pohlmann, at Ujjain with Scindia,
> Second Brigade currently commanded by George Hessing, with Perron at Koil and around Alighur.
> Third Brigade commanded by Major Louis Borquien, in and around Delhi and watching the Sikhs.
> Fourth Brigade commanded by Colonel Dudrenec, on the march between the Deccan and Hindustan, eventually to return to Agra.
> Fifth Brigade commanded by Major Brownrigg, near Poona but shortly to march north back to Hindustan.
> Hindustani Horse commanded by Captain Fleury, around Koil with Perron and roughly 5,000 strong with at least 12 galloper guns.

There was also, in addition, the remnants of Filose's brigade under a Dutch officer called Dupont, and of course the *Begum* Somru's corps commanded in the field by one Colonel Saleur, a French officer. Both of these brigades were with Pohlmann's First Brigade about to invade the territory of the Nizam of Hyderabad who was, of course, now an ally of the British. This army along with about 35,000 Maratha horse was nominally commanded by Daulat Rao Scindia and his ally Rhagoji Bhonsla, *Raja* of Berar. These two had tried to form an alliance of all the members of the Maratha Confederacy, great and small, and at first such an alliance had looked more than possible. But true to his past schemes, Jaswant Rao Holkar had pulled back at the last minute over territories disputed between himself and Scindia. Holkar would watch the coming war from the side-lines, awaiting any opportunity that arose.

The Campaign in the South and the Battle of Assaye

In later years, full of age and honours, the famous Duke of Wellington was, more than once asked what had been the hardest fighting he had ever experienced. The civilians in question, doubtless expecting the Duke to answer 'Waterloo', would be transfixed by the Duke's uncompromising stare, and looking down his impressive prow of a nose, Wellington would bark the single word 'Assaye' at his discomfited questioner. Assaye was the battle that the young Arthur Wellesley would fight against the First Brigade of the Army of Hindustan.

When the war between the British and the allied Maratha leaders finally erupted on 6 August 1803, the major British military objectives were to disperse the forces of Scindia and Bhonsla of Berar, taking particular account of the supposedly French trained infantry and guns.

Wellesley's campaign has over the years received far more attention than that of Lake, mostly because Wellesley was at the beginning of what was to become a famous career and the 60-year-old Gerard Lake was near the end of his. This is not to diminish Wellesley's achievements in the Assaye campaign but rather, as we shall see, to set it into a wider context.

Wellesley's military objective was simply to disperse Daulat Rao Scindia's and Bhonsla of Berar's forces, giving special attention to the trained brigades. Straightforward enough in essence, but as Clausewitz would teach a decade or so later, in war the simplest things become difficult.

The army that would face Wellesley at Assaye was neither homogenous nor entirely reliable. The bulk of the force, 35,000 Maratha cavalry, were of the usual variable quality to be expected of such a horde. A small minority would

A Sepoy of the British East India Company's Madras Army around 1803. This was the uniform worn by Wellesley's Indian Infantry for the Assaye campaign. Lakes Indian Infantry wore a similar dress except for their headdress which was a 'sundial turban'. (Public Domain)

fight, perhaps a few thousand, but the rest would be at best noisy spectators and most would flee quite early in the day. The core of the Maratha force was, of course, the trained brigades of infantry and guns, but even here the quality was variable. A report by a 'Mr Stuart' serving with the First Brigade under Pohlmann (there is a Captain Stuart on Smith's list) to Colonel Barry Close gives the state of the troops he saw immediately before requesting his discharge on 12 September 1803:

> The force at Edilabad was then as follows,
> 8 battalions of the First Brigade
> 4 Battalions of Begum Somru
> 4 battalions of the Brigade of the late Filose commanded by M. Dupont, a person of Dutch extraction born in Ceylon
> 4 or 5 battalions of the fifth brigade commanded by Major Brownrigg.
> 6 or 7 battalions of the fourth brigade commanded by the Chevalier Dudrenec.

Stuart continues to detail the ordnance:

> With the first brigade there were five guns to each battalion besides a park to the brigade consisting of eight or ten pieces 18 or 12 pounders. The ordnance of the other brigades was not quite so numerous, probably about three to each battalion, besides which was Daulat Rao Scindia's own park called the Jinsee under Man Singh Chaudari about forty or fifty pieces.[13]

Indeed, when Wellesley met Colonel Collins near Poona shortly before active operations began that wise old diplomat gave his own considered opinion of the forces the General would shortly be facing: 'I tell you General, as to their Cavalry you may ride over them whenever you meet them; but their infantry and guns will astonish you.'[14] Collins was of course correct.

Once Brownrigg and Dudrenec had begun their march north to Hindustan, Daulat Rao and Rhagoji Bhonsla were left with three brigades of European led regular infantry, plus Bhonsla's own 'ragamuffin battalions' of semi-regulars, which, assuming the usual pattern of such units was followed, would be badly equipped and worse paid. Largely incapable of battlefield manoeuvre, but not without courage and some determination, their best use was in defending fortified places. Smith gives Bhonsla 15 such battalions along with 60 guns though how many of these were actually at Assaye is quite another matter.[15]

Nevertheless, the three regular brigades were, in theory, formidable enough, though hardly as numerous as the usual 15,000 regulars attributed to the Marathas at Assaye.[16] Even given full strength battalions with no

---

13 A. Bennel, *The Maratha War Papers of Arthur Wellesley* (London: Army Records Society, 1998), Letter no. 343, pp.333–334.
14 Captain John Blakiston, *Twelve Years Military Adventures in Three Quarters of the Globe* (London: Colburn, 1829), p.144.
15 Smith, *Regular Corps*, p.64.
16 Weller, *Wellington in India*, p.171.

campaign wastage, Pohlmann's First Brigade of eight battalions would be no more than 6,000 strong with its 50 guns, to which might be added the brigade cavalry of around 300 Hindustani horse. Somru's five battalions would be unlikely to add more than 2,500 and probably less, while Dupont with the four battalions of Filose's *compoo* no more than 2,000. If Stuart's eyewitness statement, quoted above, of around three guns per battalion for units outside the First Brigade is accepted, then the 15,000 regulars with 95 guns very quickly shrinks to a maximum of 10,500 regulars with perhaps 80 guns. The total could well be below 10,000 once we factor in campaign wastage such as disease and desertion. This is still a formidable force of 17 battalions but it was further weakened by having four of the Begum Somru's battalions detached from the main force to guard the baggage and for Scindia's personal security.[17] So the actual force of regular infantry available for the battle would be 13 battalions, which even with generous estimates cannot have been much more than 7,000 bayonets, with only those of the First Brigade being of the best quality, given Major Lewis Ferdinand Smith's strictures on the other two *compoos*.[18] Of course, whatever the precise strength of the regular infantry in terms of bayonets the number of guns their battalions brought into the field was truly formidable, and as ever, it would be the guns and their crews who would bear the brunt of the action.

Although by no means all of the European officers had deserted their men there was a distinct air of unease and mistrust in the Maratha camp. To add to the disappearance of some of their officers the men had not been paid. So, on the morning of 23 September the regular brigades staged a *dharma* or 'coercive demonstration against their employers for their due pay and rations.'[19] The British were also doing their best to subvert the mercenary brigades:

> There was besides a secret reason for General Wellesley's confidence, in at once hastening with his own small force to give battle to the myriads of the full Maratha army. The far sighted diplomacy of the Governor-General had contrived that Begum Somru's five battalions, now with Scindia in the Deccan, would come over to the English as soon as they could separate themselves from him with safety.[20]

There is also some question as to Pohlmann's actual role in the battle. Compton doubts his presence there at all.[21] Especially as he was later employed by the British to command an irregular corps.[22] Fortescue accuses him of treachery to his master. Sarkar opines that Pohlmann had already made up his mind to accept the Governor General's 'very liberal promise of bounty.'[23] Whatever the precise truth, that experienced Hanoverian soldier, the victor of Malpura, was certainly not on form at Assaye.

---

17 Compton, *Particular Account*, p.387.
18 Smith, *European Mercenaries*, p.54–55.
19 Sarkar, *Fall of the Moghul Empire*, Vol.4, p.272.
20 Sarkar, *Fall of the Moghul Empire*, Vol.4, p.271.
21 Compton, *Particular Account*, p.382.
22 Cardew, *Bengal Native Army*, p.100.
23 Sarkar, *Fall of the Moghul Empire*, Vol.4, p.271

THE CAMPAIGN IN THE DECCAN

As Wellesley's army crossed the Kailna river at the Peepalgaon ford he was under the impression that the Maratha regulars would not be capable of any manoeuvre to counter his out flanking move.[24] His army consisted of two King's infantry regiments, the 74th and 78th foot; with a single King's cavalry regiment, the 19th Light Dragoons. He also had four EIC Madras Native Infantry battalions; the 1/4th, 1/8th, and 1/10th Regiments, plus the 2/12th. His other battalion, the 1/2nd Madras Native Infantry, and some other detachments had been left to protect the camp and heavy baggage from the likely interference of Maratha cavalry raiders. This was also true of the allied Mysore cavalry, who were left south of the Kailna to protect Wellesley's rear from the marauding Maratha light horse. Of the Madras Native Cavalry, Wellesley had three regiments; the 4th, 5th and 7th. In total Wellesley fielded 5,170 infantry, 1,731 cavalry, and 22 guns.[25] Though still outnumbered the disparity between what might be termed the combat elements of the two rival armies was by no means as serious as the reported numbers might suggest.

It was probably the *dharma* or demonstration for back pay that Wellesley saw when he observed the Maratha army in its eight-mile-long encampment. The regular troops were in their ordered lines, closest to the ford that Wellesley meant to use to turn their flank, already drawn up in their battalions with their guns, but apparently facing away from the British toward the interior of their camp. Wellesley may have been under the impression that the Maratha forces were breaking camp.[26] The masses of the Maratha cavalry and useless irregular infantry were scattered about in nothing remotely close to order or readiness, in amongst the usual detritus and disorder of an Indian encampment. More of a migratory mass than a military force. What is clear is that the Marathas were not prepared to fight. Wellesley had achieved something of a tactical surprise.

Whilst in terms of bare numbers Wellesley appeared hugely outnumbered, he was well aware that simple numbers meant little or nothing. The vast bulk of the Maratha forces could be discounted; the irregular infantry and the

Rear view of an East India Company sepoy. (Anne S.K. Brown Military Collection)

---

24   Col. John Biddulph, *The Nineteenth and their times. Being an account of the Four Cavalry Regiments of the British Army that have borne the number Nineteen and the Campaigns in which they served* (London: Murray, 1899), p.140.
25   Simon Millar, *Assaye 1803* (Oxford: Osprey, 2006), p.27, but see also Fortescue, *British Army*, Vol. V, p.24, and Wilson, *Madras Army*, Vol.3, p.111, for precise details of unit strengths.
26   Weller, *Wellington in India*, p.174.

30,000 or so light cavalry were of no account in a pitched battle. Many would be too far away from the point of the action, even assuming their chieftains could induce them to fight, to have any influence on the coming combat. The two main leaders, Scindia and Berar, were not only camped several miles apart but would flee the field almost as soon as the shooting started. Berar being almost the first to flee. All that really mattered in the coming action were those 13 battalions of regular troops and their artillery, the rest was mere window dressing.

So, in essence Wellesley's force of around 7,000 all arms was taking on a mercenary force of non-Marathas in Maratha pay of less than 10,000 regular infantry and gunners, with a minimum of 65 guns. These troops would be supported by the garrison of Assaye, Berar's semi-regulars, with their guns – perhaps another 30 or so – and such cavalry both, Maratha and Hindustani, who could actually be brought to fight. The remaining 30,000 or more in the Maratha army would take no part.

Wellesley first had to get his army across the river Kailna so that he could actually attack the Maratha regulars. While his local guides told him no ford existed Wellesley felt certain that such a ford must be present between two villages; Peepulgaon to the south of the river and Warour immediately north of it. This indeed proved to be the case. The British were therefore able to cross the river almost unopposed. This forced the Maratha regulars to react by changing their front so that their new line rested with their left on the fortified village of Assaye and their right on the river Kailna.

Wellesley's first surprise of the day was, perhaps, the ability of Scindia's regular infantry to actually preform this feat, as Blakiston wrote:

> I observed the enemy's infantry in the act of changing their front, and taking up a new position with their right on the River Kailna and their left on the village of Assaye. This manoeuvre they were performing in the most steady manner possible, though not exactly according to Dundas; for each battalion came up into the new alignment in line, the whole body thus executing a kind of echelon movement on a large scale.[27]

The comparative clumsiness of the execution of this manoeuvre possibly points to the lack of an overall commander, but a very competent command from the native officers, *subedars* and *jemadars*, at battalion level. Normally the battalions would manoeuvre in columns – of half companies – then shake out into line as they reached their new positions. This would have been significantly faster than this 'kind of echelon movement' which was actually performed. The veteran *sepoys* of the First Brigade were certainly drilled to be able to perform such manoeuvres as we have seen from their previous battles. How well drilled the troops under Dupont's command and the single battalion from Somru's *compoo* actually were is another matter.

It also should be noted that the three elements of the battle line were not all drilled to the same system. Somru's battalion were drilled in the French

---

27 Blakiston, *Twelve Years*, p.162.

style, the brigade being originally founded by Walter Rheinhart (the original Somru, from whom the *Begum* took her name) in the late 1760s. The four battalions under Dupont were originally part of Filose's *compoo* so again drilled in the French manner, each with the battalions forming three ranks deep. The First Brigade as Smith tells us were 'disciplined according to the old English exercise of 1780' so would, in theory, still be forming in three ranks.[28] Nevertheless there were no common words of command to move the whole 13 battalions. Even so, fitting 13 battalions with a frontage of around 100 metres each into the available space was going to be a tight fit and argues a high state of individual battalion drill and discipline. There is no precise information as to where each of the three component brigdes in the Maratha line stood in relation to each other.

The regular battalions were able to execute this manoeuvre, so Wellesley's army was confronted with a solid line of 13 battalions of regular infantry, each with its guns in front of it, stretching for 1,500 metres (around a mile) between the village of Assaye, held by Bhonsla's semi-regular infantry with their guns, to the north and the River Kailna to the south. A tough nut to crack indeed.

As Wellesley led his troops across the river the Maratha regulars were changing front, both armies had just enough time to organise themselves before the British assault went in. There is no doubt that Wellesley's army was the better led and the more flexible, but the defending Maratha regulars did not need flexibility only the solidity of their infantry and gun line.

Suffice it to say that the British assault upon the trained brigade's line met an absolute storm of fire both from the guns placed in front of the defending infantry and from those placed around the defended village of Assaye.

The attackers came close to failure. Wellesley's six and a half battalions stormed the Maratha line. The half being the collected pickets of last night's camp not yet returned to their units. There was enough space for the British line to attack without approaching the defences of Assaye but the most northerly two units on the right of Wellesley's line had, by a misunderstanding of their orders, moved too close to the village. They were consequently being hammered by the Maratha artillery, both those of the regulars and the guns which were deployed around the village. Their assault faltered, the 74th and the pickets taking horrendous casualties. At this point some at least of the better Maratha cavalry attacked and the remains of the 74th formed square. This situation was rescued by Brigadier Patrick Maxwell, colonel of the 19th Light Dragoons who, on his own initiative, led a charge against the Maratha horse and drove them off.

At the southern end of the line the King's 78th Regiment advanced and delivered a volley at around 60 metres range before going in with the bayonet to take the Maratha guns in front of them, ably supported by 1/10th and 1/8th Madras Native Infantry. The other Madras infantry regiments likewise managed to achieve their objectives, though all suffered casualties.

---

28   Smith, *Regular Corps*, p.50.

'THEIR INFANTRY AND GUNS WILL ASTONISH YOU'

British Light Dragoons skirmishing with Indian horsemen. (Anne S.K. Brown Military Collection)

The Maratha regular *golandauz* fought their guns to the end, many dying under bayonet or sabre rather than surrender their beloved cannon. Even after the British line swept over the Maratha artillery and pushed the supporting infantry back, the surviving gunners re-manned their guns and turned them on the backs of the British. What is astonishing here is that these mercenaries from far away Oudh and Hindustan, with no stake in the Maratha cause, fought so well. Even after these troops lost many of their guns, they still managed to form a second line with the left anchored on Assaye but now facing south. They beat off a cavalry charge, killing Maxwell of the 19th Light Dragoons and not a few of his regiment in the process.

Although Wellesley had the victory and held the field, his battered army was in no condition to mount an effective pursuit and halted where they were. Wellesley remained at Assaye until the end of September.

Several of the Maratha regular battalions were indeed broken and dispersed. The single battalion of the *Begum* Somru's brigade that was in the battle line was destroyed, though the other four battalions on baggage guard duty a few miles away from the action with Scindia escaped virtually unscathed, eventually to return to the *Begum*'s jaghir of Sardana.[29] Dupont's four battalions seem to have been especially roughly handled and all were dispersed in the battle or soon after, with Dupont surrendering to the British at Burhanpur on 16 October along with 14 other Europeans, including at least one Englishman, ranging in rank from lieutenant down to gunner.[30] Some battalions of the First Brigade retired in good order though without most of their guns, which were left on the field. Pohlmann's brigade being reported by the British to still have 15 guns and two howitzers on 1 October.[31]

---

29 Compton, *Particular Account*, p.408.
30 Bennel, *Maratha War Papers*, p.340, letter 350.
31 Bennel, *Maratha War Papers*, p.306.

THE CAMPAIGN IN THE DECCAN

The classic and much used image of Maratha artillery in action nevertheless gives a good overall impression of the tenacity of the *golandauz* in action. (Author's Collection)

Wellesley's regiments were too shattered to mount any pursuit, so this task was taken up by that part of the army under Colonel James Stevenson which had not been with Wellesley at Assaye but had joined him on the following day. The Maratha cavalry of course got clean away, but the exhausted and unpaid remnants of the regular infantry could not move so quickly. Destroying or dispersing those that were left became Wellesley and Stevenson's top priority.

However, there was to be no glorious last stand for the First Brigade in the Deccan. Their remaining European officers and gunners were coming in to the British. Scindia and Bhonsla, who had both fled the field early in the battle, went their separate ways, and it would not be too many weeks before Scindia began to put out feelers for a negotiated peace. The remaining men of the regular brigades began to march back to Hindustan. Colonel Pohlmann was in British hands by mid-October along with other officers.[32] An otherwise unknown 'Mr Grant' is described by Colonel Collins as Pohlmann's brigade

---

32 Bennel, *Maratha War Papers*, p.340, Colonel Stevenson to Wellesley 17 October 1803.

major and seems to have been in British hands somewhat earlier, as he and a Mr McCullough had obtained their discharge from the brigade along with Mr Stuart.[33] The two latter officers both appear on Smith's list but Grant does not, and so like Brownrigg and others he must be added to the total number of Officers, NCOs and gunners who left the Army of Hindustan rather than fight the British.

Wellesley was of the opinion that only one battalion of the First Brigade actually escaped and even then he was not certain.[34] In fact when Pohlmann's line retreated, after beating off Maxwell's light dragoons and the 7th Madras Native Cavalry, the remaining battalions managed to break contact and escape. This is not to say that they were in any kind of reasonable condition. At the very least they would need rest and re-equipment. This they were not to get in any meaningful way. Colonel Stevenson quickly captured Burhanpur and Asseghur, both Maratha supply centres, before the end of October further depriving Scindia's regulars with any chance of re-equipping.[35] Indeed the First Brigade was now falling apart; unpaid, exhausted, and without most of its officers or guns. Vengeful peasants fell upon any wounded who could not keep up with the columns. Some units crossed the River Narbada together and left the Deccan, but were in no condition to fight again. The men seem simply to have wanted to go home. The First Brigade, the oldest of the Army of Hindustan, simply evaporates from history.

---

33 Bennel, *Maratha War Papers*, p.330, letter 340.
34 Bennel, *Maratha War Papers*, p.341, letter 352.
35 Weller, *Wellington in India*, p.198.

12

Things Fall Apart: The Last Campaigns of the Army of Hindustan: The Campaign in Hindustan

While Wellesley was winning his first major victory far to the south, General Gerard Lake had to contend with General Perron and all the remaining four brigades of the Army of Hindustan.

Gerrard Lake was an experienced soldier who had, as a young ensign in the British 1st Foot Guards, first seen combat in the later stages of the Seven Years War, fighting in Germany under Ferdinand of Brunswick. He had also seen service in the American War of Independence, and latterly in the war against Revolutionary France, as well as against the Irish rebels of 1798.

Lake's task, as Commander-in-Chief, in India was formidable to say the least. The four uncommitted brigades of the Army of Hindustan had a total of 32 battalions of regular infantry and something around 200 guns. There were, in addition, the garrisons of Alighur, Agra and Delhi, plus the 5,000 or so Hindustani Horse, not to mention the more irregular forces under the direct command of Maratha chieftains such as Ambaji Angria and others. These irregulars would add something in the region of 20–30,000 Maratha light horse, some, admittedly of dubious battlefield value, and numbers of irregular infantry of sometimes significantly less dubious value to the forces that ranged themselves against Lake's army.

It transpired that two of the brigades – Dudrenec's Fourth Brigade and Brownrigg's Fifth Brigade – were on the march from the Deccan in the south towards Agra in Hindustan and so would be out of immediate availability for the first part of the coming campaign. Indeed, although the two brigades had set off as early as 17 July the monsoon weather held them up so that they did not reach the seat of operations in the Agra district until the end of September. This temporary unavailability was to have serious consequences for the Maratha war effort.

Lake was aware that all was not well in the Army of Hindustan. As we have already seen, Perron's influence with his employer, Daulat Rao Scindia, was

'THEIR INFANTRY AND GUNS WILL ASTONISH YOU'

General Gerard Lake. From a portrait made after his return to England with the Title of Viscount Delhi. (Author's Copllection)

not what it had been. Equally Perron had managed to alienate many of the Maratha chieftains by his increase in power within Hindustan at their expense. Ambaji Angria especially, was now his particular enemy, as Perron had supplanted him as *Subahdar* of Hindustan. Ambaji had therefore made it his mission to destroy Perron's influence. He was not above using the British to do this and had even put out feelers to Colonel Collins as early as late 1801, but nothing came of this contact. Perron was perfectly well aware of the plots and intrigue levelled against him by his enemies at Scindia's court. The encounter with Daulat Rao in which outright bloodshed was narrowly avoided cannot have increased Perron's confidence.[1]

Despite this, when the war became increasingly likely, Perron evolved a grandiose plan which would have seen the regular brigades defending Maratha territory. In the meantime, huge hordes of Maratha and mercenary Pathan cavalry would be unleashed upon the British territories, and those of their ally the Nizam of Hyderabad, to disrupt and destroy in the old *ghamini kava* style.[2] This plan, fine though it may have been, was never put into effect. Not least because Jaswant Rao Holkar betrayed the Maratha Confederacy and stayed aloof from the 1803 campaign, but also because Daulat Rao could not make up his mind to fight or to negotiate and, as he had done in previous campaigns, wasted time in prevarication until it was almost too late.

Lake's 'Grand Army' was based at Cawnpore and had a total of eight cavalry regiments, of which three were King's regiments of Light Dragoons. The other five being Bengal Native Cavalry. There were 12 infantry battalions, plus two detachments of less than battalion strength of which only the 76th Foot was a King's regiment. The other units present being all Bengal Native Infantry. Artillery, although well served, was not over numerous with only 16 guns amongst the infantry brigades. However, each of the cavalry regiments had two 6-pounder galloper guns attached to it. More importantly, the cavalry had spent several months training with the guns, and with the other regiments of the army, in the manoeuvring of large bodies of cavalry. In all Lake's army was a little over 10,000 strong. Not overly large for the task ahead of it.

The initial objective for this well-trained force would be the fortress of Alighur and the nearby town and cantonment of Koil. This was, in effect, the headquarters of the Army of Hindustan and contained the arsenal and the supply depots of the army. Alighur was fantastically strong and had a garrison

---

1   See Chapter 11.
2   See Compton, *Particular Account*, pp.288–289 for details.

of at least 3,000, including 800 regular infantry.³ Not only that but it was covered by Perron himself with 5,000 of his Hindustani Horse plus another 10,000 irregulars. Although the two available regular infantry brigades, the Third under Louis Borquien and the Second now under George Hessing were in and around Delhi. Sutherland had retired to Agra and Hessing would also shortly follow him, ostensibly as the garrison commander. Hessing did not fight the British and the Second Brigade would be commanded in the coming campaign by the otherwise unknown French officer Major Geslin.⁴

Perron seems to have been caught somewhat by surprise. Despite the fact that he had been in communication with General Lake before the official commencement of hostilities, which Perron did not learn of until 20 August, he did not recall the troops from Delhi. Though, as we have seen, the Fourth and Fifth brigades were recalled from the Deccan. Compared to his decision making in his earlier career this was unusually and suspiciously dilatory. It is true that he had threatened to leave Scindia's service and both Lake and Richard Wellesley were anxious to persuade him to do so. Perron even sent his aide, one Captain Birket or Boukett, to meet Lake face to face as Lake's forces approached Alighur.⁵ Nothing concrete came of these negotiations. However, the fact that they happened at all must have unnerved those of Perron's forces who were aware of them. Doubtless rumours of betrayal and treachery flew on wings through the 15,000 cavalry that Perron had under his command.

Quite what was going through Perron's mind at the end of August 1803 is impossible to divine, yet his first and only action against a British force was an unmitigated shambles. The 29 August skirmish outside Koil, for it cannot be dignified by the name of battle, saw 15,000 or more of Perron's cavalry break and flee from eight regiments of British and Indian cavalry who cannot have numbered more than 3,000 sabres. Some little resistance was offered by irregular matchlock armed infantry holding a village, but this was stormed, with little loss, by the infantry of Lake's vanguard. The dozen or so casualties incurred here being the only British losses of the day. The fugitive cavalry fled west ignoring the fortress of Alighur, pursued by the British cavalry whose galloper guns did some execution upon them. Perron being amongst the first to flee.⁶

We get a tiny peek at Perron's disordered state of mind from Skinner, who met him during his flight. Perron had summarily dismissed all those remaining officers of British extraction, within his reach, immediately after Captains Carnegie and Stewart, both of the Second Brigade, had resigned. Although Skinner and others protested, Perron was adamant and ordered them out of Maratha territory. Robert Skinner travelled to Sardarna to seek service with the *Begum* Somru. James Skinner and several other officers, including Carnegie and Stewart, had decided to travel to Agra. The party had stopped to rest during the heat of the day of 29 August when:

---

3   Sarkar, *Fall of the Moghul Empire*, Vol.4, p.238.
4   Compton, *Particular Account*, p.362.
5   Pester, *War and Sport*, p.152.
6   Pester, *War and Sport*, pp.150–151.

But bye and bye they saw some of the Maratha horse passing by in a disorderly manner, and in a little Perron himself, in confusion, without his hat. Skinner went up to him immediately and told him that he had come to remonstrate against his dismissal and had determined to remain and share his fortune.

'Ah no no!' replied Perron–'it is all over; these fellows [the horse] have behaved ill; do not ruin yourself, go over to the British; it is all up with us.'

'By no means' replied Skinner 'it is not so; let us rally yet, and make a stand– you may depend upon having many yet to fight for you.'

But Perron still shook his head and after a little said in his bad English,

'Ah, no, Monsieur Skinner, – I not trust – I not trust; I 'fraid you all go.'

Skinner on this got angry, and retorted saying, that in that case it was *he* who was the traitor, if he meant to proceed in that way; if, on account of one or two ingrates, he should lose, to his master the services of many faithful persons, this was the way to ruin the cause; but that, if he persevered in doing all for the best, no doubt he might hold the country and effectively serve his master. But Perron who had made up his mind on the matter, still refused to have anything more to do either with him or any of his brother officers; on which Skinner declared he would go to Scindia himself and complain. Perron answered impatiently and biding no further parley, shook his head and rode off saying

'Goodbye Monsieur Skinner; – no trust , no trust.'[7]

Perron had evidently decided to take the money and run, how premeditated this decision was can only be guessed at, despite the vicious invective of Louis Borquien's autobiography, but it became a certainty after the debacle outside Koil. In theory Scindia had deprived Perron of his position as *Subahdar* of Hindustan, replacing him once more with Ambaji Angria in return for a bribe of 25 lakhs of rupees (Rs2,500,000). This move may have tipped the balance in favour of flight, though Ambaji did not arrive in Hindustan to take over before the war began.[8] Perron now needed time and a little misdirection to effect his escape to British territory. He therefore ordered Captain Fleury to take the remaining Hindustani Horse on a raid into British territory. Meanwhile Perron moved towards Agra where his family and more of his considerable fortune were ensconced. He also sent a letter to Colonel Pedron who commanded in Alighur exhorting him to hold the fortress to the last extremity:

To Colonel Pedron.

Sir– You will have received the answer you are to make to the propositions of General Lake. I never could have believed that for an instant you could have thought of capitulation.

Remember that you are a Frenchman and let no action of yours tarnish the high character of the nation.

I hope in a few days to send back the English Commander as fast,or faster than he came. Make yourself perfectly easy on the subject. Either the Emperor's army

---

7   Baillie-Fraser, *Military Memoir*, Vol.1, pp.252–253.
8   Smith, *Regular Corps*, p.31.

or the army of General Lake shall find a grave before the fort of Alighur. Do your duty; and defend the fort while one stone remains upon another.

Once more remember your nation. The eyes of millions are fixed upon you.

I am etc.

C. Perron.[9]

Perron penned this extraordinary missive *after* his flight from Koil. Pedron received it sometime on 30 August. In the circumstances it looks like a blind to buy Perron time to flee to safety, for by 8 September Perron was in British territory and out of the war. The Army of Hindustan had lost its commander and in terms of the ongoing war Perron was now irrelevant, so we must turn to other players in the drama.

Captain Fleury's Raid

In almost his last coherent military order Perron had given Captain Fleury, the French officer in command of the Hindustani Horse, instructions to raid into British territory to disrupt their supply lines, and generally cause mayhem in the approved manner of light cavalry the world over. Since this occurred after the Koil disaster and his encounter with Skinner one is left with the feeling that Perron wanted the Hindustani Horse out of the way to enable his escape. Nevertheless, the gallant Fleury took something in the region of 5,000 cavalry with their 12 galloper guns in the direction of Cawnpore to see what could be done.

On 3 September 1803 Fleury's force attacked the British garrison and cantonment of Shikoabad held by five companies of the 1/11th Bengal Native Infantry with a single 6-pounder gun.[10] The first assault was beaten off with loss, the garrison being drawn up on the parade ground to receive the enemy. However, much of the cantonment was burnt, including the bungalows of the regiment's officers, most of whom, with the bulk of the regiment, were with Lake's army. On 5 September, Fleury's cavalry returned. The garrison resisted for a time, but they were now a mere 300 strong, with many wounded, and as their ammunition was quickly exhausted they agreed terms. They were allowed to pass into British territory with their arms and personal property. The cantonment was looted and Mrs Wilson, wife of one of the officers with Lake, was made prisoner and taken to Agra. Fleury made sure she and her children were well treated, though his own position amongst his almost mutinous troopers was none too secure. Indeed, after this operation Fleury left the Maratha service and eventually joined Perron in Calcutta. If Perron had indeed hoped to rid himself of these inconvenient cavalry he failed, as some 4,500 of them caught up with him at Mathura and he was forced to handover three lakhs of rupees (Rs300.000) to further facilitate his escape.[11]

---

9   As quoted in Compton, *Particular Account*, p.302.
10   Cardew, *Bengal Native Army*, p.82, though he gives the assault date as 2 September; Pester, *War and Sport*, p.159 says 3 September.
11   Sarkar, *Fall of the Moghul Empire*, Vol.4, p.241.

The raid did have some effect on the course of the campaign. Brigadier Richard Macan with two regiments of cavalry (29th Light Dragoons, 4th Bengal Native Cavalry) was detached from Lake's army in pursuit of Fleury's raiders. Other units not yet part of Lake's forces including the 8th Light Dragoons also joined in this operation They did not catch the raiders and although overall the disruption to Lake's campaign was minor, Fleury's raid remains the only success the Army of Hindustan had against the British.[12]

The Storming of Alighur

After the skirmish at Koil, Lake's next task was to take the immensely strong fortress of Alighur close by. He made his headquarters in the palatial residence that, a few days earlier, had been Perron's own. Negotiations were opened with Colonel Pedron who was by no means disinclined to surrender on terms despite the exhortations of Perron's letter. However, within the fortress Pedron quickly lost whatever control or authority he may have had, as the majority of the garrison under the Rajput second in command Baji Rao decided to fight. Pedron was arrested and confined, the only other European officer in the garrison escaped on 1 September.[13]

The discharge of the British officers by Perron and his subsequent flight, and Pedron's reluctance to fight, had given the garrison no reason to trust the European mercenaries. It is therefore unsurprising that Indian officers and *sardars* took command of the situation.

Alighur was the main arsenal of the Army of Hindustan, having a large stock of military supplies in its magazines, including unissued uniforms as well as powder and shot for the 300 guns. The garrison of around 3,000 included a battalion of 800 regulars, commanded by Meer Shadut Ali, and 200 *golundauz*. The remainder being Rajput and Mewati irregulars and 500 new recruits, undrilled perhaps, but courageous men inured to warfare and battle from childhood.[14] Their lack of drill would not be such an obvious disadvantage in a siege as it would have been in the open field.

As for General Lake, newly ensconced in Perron's recently vacated palace, he faced limited choices. Lake had neither the time nor the resources for a drawn-out formal siege. His heaviest guns were 18-pounders, barely adequate for the task, and Lake does not seem to have been over provided with them. He was thus left with little alternative but to storm the place. After some consideration Lake decided to send the storming column in through the front gate using a 12-pounder gun as a lock pick!

Of course, it was not quite as simple as that and the decision was not taken lightly. Lake had intelligence from Captain Lucan, who had been in Scindia's service, concerning the layout of the fort and Lucan would guide the storming party once inside the first gate. Lake could see with his own eyes the formidable strength of the place. It would be a hard nut to crack:

---

12 Pester, *War and Sport,* pp.157–159 and Fortescue, *British Army*, Vol.V, p.52.
13 Sarkar, *Fall of the Moghul Empire*, Vol.4, p.238.
14 Baillie-Fraser, *Military Memoir*, Vol.1, pp. 265–266.

THE CAMPAIGN IN HINDUSTAN

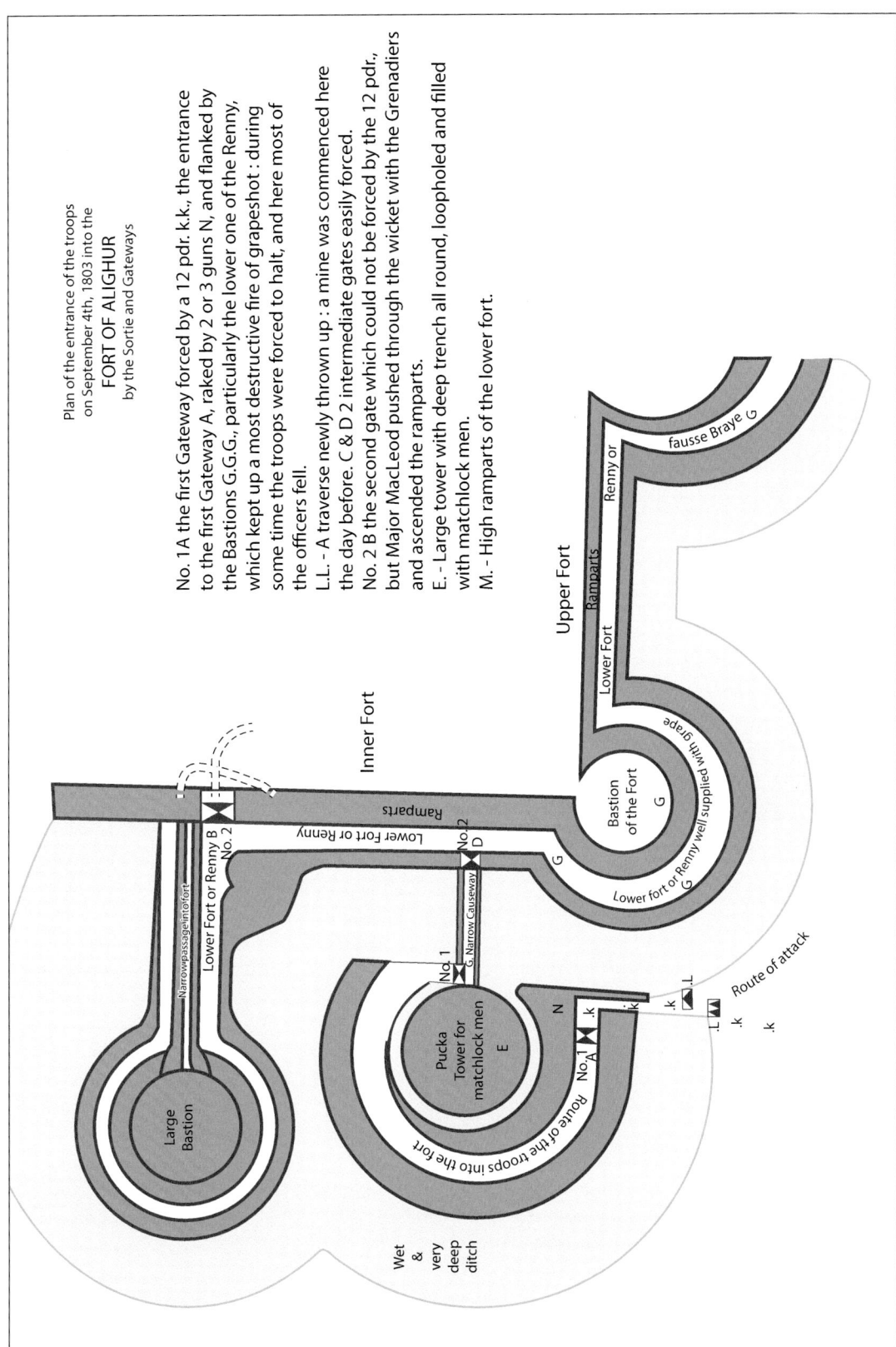

Plan of the Storming of Alighur showing the tortuous route taken by the storming party pushing their 12-pounder cannon under fire most of the way.

> As for a coup-de-main the walls were of great height and strength, not to be quickly breached by the weak artillery of Lake's Army; the ditch had a breadth varying from 100 to 200 feet; even in the dry season it had a minimum depth of 10 feet of water; the only entrance into the fort was so guarded by batteries as to be most difficult to force, and would indeed have been inaccessible had the commandant cut away a narrow bank which traversed the most and carried a roadway into the fort.[15]

This roadway would be the route the storming party would have to take. The storming party was to be commanded by Lieutenant Colonel William Monson of the 76th Foot and would comprise four companies of that regiment, including the two flank companies, the first battalion of the 4th Bengal Native Infantry, and four companies of the 17th Bengal Native Infantry, together with scaling ladders and two 12-pounder guns which were of course manhandled. The date for the attempt was set for the morning of 4 September 1803. The Rajputs, under the command of Baji Rao himself had charge of the gate and outer fort. It would be they who would bear the brunt of the coming assault.

Pester describes the events in his diary, as he was present with the column:

> The whole line was under arms by five o'clock; the storming party formed near Perron's gardens. The covering guns were run down during the night. Those destined to cover the left were three 18 pounders; those to the right four six pounders.

The covering guns were there to support the storming party by firing upon the walls to deter the enemy from engaging the stormers. Pester continues.

> The Honourable Colonel Monson, who headed the stormers, advanced steadily at the head of his column, which was preceded by Shipton and two twelve pounders, scaling ladders etc. We were at the entrance to the sortie before they could perceive us from the walls. Our first salute was from the two half moon batteries which flanked the gateway and at the same moment the whole face of the fort was illuminated by the fire of their cannon and musketry. Our covering batteries opened at the same time, and their fire, as we could perceive by the slaughter on the walls, was well directed. In addition to the heavy guns played upon us in the sortie the enemy also had heavy mortars loaded with grape and canister shot, and the leading twelve pounder of ours, was, in the hurry to carry it up to the gate, thrown into a trench which the enemy had made near the entrance of the sortie. This misfortune detained us considerably and at this time it was we lost so many of our officers and men. Never did I witness such a scene before the second gun could be hauled up, the sortie was become a perfect slaughter-house and it was with the greatest difficulty that we dragged the gun over our killed and wounded. Nothing could exceed the determined gallantry with which our troops struggled under this most destructive fire. The enemy too fought desperately and many

---

15 Col. H. Pearse, *Life and Military Services of Viscount Lake* (Edinburgh: Blackwood, 1908), p.169.

of them actually stepped out upon our own ladders, which were placed against the wall, to meet our men ascending, but British valour prevailed, and although Shipton who commanded the guns, was wounded, he kept on his legs till two rounds from the leading gun opened the gate; when our troops rushed in, and the slaughter among the enemy, in their turn was very great.[16]

This was brutal work, the column despite its losses, broke through the first gate. Rushing along the causeway, still under fire from loopholes in the base of the circular bastion, they reached the second gate. This was also forced, revealing yet another gate at the far end of another causeway also swept by musketry. This third gate was also entered only to reveal yet another gate which proved too strong for the 12-pounder. However, Major William MacLeod of the 76th forced a small wicket gate within that main gate and was followed by the remaining grenadiers of that regiment, gaining access to the rampart.[17]

Such relentless hand-to-hand combat produced a high butcher's bill. Of the garrison Baji Rao and 2,000 of his men were killed, many as they tried to escape by swimming the moat. The British lost 223 officers and men, killed and wounded. Monson, though wounded, survived. Six of the officers of the 76th were killed, and others wounded, but Alighur was now in British hands. The fort was looted, and a significant quantity of treasure and other supplies fell into the hands of the victors.

Colonel Pedron was released from his arrest but subsequently disappears from the record. He had been a mercenary soldier in India since at least 1760 so by 1803 was elderly by the standards of the time. His ultimate fate is unknown.[18]

So Alighur, that 'impregnable' fortress, had fallen to a long morning's brutal assault. Perron's overblown rhetoric had been rendered laughable by the insane courage of the storming column. Yet despite this body blow to the Army of Hindustan, Lake had not, so far engaged any of main field force brigades. That was soon to change.

Colonel Louis Bourquien and the Battle of Delhi

Louis Borquien was never the best of soldiers. He had begun his mercenary career in Lestineau's brigade, along with Perron, in 1787 and after spending some years in the *Begum* Somru's army became one of De Boigne's officers. He had arrived in India, like Perron with Suffren's fleet and before becoming a mercenary, he was a cook and then a firework maker.[19] According to his own rather garbled and self-justifying autobiography Borquien first saw mercenary service with Lestineau and fought at Tunga with that brigade as

---

16 Pester, *War and Sport*, pp.154–155.
17 Baillie-Fraser, *Military Memoir*, Vol.1, pp.269–270.
18 Compton, *Particular Account*, pp.378–379.
19 Compton, *Particular Account*, p.341.

did Perron.[20] After service with the *Begum* Somru he joined De Boigne as a lieutenant in 1794. His career was unremarkable, but he did manage to become commander of the Third Brigade under Perron's patronage after De Boigne's retirement.

This does lend some circumstantial colour to the British statements regarding the idea that Perron was attempting to create a French state in Hindustan. The real reason may have been simply that they were related by marriage, or even that Borquien bought his commission, as others certainly had. The precise truth may never be known. Command of the Third Brigade enabled him to make something of a mess of the campaign against George Thomas.[21] He received some censure from Perron for this. It may be conjectured that it was this, and other slights received because of other incidents of incompetence, that caused Borquien to conceive a poisonous hatred for Perron. This dislike would be evident in his actions and in his 'Autobiographical Sketch.'

It was during the campaign against Thomas that both Skinner and Smith served under Borquien, and neither had any faith at all in his abilities either as a solder or as a man. In his 'Autobiographical Sketch' Borquien claims credit for Pohlmann and Lackwa Dada's victory at Malpura which, while he was a junior officer in Pohlmann's brigade at the time, is scarcely credible.[22] One is left with the distinct impression that Borquien's autobiography's sole purpose is simply to justify his own actions and denigrate those of Perron.

At the beginning of the war against the British, Borquien and his Third Brigade were stationed around Delhi along with Major Geslin, now in command of the Second Brigade. These two Brigades had lost several of their officers as a result eithr of resignations or dismissals.

Once again, this loss of officers would have a profound effect upon the morale and discipline of the soldiers of the two brigades, as it had on Pohlmann's brigade far to the south. Following Perron's flight to British territory Borquien proclaimed him a traitor and took command of the two brigades in Delhi, continuing the war against General Lake. Or at least that is the way he tells it.

The departure of so many of their European officers seriously disturbed the troops. At first Borquien seems to have maintained a tenuous control over his own Third Brigade but he failed to get control over, or even gain access to, the person of the Emperor Shah Alam II. The commander of the Delhi garrison, Major Drudgeon, a Savoyard and one-time protégé of De Boigne, refused to comply with Borquien's demand for the Emperor's presence in his camp and for the public treasury until he heard from Perron. This led to the ludicrous situation of Borquien besieging the Red Fort in Delhi and bombarding the place on 9 September. The Army of Hindustan was, for a few days, at war with itself. Major Geslin, in command of the Second Brigade, also seems to have ignored Borquien at first but eventually joined his countryman as the troops of both brigades demanded to be led against the British.

---

20 Thompson, 'An Autobiographical Sketch of Louis Borquien', p.37.
21 See Chapter 9.
22 Thompson, 'Autobiographical Sketch', p.40.

At this juncture, with General Lake fast approaching, the two brigades of the Army of Hindustan were: '... in a state of indescribable ferment. At last they rose against their deceitful foreign captains and compelled them to march out for fighting the English instead of surrendering like cowards or effecting their own escape from Delhi.'[23] Faced with little choice Borquien and Geslin led the Second and Third Brigades, together with some 4,000 or more Hindustani Horse, who had returned to Delhi after Perron's escape, out of Delhi to give battle to General Lake and his approaching army.

The Battle of Delhi – 11 September 1803

After the storm of Alighur Lake needed to rest his forces, so it was not until 7 September that he began the march towards Delhi. It was on this date that Macan's cavalry brigade was sent after Fleury's raiders.[24] This formation would not, therefore, be present for the upcoming battle. Indeed, other various detachments meant that Lake's force was considerably diminished, so that by the 11th, as he neared Delhi, Lake had only eight and a half battalions of infantry and three regiments of cavalry with him. This amounted to something less than 5,000 men. Indeed, after baggage guards and other small detachments Lake would only take some 4,500 men into action.

As for the army opposing Lake there is no doubt that it was somewhat larger and had a formidable artillery element, but the notion that Lake faced 19,000 men is surely an exaggeration.[25] If both brigades were at full strength, with all 20 possible battalions and all 5,000 of the Hindustani Horse present, then the total may indeed have reached 19,000. But neither of the two brigades was at full strength. Smith gives the total of 18 battalions for the two Brigades but also tells us that only 12 battalions were actually present, with 70 guns and 5,000 horse, on the battlefield.[26] Borquien says that he crossed the river Jumna on 9 September with 10 battalions, 60 guns and 3,000 cavalry in response to the soldier's demands to be led against the English. Five battalions were left behind in Delhi watching Major Drugeon in the Red Fort, though the actual bombardment of that place by Borquien's guns had ceased. Even assuming full strength for each of the 12 battalions Smith gives as present, which is unlikely, and including 5,000 cavalry the total facing Lake cannot have been more than 14,000 and was very probably closer to 10,000, or even less if only 10 battalions were with Borquien.[27] As for guns Borquien says 60, Smith 70. This would include all of the guns held by the individual battalions plus those of each brigade's heavy guns that could have crossed the river in time.

---

23 Sarkar, *Fall of the Moghul Empire*, Vol.4, p.243.
24 Pester, *War and Sport*, p.161.
25 Fortescue, *British Army*, Vol.V, p.54, and Cardew, *Bengal Native Army*, p.82.
26 Smith, *Regular Corps*, p.35.
27 Smith, *Regular Corps*, p.51. Borquien may indeed have only had 10 battalions under his immediate hand, the plan of the battle in F.A. Hayden, *Historical Records of the 76th Hindoostan Regiment of Foot 1787–1881* (Lichfield: Johnson's Head, 1908), p.28, shows two battalions and eight guns defending the river crossing some distance behind the main Maratha line.

'THEIR INFANTRY AND GUNS WILL ASTONISH YOU'

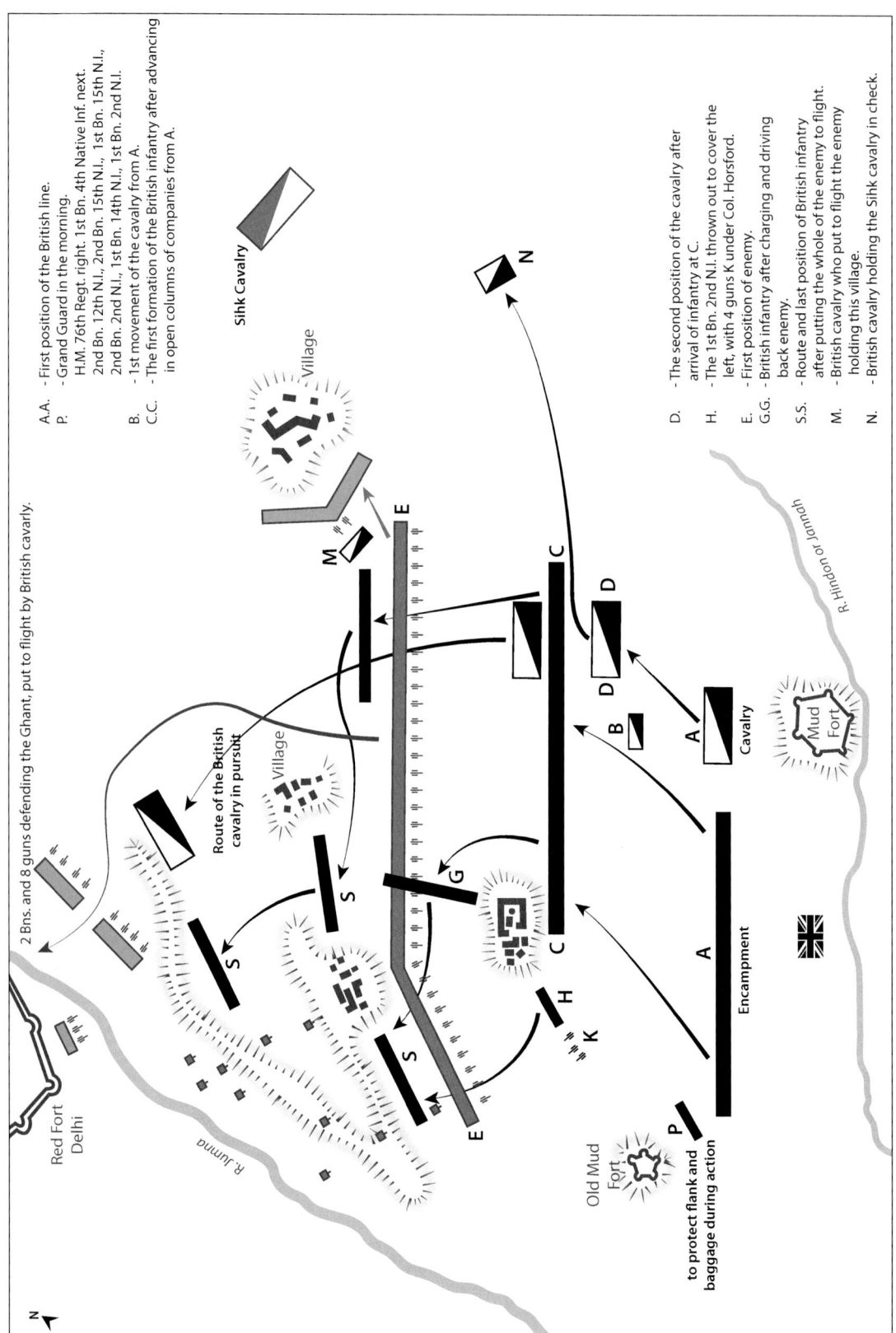

Plan of the Battle of Delhi. General Lake defeats Louis Borquien and the majority of two brigades of the Army of Hindustan.

THE CAMPAIGN IN HINDUSTAN

Lake was nevertheless outnumbered at least two to one, as well as being seriously outmatched in both numbers of guns and weight of metal when it came to artillery.

Skinner gives the chief command of the two brigades to Surwur Khan 'one of the native commandants' so we cannot be certain exactly how much command Borquien and Geslin actually had.[28]

Both of these Brigades had been in existence since De Boigne raised them for Madhaji Scindia a decade ago, so whoever was in actual charge of the army, the practised professionalism of the veteran infantry, allowed the battalion officers to deploy their men in the usual formation. In some respects, Borquien and Geslin and the other European mercenaries, having become mistrusted by their men, had made themselves irrelevant.

Geslin's brigade, being the senior, stood on the right of the line and Borquien's on the left. They drew up in line on a rising ground, guns to the front, and entrenched. The Hindustani Horse formed a second line. There they awaited the arrival of the British. Lake's approach march to the battle had not been without incident. The army rumour machine had been predicting an engagement since at least 7 September and by the 10th, despite some confusion when the camp colourmen became lost laying out the British night camp, Pester was certain an engagement would take place within the next day or so:

> I received a private note from Wemyss telling me that it was the opinion of all at Headquarters that we should have an action certainly tomorrow or the next day. Scindia's troops were said to be at this moment drawn up on the banks of the Jumna in order of battle and ready to engage us. This position said to be a very strong one supported by a numerous and formidable train of excellent Artillery.[29]

At this point it seems the British expected to have to fight to cross the river Jumna but this fortunately for them was not the case, Borquien had already crossed the river though the British did not know this for certain until the following day, as Pester tells us:

> 1803 Sept 11th.
> I left the ground soon after two this morning with the Quarter Master General. We were apprehensive of being annoyed by parties of the enemy's horse and therefore our escort was strengthened by a squadron of Dragoons. Soon after daybreak I observed two men quitting the road and endeavouring to avoid us. I pursued them with a couple of Troopers and soon came up with them. The men appeared a good deal alarmed, and readily confirmed they were from the enemy's camp. They acknowledged their surprise at meeting us as they had been led to suppose that we were not arrived at Secundra. After a few threats they proceeded to give us intelligence, which rather surprised us, as we did not suppose the enemy had left the banks of the Jumna. They told us 'that Scindia's army, composed of fourteen

---

28 Baillie-Fraser, *Military Memoir*, Vol.1, p.275.
29 Pester, *War and Sport*, p.163.

thousand men and one hundred pieces of cannon was at that moment within five miles of us, drawn up in order of battle waiting our attack.'[30]

This was, in some respects, unwelcome news. Lake had found his enemy but was still on the march. In an age of slow communications, it took some hours for Lake to be aware of this intelligence. In the meantime, the camp for the army was laid out in the usual manner by the various quartermaster's parties. The army had undergone a fatiguing march since it set out, as usual for India, in the pre-dawn cool of the day. After its march of some 18 miles from its previous camp the army expected food and rest. This was not to be.

As the outlying picquets moved to their posts to protect the camp they came under fire from the enemy picquets who were quickly reinforced. This resulted in the British picquets being driven back towards the camp. Borquien's account of the action whilst certainly magnifying his own role and laying blame elsewhere is not entirely at variance with the British accounts: 'When drawing up my line of battle I placed Major Geslin's brigade, as it was senior to mine on the right in order to make full use of the advantage obtained by my cavalry.' None of the British accounts mention any such cavalry attack though this may well have been the initial encounter between the picquets of the two armies somewhat magnified in Borquien's memory when he composed the autobiography when back in Europe. He continues:

> I intended to advance at once against the enemy, the ground between us being quite level. I wished to advance in order of battle in order to be ready for any eventuality. I gave orders accordingly but the five battalions of the right wing, instead of advancing in line chose to wheel to the right and advance in column of route (to the left) this producing a gap between the two wings. A sad foretaste of the experience I was to have of these battalions at the critical moment.
>
> It was only after much insistence on my part that they again formed line with the five battalions on their left. My intention was to form a second line but none of my battalions would take post there, so having come in sight of the enemy just as we found him in order of battle on the hitherside of a small river. On the far side of it he had previously been encamped. We advanced to within half gun-shot range and at this distance opened fire with our artillery, still advancing towards the enemy. When within grape-shot range we fired a volley which caused disorder in the English ranks and forced them to flight. We pursued up to the small river. I then prevented my troops from advancing further and rallied them on the centre to await the enemy should he return to the charge, or to continue the pursuit in good order. The English, as it happened, reformed on their supports and despite the fire of our artillery attacked our left wing in close column. This manoeuvre would have cost them dear if I had had control over my troops. I sent an order to our right wing to form quarter left and charge the enemy, in this way the English column would have been taken in flank before it could deploy and would have been between two fires, I was not listened to. I went myself along the line and found Major Geslin sword in hand motionless at the head of his wing. He

---

30 Pester, *War and Sport*, p.164.

told me his battalions refused to obey him. I harangued them. I exhorted them. I implored them, for the time for threats was past. One of the battalions changed front but remained where it was. Meanwhile the five battalions of my Brigade kept up the fight with the greatest courage for four hours they resisted the enemy and retreated unbroken to the banks of the Jumna. But finally discouraged by the inaction of the right wing, which had already withdrawn in a contrary direction towards Tappal, even more than the great losses they had endured, they yielded and scattered.[31]

Borquien's account does, despite its histrionics, largely coincide with the British accounts in its essential, if not in the precise, details. After his picquets were driven in, Lake advanced with his cavalry brigade (27th Light Dragoons, 2nd and 3rd Bengal Native Cavalry) to view the enemy position and also to give his infantry brigades time to form line and advance. These came under fire from Borquien's guns and suffered some losses before the infantry came up. Lake had a horse shot under him but, as the infantry arrived he ordered the cavalry to retire. This retrograde movement surely corresponds to Borquien's 'forced them to flight.' Borquien's men pursued, but his enemy 'reformed upon their supports' which is precisely what the British cavalry did, revealing their line of infantry. Lake's 'feigned flight' if indeed it had been such, had drawn the Maratha infantry and guns upon his own. Lake's only British infantry unit – the 76th Foot – was on his right, his other battalions were all Bengal Native Infantry and were the first and second battalions each of the 2nd and 15th, and the second battalions of the 4th and 12th, the first battalion of the 14th, and four companies of the 2nd battalion of the 17th which last seems to have been the baggage guard.[32]

Most of Lake's meagre artillery did not come up in time although four guns did advance with Lake's left wing and engaged the Maratha gun line. Once the British Infantry line advanced to contact, the action moved into its decisive phase. Despite the furious Maratha artillery fire the British advanced to within one hundred yards, fired a volley and then went in with the bayonet. At least that was the plan, and indeed on the right wing, where Lake himself was with the 76th this was what happened. On the British left wing the terrain made things a little more complex. As Pester describes: 'A village on an eminence was immediately in front of our wing and as we could not pass through it without throwing the Brigade into confusion, Colonel Blair ordered them to wheel back by sections on the right and move round it's flank in column.'[33] It was doubtless this movement that in Borquien's memory later persuaded him that the British had attacked in column.

Pester continues:

The enemy's fire was very destructive on us in clearing this village and while we were forming again after we had passed it. I was with Colonel Blair at the head of the column, receiving some orders from him, when a very heavy shot grazed

---
31 Thompson, 'Autobiographical Sketch', pp.66–67.
32 Cardew, *Bengal Native Army*, p.83.
33 Pester, *War and Sport*, pp.165–166.

> between us and most completely buried us in the dust it threw up… We escaped but the shot plunged directly into the column and killed and wounded a great many men of the leading company (The Grenadiers of the 14th Regiment)…
>
> We quickly formed our line after we had passed the village and closed again with the Corps on our right. The cannonade at this time, to a calm spectator, must have seemed tremendous and awful and the grape came literally in showers. I had the mortification to see Aldin and Harriot of our Corps fall.

At this point Pester had his horse shot from under him and was remounted on one of Colonel Blair's. The advance continued the men still with their muskets on their shoulders until they came within musket range of the Maratha line. When like their comrades of the right wing they gave a single volley and charged with the bayonet: 'The volley was instantly followed by a cheer, and the drums, striking up, they rushed on with an ardour nothing could resist, closed with the bayonet, when the enemy fled and the contest with us on the left was now decided.'[34]

Indeed, the actual fighting was over. The infantry line once again formed columns of battalions to allow the cavalry, with their galloper guns, to pass through and commence a pursuit. The 10 or perhaps 12 battalions of infantry of the two brigades of the Army of Hindustan were almost entirely dispersed or destroyed. Almost all Borquien's guns fell into Lake's hands along with ammunition tumbrils. A total of 58 guns 37 ammunition tumbrils and two 'tumbrils of treasure' were captured.[35] Casualty estimates for the defeated Marathas included some 3,000 killed and wounded while the victorious British had suffered some 485 casualties all told, over 10 percent of those engaged.[36] Much of the Hindustani Horse, never seriously engaged, escaped. Borquien and four other French officers surrendered to Lake on 14 September. Drugeon in Delhi also surrendered, and Lake entered Delhi on the same day finally responding the old blind Emperor's request to be rescued from the turbulence of the previous months.

Lake's victories at Alighur and outside Delhi had dealt a mortal blow to the Army of Hindustan yet the war in the north was by no means over. Those battalions remaining were now commanded entirely by Indian officers. All the European officers had either fled or surrendered. Some 2,000 men of the two Army of Hindustan Brigades, probably mostly from Geslin's Second Brigade, had managed to retire in reasonable order with four of their guns.[37] This group were in addition to those five or six battalions that Borquien had left in Delhi. These men now commanded by Sarwar Khan, made their way towards Agra, the last great bastion of resistance in Hindustan.

---

34 Pester, *War and Sport*, p.167.
35 Hayden, *Historical Records*, p.29.
36 Hayden, *Historical Records*, p.30.
37 Baillie-Fraser, *Military Memoir*, Vol.1, p.276.

The Fall of Agra

After his victory on the battlefield and the subsequent occupation of Delhi, Lake needed to rest his exhausted army. It was therefore not until 24 September that Lake got his army moving in the direction of the great fortress and city of Agra. In the intervening time 'eight rissalahs of Perron's Horse came over to Lord Lake.'[38] After some persuasion and an assurance that he would not have to bear arms against his former employer Skinner was placed in command of these men.

All was not well in Agra. The garrison was, in theory, commanded by Colonel George Hessing but the news from Alighur and then more recently from Delhi had set the 5,000 or so Sepoys in the garrison in something of a ferment. Once again, the issue came down to trust. The Europeans, at least those in a position of wealth, preferred to take the money and run rather than fight for their employer. There was also the problem of the huge amount of treasure stored in Agra fort. The soldiers of the garrison knew of this treasure and there is no doubt that some wished for their share. The troops were divided into two parties, those wishing to make terms and those wishing to fight on. Those Europeans remaining in Agra sided with the peace party. This group included both Hessing and Sutherland. Although these Europeans were placed in confinement, they still seem to have had at least some communication with the outside world. Despite the removal of Hessing from his post no Indian officer seems to have taken command, as had happened at Alighur or indeed as Sarwar Khan had done with the troops who had survived the Battle of Delhi. The net result was a total lack of stability within Agra fort. This was not helped by the appearance of seven battalions who had marched from the Deccan and encamped on the glacis of the fort. The garrison refused them entry lest they plunder the treasure stored in Agra.[39] These seem to have been from Brownrigg's Fifth Brigade with possibly three battalions from Delhi, though Brownrigg himself and his other officers were confined with the rest of the Europeans in Agra.[40] These seven battalions had at least 26 guns with them.[41]

Meanwhile General Lake's army that had fought at Delhi had been reunited with some of his detachments, most notably that of Colonel Vandeleur who had taken Muttra and it was here that Lake met him on 2 October. This added three cavalry regiments (two being King's regiments of Light Dragoons) and two and a half infantry battalions to Lake's army.[42] Colonel Vandeleur also had with him three European officers from the Fourth Brigade who had surrendered to him at Muttra on 30 September. These were the brigade commander Colonel Dudrenec, Major Lewis F. Smith his second in command, and Lieutenant Lapenet.

---

38 Baillie-Fraser, *Military Memoir*, Vol.1, p.276
39 Grant Duff, *History of the Marathas*, Vol.2, p.284.
40 Compton, *Particular Account*, p.343.
41 Compton, *Particular Account*, p.315.
42 Pester, *War and Sport*, p.188.

Lake came within sight of Agra on 4 October 1803 and immediately came under sustained fire from the heavy guns in the fort. He sent in a summons on the 5th but the garrison were resolved to resist. There were a number of skirmishes and affairs of outposts over the next few days as the British sought to establish themselves for siege operations. These included driving out an enemy garrison from the Taj Mahal and replacing them with five companies of Bengal Native Infantry and two guns, though one gun appears to have been later withdrawn.[43] On 10 October Lake decided to storm the town of Agra, but not the fort, and also to clear the ravines and glacis of those of Scindia's regular battalions encamped there.

The seven or possibly eight battalions of the Army of Hindustan stranded on the glacis of Agra fort cannot have been in the best of condition. Those from Brownrigg's Fifth Brigade had marched all the way from the Deccan. The other three battalions were from Delhi and must have been aware of the defeats of their comrades in the fighting there and at Alighur. They were certainly aware of the desertion of their European officers. Indeed, the Delhi battalions may have been those who escaped from the battle, or three of Sarwar Khan's battalions who had remained in Delhi during the battle, but which is by no means certain. At all events these battalions with their 26 guns do not seem to have had an overall commander. At full strength seven battalions would have been around 5,000 strong, infantry and gunners together. There is no suggestion in any of the sources that this force was close to that total. The recent upheavals within the brigades as previously trusted officers fled the service must have taken its toll in desertions and Brownrigg's march from the Deccan must also have thinned the ranks from sickness and fatigue. Consequently, the seven or eight battalions encamped forlornly on the glacis, not allowed into Agra fort by one time comrades and deserted by their European officers, were probably 3,500 or 4,000 strong at the most.

Lake's force sent to attack these battalions consisted of three Bengal Native Infantry units; the first battalion of the 14th BNI and both battalions of the 15th. This was considered sufficient for the task and despite heavy artillery fire, both from the guns of the stranded battalions and some fire support from the heavy guns in the fort, the three battalions were enough to clear the ravines and capture the Maratha guns. The battalions on the glacis being taken somewhat by surprise. A second column of two and a half battalions (2/9th BNI, 1/12th and six companies of the 16th) assaulted the city and after some serious street fighting drove the city garrison into the fort.[44] The twin actions cost the British some 228 casualties and the regular battalions of the Fifth Brigade some 600 men, though this figure may include those lost by the garrison of Agra in the street fighting.[45]

The remnants of those Army of Hindustan battalions defeated on 10 October, some 2,500 men, came over to the British en masse on 13 October.[46] The Fifth Brigade had ceased to exist.

---

43 Pester, *War and Sport*, p.195.
44 Williams, *Bengal Native Infantry*, p.284, & Pester, *War and Sport*, pp.197–198.
45 Pearse, *Lord Lake*, p.215.
46 Cardew, *Bengal Native Army*, p.84.

There was to be no blood-soaked storming of Agra and although almost continuous firing between the guns of the fort and the British batteries continued, the garrison began to negotiate for a formal surrender. The British were well aware of Scindia's treasure in the fort, and while they were prepared to allow the garrison to march out with the honours of war, they were equally determined that they should not be allowed to fill their pockets before they left. Equally the European officers, imprisoned inside the fort, informed the garrison that 'if the money was lost, their lives would answer for it.'[47] Eventually, on 18 October 1803 the garrison marched out being allowed personal weapons and property. Agra, the much-vaunted key to Hindustan, was in British hands together with Scindia's treasure; some 24 lakh of rupees (Rs2,400,000). Scindia's cause, both in the Deccan and now in Hindustan, was in ruins.

The Final Tragedy: The Battle of Leswaree – 1 November 1803

Despite the British victories at Delhi and Agra the war was not over. Ambaji Angria, Perron's replacement as *Subahdar* of Hindustan, had finally made his presence felt. Ambaji was no Maratha patriot but merely another chieftain intent on carving out a state for himself as Madhaji Scindia had done.[48] Since he had those battalions which had been Dudrenec's Fourth Brigade at his back, he had the wherewithal to attempt this.

The Fourth Brigade was, by mid-October 1803, the last full formation of the Army of Hindustan still in existence. The First had died at Assaye, the Second and Third at Delhi and the never completed Fifth under the walls of Agra. The Fourth Brigade would be joined by other battalions, refugees from Delhi, under Sarwar Khan. In the end this last Maratha army would have 12 trained battalions and some 74 guns.[49] It was however, notably weak in cavalry, having only some 1,200–1,500 Deccani horse. Smith writes:

> General Lake Marched on the 27th of October, with the British Army to attack twelve battalions of Scindia's army which were ravaging the country between Fattehpoor and Meerut: they consisted of seven battalions of Perron's fourth brigade which had arrived from Deccan and the three remaining battalions of the six which had escaped from Delhi; also two which had been formed out of the fugitives from the battle of 11th September near Delhi and the action of the 10th October under Agra with seventy four pieces of cannon and twelve or one thousand five hundred Maratha horse. These twelve battalions were stronger than ever from the accession of all the fugitives from the war and amounted at least to eight thousand infantry.[50]

---

47 Smith, *Regular Corps*, p.38.
48 Sarkar, *Fall of the Moghul Empire*, Vol.4, p.248.
49 Fortescue, *British Army*, Vol.V, p.58, give the total as 17 battalions but this seems to ignore the losses in the action under the walls of Agra and overestimates the number of battalions originally sent from the Deccan. Smith's total of 12 or Sarkar's of 13 are the most likely.
50 Smith, *Regular Corps*, p.40.

This was the last 'Maratha' army in the field, yet very few of the men in it were Marathas. Only the 1,500 or less Deccani Horse could be classed as Maratha. The infantry and artillery were all Hindustani from the traditional recruiting grounds of the Army of Hindustan and indeed the *sepoy* battalions of Lake's British Army. The Army of Hindustan would fight its final battle against men who, like them, were mostly mercenaries fighting for pay and sometimes for the honour and respect of their chosen profession. They were veteran troops, many with several years of constant campaigning behind them. Their European officers had betrayed and deserted them but their Indian officers remained, and while their higher command abilities were suspect due to lack of experience, their battalion and company command structures remained intact. The last of the Army of Hindustan was not to be taken lightly.

Despite Ambaji's call for local rulers to join him once he was in Hindustan almost none did, simply because his troops were ravaging the country in default of being paid. De Boigne's financial system had entirely broken down. Rather than join Ambaji, numbers of cavalry supplied by local rulers including a contingent from the *Raja* of Bhurtpore, which may have been 5,000 strong, actually joined Lake's army as allies and scouts and were able to inform him of Ambaji and Sarwar Khan's movements. When Lake left Agra on 27 October his army was considerably larger than that which had fought at Delhi. Initially he led nine and a half infantry battalions and eight cavalry regiments. These included the King's 76th Foot and three regiments of Light Dragoons. He dropped of his heavy baggage and guns at Fatehpur-Sikri with a baggage guard of two battalions, before setting off in earnest pursuit of the last of the Army of Hindustan.

Ambaji Angria and the Maratha commanders do not seem to have had any kind of coherent strategy in mind other than to avoid the British and keep their army in being. Ambaji's own objective was simply to carve out an independent state for himself and enjoy the fruits of his rapacity, So, rather than attack Lake while the British were engaged in the siege of Agra, he busied himself with looting the villages in his path.[51]

Lake finally caught up with the fugitives on 1 November 1803 after a series of long marches by both foot and horse. This culminated in an overnight forced march with his cavalry of some 25 miles. He had all eight of his cavalry regiments with him, but his infantry had been left behind to eat and rest so were marching to catch up as Lake came upon his quarry. The coming battle would not see quite the usual disparity in numbers between the two sides. Lake's army must have mustered at least 6,500 men and possibly somewhat more. Of his eight cavalry regiments only three had seen serious action at the battle of Delhi and despite some hard marching must have totalled some 2,500–3,000 sabres. Bengal Native Cavalry regiments had a theoretical strength of 600 all ranks, so even allowing for wastage and casualties the five regiments must have been at least 2,000 strong between them, before adding the three Light Dragoon regiments (8th, 27th and 29th) of which the 27th had seen hard service at Delhi.

---

51 Sarkar, *Fall of the Moghul Empire*, Vol.4, p.248.

THE CAMPAIGN IN HINDUSTAN

General Lake and his son at Leswaree. During the fierce fighting Lake had his horse shot from under him. His son, serving on the staff, was badly wounded while giving his own horse to his father. (Author's Collection)

Of the infantry the 76th were looking a little thin in numbers. They had started the campaign 804 strong but had lost heavily at Alighur and Delhi so it is unlikely that they were more than 400 strong at this point.[52] A Bengal Native Infantry battalion's paper strength at the start of the campaign would have been a theoretical 900 privates plus officers and NCOs each, and while none of Lake's six and a half Bengal Native Infantry battalions would have been even close to this, an average of 500 men per battalion is not unreasonable. So, it is likely that Lake had perhaps 3,500 infantry. Lake

---

52 Hayden. *Historical Records*, p.21.

only had his light artillery with him, the cavalry had their gallopers and the infantry 'brigade and battalion field pieces.'[53]

The army he faced was not more than 10,000 strong and much weaker in cavalry than was usual for a Maratha army having, as we have seen, no more than 1,500 horse. Once again, the Army of Hindustan would rely on superb artillery backed by seasoned infantry for the coming engagement. These last battalions of the army founded by De Boigne were at near full strength 'strong battalions' as Smith has it, so his figure of 8,000 infantry tallies pretty closely to 12 battalions of De Boigne's organisation.

Thus, Lakes army of around 6,500 or more, would face probably less than 10,000 Marathas. The cavalry of Lake's allies do not seem to feature in the battle, except as plunderers once the fighting was finished. Although the *Raja* of Macheri provided detailed information as to Ambaji's whereabouts. Lake came upon Ambaji's army on the morning of 1 November 1803, as it appeared to be retreating. Lieutenant William Thorn, with the 29th Light Dragoons, takes up the story:

> On our approach it appeared that the enemy were upon the retreat, and that in such confusion as to induce the British General to make an instant attack upon them, without waiting for the arrival of the infantry. The enemy, on their part were not wanting in adopting measures for their defence, and the annoyance of our troops. With this view by cutting the embankment of a large tank or reservoir of water, the road was rendered extremely difficult for the passage of cavalry, a circumstance, which while it impeded our progress, gave them an opportunity of choosing an advantageous position, their right being in front of the village of Laswaree and thrown back upon a rivulet, the banks of which were so very steep as to be extremely difficult of access; while their left was upon the village of Mohulpoor and their entire front, which lay concealed from view by very high grass was defended by a most formidable line of artillery.[54]

Lake was further impeded by the immense cloud of dust thrown up by the movements of his own cavalry so that discerning the precise location of the enemy positions over their front of roughly 2,000 yards became extremely difficult. The breaking of the embankment gave Ambaji and Sarwar Khan time to put their forces in a defensive posture, even chaining some of the guns together to impede the expected charges of the British cavalry. These were not long in coming. Lake sent in his three cavalry brigades with the intention, it seems, of pinning the Maratha forces until his infantry could come up in support. The eight regiments made repeated charges upon the Maratha line under a storm of fire both from the superbly served guns and the supporting infantry. As Thorn writes:

> But notwithstanding the shock of this iron tempest and the awful carnage produced by it in our ranks, nothing could suppress the ardour of the cavalry, whose velocity overcame every resistance and bore down with impetuous fury,

---

53 Pester, *War and Sport*, p.219.
54 Major William Thorn, *Memoir of the War in India* (London: Egerton, 1818), pp.212–213.

THE CAMPAIGN IN HINDUSTAN

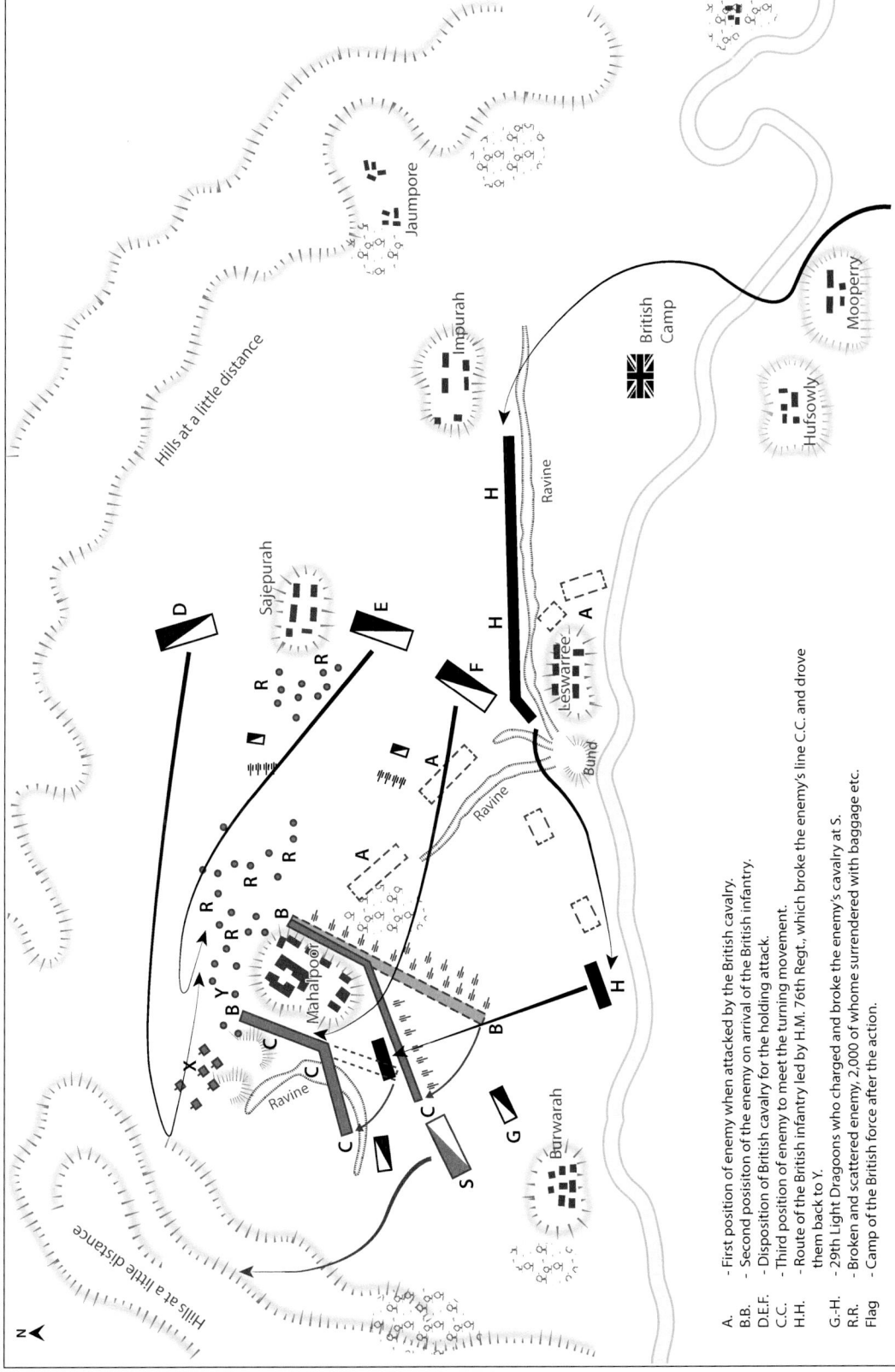

A. - First position of enemy when attacked by the British cavalry.
B.B. - Second posisiton of the enemy on arrival of the British infantry.
D.E.F. - Disposition of British cavalry for the holding attack.
C.C. - Third position of enemy to meet the turning movement.
H.H. - Route of the British infantry led by H.M. 76th Regt., which broke the enemy's line C.C. and drove them back to Y.
G.-H. - 29th Light Dragoons who charged and broke the enemy's cavalry at S.
R.R. - Broken and scattered enemy, 2,000 of whome surrendered with baggage etc.
Flag - Camp of the British force after the action.

Plan of the Battle of Leswaree. After and extremely hard-fought engagement Lake finally defeats the last organised battalions of the Army of Hindustan.

197

the accumulated obstacles and fearful odds with which they had to contend. Having penetrated through the enemy's line, they immediately formed again and charged backwards and forwards three times, with surprising order and effect amidst the continued roar of cannon and an incessant shower of grape and chain shot.[55]

Despite Thorn's purple prose and the undoubted courage of the Light Dragoons and Bengal Native Cavalry these repeated charges, while pinning the infantry of the brigades in place, were not really doing much more than damaging Lake's cavalry. Each charge captured some enemy guns but as soon as the cavalry had passed the *golandauz* of the Fourth Brigade and the other battalions came out from under the guns and tumbrils, where they had taken refuge from the cavalry sabres and, like the professionals they were, commenced firing again.

After about an hour or so of mutual carnage, Lake pulled his tired and bloodied cavalry out of range of those terrible guns. Vandeleur's brigade alone had lost 83 men and 191 horses in the fighting, including the brigade commander. Lake needed to wait for his infantry who were coming up at a forced march rate, together with such artillery as could keep up.

Upon seeing the arrival of the British infantry, in column of march, from his post atop his elephant, Ambaji Angria and Sarwar Khan (who seems to have been the operational commander) had a golden chance to go upon the offensive and deal the British army a telling and possibly destructive blow, yet they either could not or would not. Could not, because their army was arrayed defensively and it would take time to transmit orders and evolve a plan of attack. Would not, because that was not part of Ambaji's limited objective, which was merely to ensure his own survival as an independent ruler. Sarkar, following Baillie-Fraser, says that the British cavalry had only fought four of Ambaji's battalions and that during the lull in the fighting following the cavalry's repulse the other nine battalions that Ambaji and Sarwar Khan possessed returned from their 'way to Mewat' to the battlefield.[56] No other British source mentions this and surely the appearance of 'nine battalions and cavalry force' would have merited some comment by those present at the battle.

Nevertheless, during this lull in the fighting, which lasted two or three hours, Lake's infantry took time to rest and eat and Ambaji decided to try to negotiate, offering to surrender his guns if he was allowed to go on his way. While these negotiations progressed Sarwar Khan re-aligned the army around the village of Mohulpoor, where the army's baggage and bazar's were encamped. He placed the remaining battalions of the Second and Third Brigades, those who had escaped from Delhi, on the right of his double line and the Fourth Brigade on the left.[57]

---

55 Thorn, *Memoir of the War in India*, p.215.
56 Sarkar, *Fall of the Moghul Empire*, Vol.4, p.253, and Baillie-Fraser, *Military Memoir*, Vol.1, p.304–305. The latter has the Deccani horse with the four battalion rear guard.
57 Compton, *Particular Account*, p.319.

Lake picked his point of attack with some care. He intended to turn his opponent's right wing and to that end led a column headed by the 76th Foot to attack Sarwar Khan's right. A second column was directed to support the first while two of the cavalry brigades were ordered to demonstrate against the enemy centre and left. Such guns as were available, mainly cavalry gallopers, but including 'as many field pieces as could be brought up' were with the infantry columns divided into four distinct batteries.[58] Lake's route ran along the banks of the nullah to the rear of Leswaree was a slow approach due to the roughness of the terrain. To begin with the columns were concealed by high grass but as soon as Sarwar Khan perceived the British movement he threw back his right wing so that his position around Mohulpoor was now L shaped with one limb of the L facing the British advance and the other facing the British cavalry. As the British infantry column debouched from the high grass and began to deploy into line, they once again faced a storm of shot from Ambaji's guns. Not only that, but the Deccani Horse, covering the right wing of the Maratha line attempted to charge the 76th as that sorely tried regiment continued its advance, ably supported by the 2/12th Bengal Native Infantry and six companies of the 16th. The charge was beaten off but the Maratha cavalry, rather than flee, as would have been usual, rallied back with their infantry and even looked to make a second charge. In response to this move Lake sent in the 29th Light Dragoons who formed up on the left of the 76th. Lieutenant Thorn writes:

> On forming up on the outer flank of the seventy-sixth regiment the cavalry were greeted with three cheers, which gratulatory sound was heartily re-echoed by the Dragoons, on whose sudden appearance the enemy's horse, after having advanced to charge our infantry made a precipitate retreat. An awful pause of breathless expectation now ensued, the numerous artillery of the enemy seeming to watch an opportune moment to frustrate the meditated attack by pouring destruction upon their assailants.[59]

At this point General Lake had his horse shot under him and his son, Major George Lake, was wounded while remounting his father on his own horse. Nevertheless, the Light Dragoons continued the charge into the Maratha line:

> The Twenty-Ninth … Pierced with the impetuosity of lightning through both lines of the enemy's infantry, in the face of a most tremendous fire of grapeshot and a general volley of musketry. This advantage was followed up instantly by our veteran chief who at the head of the seventy-sixth regiment, supported by the twelfth, fifteenth and a detachment of the sixteenth regiment of native infantry, seized the guns from which the enemy had just been driven.[60]

This follow up attack by Lake's infantry pushed the Marathas back into the village and as more of Lake's infantry came up to support this initial thrust

---

58 Thorn, *Memoir of the War in India*, Vol.1, p.217.
59 Thorn, *Memoir of the War in India*, Vol.1, p.220.
60 Thorn, *Memoir of the War in India*, Vol.1, p.220.

the Maratha reserve in their second line became engaged. At this point Major General Charles Ware, Lake's second in command, was killed, having his head removed by a round shot. The fighting was savage, almost hand-to-hand. The Army of Hindustan would not die easily, as Thorn relates:

> The enemy persisted with determined obstinacy defending their position to the last, contending every point inch by inch and refusing to give way until they had lost the whole of their guns, and even then, when their situation was become desperate, they still continued to manifest the same courageous disposition, their left wing endeavouring to effect their retreat in good order.[61]

The surviving battalions of the Fourth Brigade attempted a retreat but were caught by the British cavalry and roughly handled, some 2,000 being finally forced to surrender. The only part played in the battle by the local allied cavalry that were with Lakes' army seems to have been this pursuit, and the plundering of the Maratha baggage.[62] The battle of Leswari had cost the British over 800 casualties, over 10 per cent of Lake's force. They captured all the Maratha guns and all their baggage and ammunition. Ambaji escaped, at first on his elephant and then on a swift horse as the British pursuers closed. The Maratha force was almost completely destroyed, with only some of the cavalry escaping. The Army of Hindustan was no more.

---

61 Thorn, *Memoir of the War in India*, Vol.1, p.221.
62 Sarkar, *Fall of the Moghul Empire*, Vol.4, p.259.

13

What Came After: 'Sometimes Pleasure, Sometimes Pain, In The Service of the English'

The Army of Hindustan was no more. That army so carefully built by Benoit De Boigne and Madhaji Scindia had died hard on the fields of Assaye and Delhi, and among the bloody grass of Leswari. In the years since De Boigne raised the first two battalions in 1785 the Army of Hindustan had achieved an almost unbroken run of victories. From the early reputation building battles of Tunga and Chaksana, to the victories of Agra, Patan, Merta and Lakahiri, De Boigne and Madhaji Scindia had built an instrument of war that was fit for its purpose. Only after Madhaji's death and De Boigne's retirement did the system begin to fracture, and even then the list of victories continued. It is no wonder that the British made the destruction of this formidable force of trained mercenaries one of the main objectives of the war of 1803.

Yet the age of trained mercenary troops in India was not, of course, by any means over. Even in the immediate aftermath of the campaigns of 1803 more troops were needed to fight the campaigns of 1804 and 1805. Jaswant Rao Holkar, who had so easily betrayed the Confederacy for his own ends, now took the field in pursuit of immediate advantage, hoping to pick up the pieces of the Maratha Empire. He would prove a formidable opponent and the British would need all the troops they could get.

Several of the officers who had been in the Army of Hindustan now took service with the East India Company. The most famous of these were the brothers Skinner, James and Robert. James Skinner, with the rank of captain, was given command of eight *rissalahs* of the Hindustani Horse, who had come over to the British soon after Perron had fled. This force with only one other European officer, also late of Scindia's service, a Lieutenant Scott, would rise to around 2,000 men. It was at first used to pacify the country between Delhi and Alighur, but would also fight against Holkar in the campaigns of 1804 and 1805 which are outside the scope of this book. This body would become the yellow coated Skinner's Horse possibly the most famous of

Officers of Skinners Horse with troopers of the regiment in the background. Most of these men had served in the Army of Hindustan before entering British service. (Authors Collection)

Indian Army regiments. Skinner would retire a lieutenant colonel (in the British army rather than the forces of the East India Company) with a string of awards including a CBE. He would die at his home in George Thomas's old capital of Hansi in December 1841. His regiment would continue to exist even after Indian independence in 1947.

Another former mercenary also raised a regiment for British service. William Gardner, who had been in Holkar's service and had escaped that chieftain's bloody revenge on the other British mercenary officers under his command, raised the green clad Gardner's Horse in 1809 again largely from former Hindustani Horse troopers. Other officers also took service with the British, often bringing with them their men, late of the Army of Hindustan. Major Brownrigg was reunited with many of his soldiers from the Fifth Brigade for the campaign against Holkar and would fall in action in February 1804.[1] Captain Lucan who had also served under Perron and took advantage of the British proclamation to join Lake was the officer who acted as guide to Colonel Monson's storming column at the taking of Alighur, for which he received a Kings commission in the 76th Foot as lieutenant and a lump sum of Rs 24,000, he does not seem to have done much duty with the 76th as he was in command of a body of irregular horse during Colonel Monson's defeat by Holkar and Amir Khan, and was wounded in action and then captured. He died of his wounds in captivity.[2]

Colonel Pohlmann had command of an irregular force consisting of 'a battalion of irregular infantry and a body of horse (formerly in the service of

---

1 Compton, *Particular Account*, p.344, and Cormack, *Maratha Wars*, p.54.
2 Compton, *Particular Account*, p.370.

Scindia).'³ This force was in action until at least April 1805 as part of a mixed force of ex-Scindian troops and EIC soldiers under a Captain Royle of the 10th Bengal Native Infantry.⁴ It is very likely that at least some of these men were veterans of the First Brigade, serving the British under a commander they knew. Pohlmann of course did not retain the rank he had achieved while in Maratha service.

Other officers mentioned in this narrative also took service with the British. Captain Carnegie was in the garrison of Delhi during Holkar's eight-day siege of that place during October 1804 and, along with Lieutenant Ross (or Rose), led out a sortie of 350 men to spike the guns of their main battery. The raid was successful and Holkar gave up the siege after a rather half-hearted attempt at an assault. Carnegie, however, although he survived the siege, would, like his mentor Colonel Robert Sutherland, (not to be confused with his brother, the Major Sutherland who appears in Smith's list) would never see Scotland again.⁵ Both would die from disease in India; Carnegie of hepatitis in July 1805.⁶ Colonel Sutherland's daughter remained with the Carnegie family back in Scotland.

Of the French officers, Perron of course, returned to France via Hamburg in 1805 with a sizable fortune, despite having to leave almost a quarter of a million rupees he had stashed in Agra to fall into the hands of the British. He tried to claim back 'his' property but needless to say the East India Company and the British prize agents were not listening. They viewed the treasure as a legitimate prize of war. Nevertheless, Perron still possessed sufficient wealth to buy himself a substantial estate near Vendome.

Louis Borquien also arrived in Hamburg with a substantial fortune while General Perron was still there. They each blamed the other for their respective defeats and despite being one-time comrades there was a significant level of hatred between them. Borquien penned a short autobiography which is about as self-serving as one would expect from such a document, sections of it being little more than an abusive tirade against Perron and the British.⁷

Others, especially those of the lower ranks, sergeants and gunners, simply sank back into the mass of Indian society. Very little information on these people survives. Those who wished to remain soldiers may have joined other princely forces or even remained in the smaller Maratha armies that survived after the end of the war. Of the ordinary soldiers many must have joined EIC regiments as the army expanded, but again precise numbers are unknown. Nevertheless, the three presidency armies of the Company continued to expand. This was especially true of the Bengal Army which would bear the lion's share of the campaigning in the coming decades. This same Bengal Army took over the recruiting grounds in Oudh and Hindustan which had

---

3 Cardew, *Bengal Native Army*, p.100.
4 Cardew, *Bengal Native Army*, p.102.
5 Cormack, *Maratha Wars*, p.57.
6 Cormack, *Maratha Wars*, p.70, letter from Nicolas Carnegie to his foster mother Susan in Scotland.
7 Compton, *Particular Account*, pp.328–329, and Thompson's translation of Bourquien's 'Autobiographical Sketch.'

been the nursery of De Boigne's brigades, so it is inconceivable that some of the expansion did not include former soldiers of the Army of Hindustan.

The British would fight the Marathas twice more. The Third Maratha War, also known as the Maratha and Pindari War of 1817–18, saw the British break up the Confederacy after a difficult campaign with some occasionally hard fighting. Two decades later the so-called One Day War of December 1843 – also known as the Gwalior War – marked the point that the British finally extinguished the remains of the house of Scindia. It was a short but bloody campaign where the two major engagements were, coincidentally, fought on the same day many miles apart. The Marathas still had trained brigades in something of the old style. In the days before the campaign began these trained infantry were commanded by Jean Baptiste de la Fontaine Filose, younger son of Michael Filose. Jean Baptise was, therefore, the longest serving European officer in Scindia's service. A man whose father had served with De Boigne.[8]

In the final analysis De Boigne and Madhaji Scindia had, between them, created an army which had been able to reverse the effects of the disaster of Panipat and indeed give Madhaji control of the rump of the Mughal Empire for the last years of the eighteenth century. De Boigne's formidable organisational skills and the availability of European adventurers such as Perron and 'country-born' British officers such as Skinner had allowed the creation of the first true European style army to be used by an Indian ruler. There had been individual battalions and small brigades in the preceding years, but De Boigne's three brigades, totalling over 30,000 men, together with the two more brigades that Perron would add, gave the house of Scindia the most potent military force outside of those territories controlled by the British. Not until the Army of Hindustan had been destroyed could the East India Company and the British Government really claim the paramountcy that they would hold in India for the next century and a half.

---

8   Compton, *Particular Account*, pp.352–354.

Appendix I

Officers of the Army of Hindustan

The list below gives the names of all the European mercenary officers who served with the five brigades of the Army of Hindustan that the present author has been able to discover so far. They are listed by brigade and includes, where known, their full name and nationality. Officers did move between brigades. Robert Sutherland served with both the First and Second Brigades, the Skinners with the First, Second and Third. Where a rank is given, it is the highest that each officer attained in the service, though some are listed more than once where different ranks in different Brigades are known.

Lewis Ferdinand Smith gives a list of 37 officers who had been in Maratha service and who were 'British Subjects.' Not all of these had served with the Army of Hindustan and of those not all can be assigned to a specific brigade. Major Gardner, for example, had served with Holkar's regulars and had been very lucky to escape with his life when Jaswant Rao murdered those officers who wished to end their service. Captain Lucan, who guided the British storming party into Aljghur served with either the Second or Third Brigade and possibly both. Smith's list does not by any means include all the Europeans who served in the brigades. Skinner adds a few names and a few others appear in other sources, some had died of disease or in combat. The names of some are simply unknown.

General Officers

There were only two officers who held the rank of general. De Boigne himself and his successor Pierre Cuillier Perron. The rank of general only seems to have appeared once the Second Brigade was raised. Perron had supreme command of the army from late 1796 after De Boigne's retirement until the commencement of the war with the British in 1803.

Officers who served with the First Brigade 1788–1803

Succession of Brigade Commanders

From 1788–1792 De Boigne commanded the Brigade himself.

1792	Major Fremont, French, died in 1794.
1794	Major Pierre Cuillier Perron, French.
1797	Colonel Drugeon, Savoyard.
1798	Colonel Duprat, French.
1799	Colonel Robert Sutherland, British.
1802	Colonel Pohlmann, Hanoverian.

Other officers who served with the First Brigade

1788	John Hessing, Dutch. One of De Boigne's first battalion commanders Smith refers to him as 'De Boigne's oldest officer.' Later has his own *compoo*. Died in India in July 1803 aged 63. His son George would follow his father as commander of his own *compoo* until that command was taken over by Perron as the foundation of the Fifth Brigade.
1790	Major Baours, French, killed in action at Patan 1790.
1790	Captain Bulkely, Irish, killed in action 1792.
1790	Mr De la Fontaine, French,
1790	Michael Filose, Neapolitan, will eventually command his own *compoo* and will have two sons who will both follow him into the family business.
1790	Mr Hunter, possibly British. His name appears in the Persian correspondence as one of De Boigne's original officers for the First Brigade.
1790	Lieutenant Pedron, French. This officer will buy his majority and later command the Third Brigade, ending his career as Governor of Alighur.
1790	Lieutenant Roberts, British, died of wounds after the Battle of Merta.
1790	Captain Rohan, French, wounded at the Battle of Merta.
1792	Captain Chambaud, French, commanded a battalion in 1792
1792	Captain Drugeon, Savoyard, would command the Brigade in 1797.
1800	Lieutenant George Carnegie, British, a protégé of Sutherland. Moves with him to the Second Brigade.
1801	Captain Brownrigg, Irish, would later command the Fifth Brigade.
1801	Captain Gautier, French.
1801	Lieutenant Rowbotham, British, killed in action in Brownrigg's battle with Holkar.
1802	Captain Dawes, British, killed in action at the Battle of Hadaspar.
1802	Captain Lieutenant Catts, probably British, killed in action at the Battle of Hadaspar.
1802	Ensign Douglas, British, killed in action at the Battle of Hadaspar.
1802	Mr Stuart, possibly the Captain Stuart on Smith's list, resigned and surrendered to the British before the Battle of Assaye.

APPENDIX I

The Second Brigade 1792–1803

Succession of Commanders

1793   Major Perron, promoted to this command after the Siege of Kanaoud where he lost a hand. Takes over the First Brigade after Fremont's death.

1794   Major Gardiner, British, not to be confused with William Lineaus Gardner who does not seem to have served in the Army of Hindustan.

1795   Major Robert Sutherland, British, cashiered King's officer. Will later command the Brigade as Colonel.

1799   Major Pohlmann, Hanovarian.

1803   Colonel George Hessing, son of John Hessing. Ended career as Governor of Agra. Refused to fight the British.

1803   Major Geslin, French, fought at the Battle of Delhi. He had previously commanded a battalion in the Second Brigade.

Other officers who served with the Second Brigade

1794   Major Drugeon, promoted and moved from the First Brigade, returned to command the First in 1797.

1794   Captain Butterfield, British. He may have joined the Second Brigade when it was raised.

1795   James Skinner, British, begins his military career as an ensign in a battalion in this brigade commanded by the then Captain Pohlmann.

1800   Captain Donelly, possibly Irish. Killed in action at the siege of Jahazpur.

1800   Lieutenant Exshaw, possibly British. Killed in action at the siege of Jahazpur.

1800   Lieutenant Turnbull, British, wounded in action at the siege of Jahazpur.

1800   Robert Skinner, British, younger brother of James.

1800   Captain Symes, British, year of commencement of service uncertain, commanded a Najib battalion. Later in the Fourth Brigade.

1800   Lieutenant Vickers, British. Later in Holkar's service as major with his own command. When he refused to fight the British in 1804 Holkar had him beheaded.

1803   Captain Stewart, British, resigned from the service at the beginning of the war with the British in 1803. Possibly the same Mr. Stuart who had served in the First Brigade.

1803   Captain George Carnegie, British. Resigned from the service at the same time as Stewart. Had previously served in the First Brigade.

The Third Brigade 1795–1803

Succession of Commanders

1795   Colonel Pedron, French.

1801   Major Louis Borquien, French.

Other officers who served with the Third Brigade

- 1801   Major Augustine Bernier, French, had previously served in the Begum Somru's *compoo*. Killed in action at the storming of Hansi December 1801, aged 32.
- 1801   Lieutenant MacKenzie, British, wounded at the storming of George Thomas's fortress of Hansi.
- 1792   (date uncertain) Captain Lewis Ferdinand Smith, British. Had been in service for several years, and had known De Boigne personally. Promoted to Major and moved to the Fourth Brigade.
- 1800   Captain James Skinner, British, moved to the Third and served under Borquien for whom he had no respect at all.
- 1801   Captain Oliver, possibly French, wounded at the Battle of Georgegargh.
- 1801   Captain (possibly) Rabella, probably French, wounded at the Battle of Georgegargh.
- 1801   Lieutenant M'Culloch, British, killed at the battle of Georgegargh.
- 1801   Lieutenant Mackenzie, British.

Skinner also lists E.F. Smith as an officer in the Third rather than of the Hindustani Horse. The first three Brigades were all raised while De Boigne was in command of the Army. The remaining two under Perron's tenure as General.

The Fourth Brigade 1801–3

Succession of Commanders
- 1801   Colonel Dudrenec, French. Dudrenec had a long career as a mercenary and had commanded a *compoo* of his own which De Boigne defeated at Lakahairi. His second command was badly mauled at the Battle of Malpura.

Other officers who served with the Fourth Brigade
- 1802   Major L.F Smith, British. Date of service uncertain.
- 1801   Captain Paish (or Parrish), British, wounded at the Battle of Seondha in 1801.
- 1801   Captain Symes, British, killed at Seondha. Previously in the Second Brigade.
- 1801   Lieutenant Arnold, British, also killed at Seondha.
- 1803   Lieutenant Lapenet, probably French. Surrendered to Colonel Vandeleur along with Dudrenec and Smith 30 September 1803.

The Fifth Brigade 1803

Succession of Commanders
- 1803   Major Brownrigg, Irish, was confined in Agra by the garrison during Lake's siege and after joining the British was killed in action,

commanding some of his old troops in the war against Holkar in 1804.

Other officers who served in the Fifth Brigade

1803   Captain Harriot, British, also one of the officers confined at Agra along with Brownrigg, George Hessing and Robert Sutherland.

The Hindustani Horse

1800   Captain Emilius Felix Smith, British, younger brother to L.F.Smith. Died of wounds received at the battle of Georgegargh aged 24.
1803   Captain Fleury, French.

Other officers who served in Army of Hindustan

There is not sufficient information to tie these officers to a specific brigade.

1803   Captain Lucan, Irish, this was the officer who guided Lake's storming party at Alighur.
1803   Lieutenant Scott, was second in command to James Skinner in 1804 in British service but had previously served in Scindia's forces.

Sir Arthur Wellesley in a letter to Colonel Collins, the British Resident at Scindia's *durbar* lists 11 other officers 'made up by taking from a few leaves from an old orderly book the names of officers ordered for duty.'[1] These officers were:
Brigade Major Grant.
Brigade Major D'Orton.
Captain Gautier.
Captain Lieutenant Mercier.
Captain Lieutenant Honore.
Ensign Wroughton.
Ensign Perrin.
Ensign Mars.
Ensign Cameron.
Ensign Brown.
Cadet Songster.

Some of these may have fought at Assaye since at least one European is noted as being killed there fighting in Scindia's cause. Some must have also served in the battalions belonging to Begum Somru that were at Assaye.

As can be seen, the majority of the officers were either of British or French extraction, though other nationalities do feature. All that can be said with certainty is that they mostly served Scindia well, many dying in action in the almost constant campaigning.

---

1   Bennel, *Maratha War Papers*, letter 320, and Compton, *Particular Account*, p.324.

Appendix II

A Selection of Other Trained Brigades

Although the Army of Hindustan was the largest and best trained of the formations commanded by the various military adventurers there were many others. Some existed only for a few years. Some were absorbed by the Army of Hindustan, and some were never in the service of the Marathas at all. Also, some Brigades changed employers as a war ended or the money ran out. The following list gives strengths and commanders of some of these Trained Brigades that were such a feature of Indian military forces in the later eighteenth century. The list is by no means complete there were many others of whom there is little or no information.

Ibrahim Khan Gardis Brigade 1752–1761

Given that many of the military adventurers were Europeans it is significant that the first large formation of European style mercenary infantry was raised by an Indian. Ten battalions with 50 guns at their strongest, and armed with European style muskets and bayonets. Trained in the French style, as Gardi had learned his trade under Bussy. Despite their destruction at the Battle of Panipat in 1761. This force was a pattern for many of the subsequent mercenary brigades raised for the service of the various Indian rules (see Chapter 2).

The Begum Somru's Brigade 1768–1805

This Brigade was first raised by Walter Rheinhardt, nicknamed Sombreor Somru for his dark and sometimes bloody disposition. When he died in 1778 the brigade was taken over by his widow the *Begum* Farzana and at the time was in the service of the Emperor Shah Alam II, who had given the *jaghir* of Sardhana to Sombre for the formation's upkeep. The *Begum* employed European officers of many nations to command this formation including George Thomas, though the majority of the officers seem to have been French.

For most of its existence the brigade hovered between four or six battalions, a 400 man cavalry regiment and a train of artillery of around 30 guns. The brigade's headquarters at Sardhana boasted an armoury and a cannon foundry. Although never part of the Army of Hindustan part of the brigade was present at Assaye guarding the Maratha baggage, from where it managed retreat to Sardhana. The brigade continued in reduced form, even after the *Begum* submitted to the British, as the security force for the *Begum*'s state of Sardharna. Indian illustrations show them dressed in Persian style with long dark blue coats, red sashes and turbans, black or white cross belts and European muskets. The battalion standards appear to have been red.

Lestineau's Brigade 1786–1790

A three battalion formation with 15 guns. Trained in the French style. Lestineau served Madhaji Scindia and the Raja of Bhurtpore. The brigade fought at Tunga, Chaksana and Agra. When Lestineau deserted with his troops' back pay and the loot of Ghulam Kadir's saddlebags the brigade was disbanded but many of the men joined De Boigne's First Brigade. Both Perron and Louis Borquien served with Lestineau.

Chevalier Dudrenec's Brigades 1791–1802

The son of a French naval officer, Dudrenec had a long career as a mercenary serving as a junior officer in Rene Madec's corps and later as an officer in the *Begum* Somru's brigade. In 1791 he entered the service of Tukaji Holkar raising four battalions which were destroyed by De Boigne at the Battle of Lakheri (see Chapter 6). Tukaji then advanced Dudrenec more money to raise a second brigade of four battalions and 20 guns. This force survived somewhat longer but was badly mauled at the Battle of Malpura (see Chapter 8) whilst still in the service of the house of Holkar. Dudrenec left Jaswant Rao Holkars service in 1802 but his troops remained, the command eventually falling to the Englishman Major Vickers who had previously been an officer in the Second Brigade. In early 1803 Dudrenec was given command of the Fourth Brigade.

Colonel Hessing's Brigade 1792–1803

Colonel John Hessing was Dutch and despite being De Boigne's oldest officer quarrelled with him after the Battle of Patan, leaving the First Brigade at this point. He was commissioned to raise a bodyguard for Madhaji Scindia which over time became a brigade of four battalions. By 1800 the brigade was in the hands of his son Colonel George Hessing who doubled the size of the formation to eight battalions with 40 guns. Four of these battalions were destroyed by Jaswant Rao Holkar and Amir Khan at Ujjain where they lost 11 European officer or gunners. The other four battalions had been sent to Agra where John Hessing was Governor, although he died in July 1803. George Hessing commanded the Second Brigade for a very short period in 1803 but his four battalions seem to have become the foundation of the Fifth Brigade as he took over the Governorship of Agra from his late father. He did not fight the British and died in Calcutta in 1826.

General Michal Joachim Marie Raymond's Brigade 1786–1798

Raymond first came to India as a merchant in 1775 and was at Pondicheri when it fell to the British in 1778. He then took service with Haidar Ali of Mysore before transferring his allegiance to the Nizam of Hyderabad. This brigade, in the service of the *Nizam* of Hyderabad, was the only one other than the Army of Hindustan, worthy to be called an army, having at its largest some 14,000 infantry in 17 battalions and 600 cavalry, plus at least 50 guns with a train of equipment that needed 5,000 bullocks to move the guns and tumbrils. They were drilled in the French style. Mostly they were used to suppress disorder in the *Nizam's* dominions. The only time they fought an external enemy was the Khardha campaign of 1795 where they were narrowly defeated by Perron (see Chapter 7). When Raymond died the corps was taken over by his second in command Colonel Piron (not to be confused with Perron). This officer espoused the values of the French Revolution, even having the troops carry the Tricolour. The British therefore forced the disbandment of the corps in 1798 without firing a shot.

Major George Sangster's Battalion 1788

Raised in Agra in 1788 for the *Rana* of Gohad. 1,000 strong with artillery. The *Rana* being short of funds, the battalion was disbanded, many of its men probably joining the First Brigade. Sangster was Scottish. He oversaw the creation of the arms industry which supplied the Army of Hindustan. Compton mentions a son who trained a battalion for Lakwa Dada in 1801. There was also a Cadet Songster who surrendered to Wellesley after Assaye who may have been another relative.

Colonel James Shepheard's Brigade 1799–1805

Five battalions with 25 guns and 500 cavalry. Initially in the service of Ambaji Angria. Saw action during the Widows War, most notably at Seondha where four of his European officers were killed. When the war with the British broke out in 1803 he took his brigade into the East India Company's service where he rendered valuable service in the 1804 campaign twice defeating the Pathan mercenary Amir Khan. By this time his brigade numbered 3,180 men.[1]

Colonel J.P. Boyd's Brigade 1795–1797

Boyd was unique amongst the military adventurers in that he was American. He was in the service of the *Nizam* of Hyderabad with a corps of 1,800 infantry (possibly three battalions) by 1795 and served at the Battle of Khardla in that year. However, Raymond seems to have intrigued against him and Boyd therefore took his battalions into the service of the Maratha *Peshwa* in Poona where he was instrumental in securing Baji Rao's place on the throne during the succession squabbles of 1796. He also helped to put down disturbances by Arab mercenaries in 1797. His ultimate fate is unknown.

---

1 Compton, *Particular Account*, p.389.

Glossary

Beldars	Skilled labourers adept at digging earthworks and gun positions. In European terms Pioneers or Sappers.
Compoo	Or *campoo*. A brigade of trained battalions. Usually mercenaries often, but not always, commanded by Europeans.
Gardi	Or *gardis*, term used by the Marathas to denote trained infantry. From Ibrahim Khan Gardi.
Golandauz	Trained artillerymen. Gunners.
Havildar	Indian NCO, equivalent to sergeant.
Havildar Major	Senior Indian NCO equivalent to sergeant major.
Jaghir	A grant of land in return for service which was not always military. Not hereditary though many became so in the crumbling Mughal Empire.
Jaidad	Grant of revenue or land specifically to support troops. Similar to, but distinct from, a *Jaghir*.
Jemadar	Indian officer, in the Army of Hindustan a platoon commander.
Kelasis	Skilled labourers who manhandled the guns in action after the gun had been unlimbered. Often rendered as *clashies* in European sources.
Killadar	Or *khilladar*, governor of a fortress.
Naik	Or *naigue*. Indian NCO equivalent to corporal.
Najib	Semi-trained matchlock musketeer. Often a Rohilla.
Paltan	A battalion of trained infantry. Corruption of Battalion. Several *paltans* make a *compoo*.
Rissalah	A body of trained cavalry with roughly 80–120 *sowars*, though sometimes stronger.
Rissaldar	Commander of a *rissalah* of cavalry.
Raisaldar	Second in command of a *rissalah* of cavalry.
Rohilla	Tribesmen of Pathan origin who had settled in Hindustan. Fought both for and against the Mughals. Often found as mercenaries. In theory specialised in the defence of fortresses.

GLOSSARY

Telinga	Term used to describe European trained infantry. The First Brigade would initially have seven battalions of *telingas* and three battalions of *najibs*
Top Khana	Artillery park.
Sardar	Generic term for chieftain or military commander.
Sepoy	Indian soldier specifically, a trained infantryman.
Sowar	A cavalry trooper.
Subahdar	Controller of a *subah* or district, which could be a single village or a whole province. De Boigne was *subahdar* of the whole of Hindustan under Madhaji Scindia.
Subedar	Indian officer rank, in the Army of Hindustan a commander of an infantry company.
Zemindar	A landowner, the more powerful aspired to independent status. Much effort was expended in collecting taxes from refractory *zemindars* by the Army of Hindustan. The British would have similar problems.

Indian place names

Throughout the narrative the names familiar to the people who were there at the time have been used. However, in the modern age some Indian place names have changed considerably though others such as Agra, Gwalior and Ujjain have remained the same. Here are some of the changes to places mentioned in the text.

Bombay	Mumbai
Calcutta	Kolkata
Cawnpore	Kanpur
Koil	Alighar.
Madras	Chennai
Pondicherry	Puducheri
Poona	Pune

Bibliography

Primary Sources

The Asiatic Annual Register (London: Debrett, 1799–1805)
Baillie-Fraser, Major James (ed.), *The Military Memoirs of Lt.-Col. James Skinner C.B.* (London: Smith Elder & Co, 1851)
Bennel, A, S. (ed.), *The Maratha War Papers of Arthur Wellesley. January to December 1803* (Sutton: Army Records Society, 1998)
Blakiston, Captain John, *Twelve Years Military Adventures in Three Quarters of the Globe* (London: Henry Colburn, 1829)
Cormack, A.A, *The Mahratta Wars 1797–1805 Letters from the Front by Three Brothers Nicholas, George and Thomas Carnegie* (Banff: Privately Published, 1971)
Dundas, Col. David, *Principles of Military Movements* (London: T. Cadell, 1788)
Dirom, Major Alexander, *A Narrative of the Campaign in India which Terminated the War with Tipoo Sultan in 1792* (New Delhi: Asian Educational Services, 1985)
Foster, William (ed.), *History of the Indian Wars by Clement Downing* (London: Oxford University Press, 1924)
Francklin, Lieutenant Colonel William, *The Military Memoirs of George Thomas* (Calcutta: Hukaru Press, 1803)
Haley, Arthur (ed.), *The Munro Letters* (Liverpool: Bullfinch Publications, nd)
Joshi, Dr P. M. (ed.) & Sarkar Jadunath (trans.), *Persian Records of Maratha History; Volume 2, Scindia as Regent of Delhi 1787 and 1789–91* (Bombay: Director of Archives, Government of Bombay, 1954)
Moore, Lieutenant Edward, *A Narrative of the Operations of Captain Little's Detachment and of the Mahratta Army Commanded by Puseram Bhow during the Late Confederacy against the Nawab Tipu Sultan Bahadur* (London: George Woodfall, 1794)
Orme, Robert, *A History of the Military Transactions of the British Nation in Indostan* (New Delhi: Today and Tomorrow's Printers and Publishers, 1985)
Pester Lieutenant John, *War and Sport in India 1802–1806* (London: Heath Cranton & Ouseley Ltd, 1912)
Raikes, Charles, *Notes on the North Western Provinces of India* (London: Chapman and Hall 1852)
Rawlinson, H.G., *An Account of the Last Battle of Panipat and the Events Leading up to it. Written in Persian by Casi Raja Pundit who was present at the battle* (London: Oxford University Press, 1926)
Sinh, Maharaj Ragubhir, Sardesai, G.S. and Sarkar, J. (eds.), *English Records of Maratha History. Poona Residency Correspondence* (Bombay: Government Central Press, 1939–1945)
Smith, Captain Lewis Ferdinand. *A Sketch of the Rise, Progress and Termination of the Regular Corps formed and Commanded by Europeans in the Service of the Native Princes of India* (Calcutta: Greenway, 1805)
Todd, Lieutenant Colonel J., & Crooke, W., *Annals and Antiquities of Rajasthan* (Delhi: Motilal Banarsidass, 1987)
Thompson, J.P. (trans.), 'An Autobiographical Sketch of Louis Borquien', *Journal of the Punjab Historical Society,* Vol.IX, Part 1 (1923), pp.36–70
Thorn, Major William. *Memoir of the War in India Conducted by General Lord Lake Commander in Chief and Major-General Sir Arthur Wellesley* (London: Egerton, 1818)

Tone, William Henry, *Some Institutions of the Mahratta People* (Calcutta: Times Press, 1818)
Williams, Captain John, *An Historical Account of the Rise and Progress of the Bengal Native Infantry from its first formation in 1757 to 1796* (London: John Murray, 1817)

Secondary Sources

Abbot, Peter, *Rivals to the Raj* (Nottingham: Foundry Books, 2010)
Bidwell, Shelford, *Swords for Hire. European Mercenaries in 18th Century India* (London: John Murray, 1971)
Biddulph, Colonel John, *The Nineteenth and their times. Being an account of the Four Cavalry Regiments of the British Army that have borne the number Nineteen and the Campaigns in which they served* (London: John Murray, 1899)
Blackmore, David, *Destructive and Formidable, British Infantry Firepower 1642–1765* (London: Frontline Books, 2014)
Cardew, Lieutenant F.G., *A Sketch of the Services of the Bengal Native Army to the Year 1895* (New Delhi: Today and Tomorrow's Printers and Publishers 1971)
Chartrand, Rene. *Napoleon's Overseas Army* (Oxford: Osprey, 1989)
Compton, Herbert, *A Particular Account of the European Military Adventurers of Hindustan* (London: T Fisher Unwin, 1892)
Cotton, Sir Evan, 'Benoit De Boigne', *Indian Historical Records Commission Proceedings of Meetings*, Vol.IX (1927)
Daniels, Major A.M., *Skinners Horse: The History of the 1st Duke of York's Own Lancers* (Uckfield: Naval & Military Press, 2006)
Dalrymple, William, *White Mughals* (London: Bloomsbury, 2009)
Dalrymple, William, *The Anarchy* (London: Bloomsbury, 2019)
Deodar, V.N., *Nana Phadnis and the External Affairs of the Maratha Empire* (Bombay: Popular Book Depot, 1962)
Duff, James Grant, *History of the Mahrattas* (New Delhi: Associated Publishing, 1982)
Fregosi, Paul. *Dreams of Empire. Napoleon and the First World War, 1792–1815* (London: Hutchinson, 1989)
Fortescue, John, *A History of the British Army* (London: MacMillan & Co., 1921)
Haider, Dr Sayed Zafar, *Islamic Arms and Armour of Muslim India* (Lahore: Bahadur Publishers, 1991)
Hayden, Lieutenant Colonel F.A., *Historical Records 76 Hindoostan Regiment of Foot 1787–1881* (Lichfield: The Johnson's Head, 1909)
Hennessy, Maurice, *The Raja from Tipperary* (New York: St. Martin's Press, 1971)
Holmes, Richard, *Wellington, The Iron Duke* (London: BBC books, 2001)
Howard, Martin R., *Wellington and the British Army's Indian Campaigns 1798–1805* (Barnsley: Pen & Sword, 2020)
Hughes, Major General B.P., *Firepower, Weapons Effectiveness on the Battlefield 1630–1850* (Staplehurst: Spellmount, 1997)
Hutchinson, Lester, *European Freebooters in Moghul India* (London: Asia Publishing House, 1964)
Irvine, W., *The Army of the Indian Moghuls* (London: Luzac & Co. 1909)
Kadam,V.S., *Maratha Confederacy – A study in its Origin and Development* (Delhi: Munshiram Manoharlal Publishers, 1993)
Kantak, M.R., *The First Anglo-Maratha War, 1774–1783* (Bombay: Popular Prakashan, 1993)
Keane, H.G., *Hindustan under Free Lances 1770–1820* (London: Brown, Langhan, 1907)
Keane, H.G., *The Fall of the Moghul Empire of Hindustan* (Driffield: Leonaur, 2009)
Keay, Julia, *Farzana, The Woman Who Saved an Empire* (London: Tauris, 2014)
Kirkwood, Major W.C., *The Story of the 97th Deccan Infantry* (Hyderabad: Government Central Press, 1926)
Klassens, J., *European Mercenaries in the Armies of Post Mughal Successor States 1775–1849* (University of Lieden, Doctoral thesis, 2007)
Kulkarni, G.T. & Kantak M. R., *Battle of Karda, Challenges and Responses* (Pune: University of Pune. 1980)
Lall, John, *Begam Samru* (New Delhi: Roli Books, 1997)
Lawford, Colonel J.P., *Britain's Army in India – from its Foundation to the Conquest of Bengal* (London: Allen & Unwin, 1978)

Malleson, Colonel G.B., *The Decisive Battles of India* (London: W.H. Allen, 1883)
Malleson, Colonel G.B., *History of the French in India* (Edinburgh: John Grant, 1909)
Mason, Philip. *A Matter of Honour, An account of the Indian Army, Its Officers and Men* (London: Jonathan Cape, 1974)
Mollo, Boris, *The Indian Army* (Poole: Blandford, 1981)
Millar, Simon, *Assaye 1803* (Oxford: Osprey, 2006)
Nicolle, David, *Mughul India* (Oxford: Osprey, 1993)
Pant, Dr, G.N. & Sharma, K.K., *Indian Armours in the National Museum Collection – a Catalogue* (New Delhi: National Museum, 2001)
Pant, Dr, G.N., *Indian Arms and Armour* (New Delhi: Army Educational Stores, 1981)
Parihar, Dr G.R., *Marwar and the Marathas* (Jodhpur: Hindi Sahitya Mandir, 1968)
Pearse, Colonel H., *Life and Military Services of Viscount Lake* (Edinburgh: Blackwood, 1908)
Roy, Kaushik, *War, Culture and Society in Early Modern South Asia* (London: Routledge, 2011)
Roy, Kaushik, *From Hydaspes to Kargil, A history of Warfare in India 326 BC to AD 1999* (New Delhi: Manohar, 2004)
Roy Tirthankar, 'Rethinking the Origin of British India. State formation and Military Fiscal Undertakings in an 18th century World Region', *Modern Asian Studies*, Vol.47, No. 4 (2013), pp.1125–1156
Sarkar, Sir Jadunath, 'General De Boigne in India', *Indian Historical Records Commission, Proceedings of Meetings,* Vol.XV (1937), pp.9–12
Sarkar, Sir Jadunath, *The Fall of the Moghul Empire* (Hyderabad: Orient Blackswan Publishing, 2019)
Sarkar, Sir Jadunath, 'The Battle of Merta', *The Modern Review*, Vol.LXXV (January 1944), pp.17–23
Sarkar, Sir Jadunath, 'The Battle of Lakheri or Campoo versus Campoo', *The Modern Review*, Vol.LXXV (1944), pp.97–104
Sensarma Major P., *The Military History of Bengal* (Calcutta: Naya Prokash, 1977)
Saroop, Narindar, *A Squire of Hindustan* (London: Nottingham Court Press, 1983)
Saxena, R.K., *The Army of the Rajputs* (Udaipur: Saroj Prakashan, 1989)
Sen, Surendra Nath, *The Military System of the Marathas* (Delhi: K.P. Bagchi & Co., 1979)
Sen, S.P., *The French in India 1760–1816* (New Delhi: Munshiram Manoharlal, 1971)
Singh, K. Natwar, *Maharaja Suraj Mal 1707–1763* (London: George Allan &Unwin, 1981)
Verma, Abhas, *Third Battle of Panipat* (Delhi: Bharatiya Kala Prakashan, 2013)
Weller, Jac, *Wellington in India* (London: Greenhill, 1993)
Wickremesekera, Channa, *Best Black Troops in the World, British Perceptions and the Making of the Sepoy, 1746–1805* (New Delhi: Manohar, 2002)
Wilson, Colonel W.J., *History of the Madras Army* (Madras: Government Press, 1888)
Young, Desmond, *The Fountain of the Elephants* (London: Collins, 1959)
Yule, Colonel H., & Burnett A.C., *Hobson-Jobson, A Glossary of Colloquial Anglo-Indian Words and Phrases* (London: Routledge and Keegan Paul, 1985)